AF608164

Arabic Second Language Learning and Effects of Input, Transfer, and Typology

Arabic Second Language Learning
and Effects of Input, Transfer, and Typology

MOHAMMAD T. ALHAWARY

Georgetown University Press / Washington, DC

Library of Congress Cataloging-in-Publication Data

Names: Alhawary, Mohammad T., author.
Title: Arabic second language learning and effects of input, transfer, and typology / Mohammad T. Alhawary.
Description: Washington, DC : Georgetown University Press, 2019. | Includes bibliographical references and index.
Identifiers: LCCN 2018018065 (print) | LCCN 2018029494 (ebook) | ISBN 9781626166486 (ebook) | ISBN 9781626166479 (pbk. : alk. paper) | ISBN 9781626166462 (hardcover : alk. paper)
Subjects: LCSH: Arabic language—Morphosyntax. | Second language acquisition.
Classification: LCC PJ6331 (ebook) | LCC PJ6331 .A445 2019 (print) | DDC 492.7/5—dc23
LC record available at https://lccn.loc.gov/2018018065

∞ This book is printed on acid-free paper meeting the requirements of the American National Standard for Permanence in Paper for Printed Library Materials.

20 19 9 8 7 6 5 4 3 2 First printing

Printed in the United States of America

Cover design by Debra Naylor.
Cover image by Shutterstock.com.

In Memory of My Parents

Contents

Acknowledgments

I owe a debt of gratitude to numerous individuals, too many to count or list here, who helped in various ways with this book and the research on which it is based. My utmost gratitude goes to all the students who participated in this research on different campuses in China, Russia, and Taiwan. Without their gracious volunteering and participation, this book would not have been possible. I would also like to express my gratitude to all faculty and students who helped with recruiting the participants, including Professor Yafia Yusif Jamil, Professor Ramazan Mamedshahov, Professor Valentina Semyonova, Professor Ruzana Pskhu, Professor Huey-Tsyr Jeng, Kai Hu, Levi Chen, Professor Suleiman Zhou, Professor Zhang Hong, Professor Jiang Chuan Ying, and Professor Zhang Chongzhi. I am extremely grateful to Hope LeGro at Georgetown University Press for believing in this project and for her personal care and generous attention from the anonymous review stage to the very last stage of printing. My thanks are extended to Patti Bower for her excellent editorial work in copyediting the book manuscript as well as her numerous excellent suggestions. My thanks also go to the editorial and production coordinator at Georgetown University Press, Kathryn Owens, for her attention to details and for pushing the book through production without any delays. Last but not least, I am forever grateful to my wife and children for putting up with the countless hours taken away from them while conducting this research and completing the writing of the book. Their tremendous support and enthusiasm kept me going, especially during the time when I experienced the greatest personal loss, the passing away of both my parents. The final time I saw my parents, when I was last in Damascus, coincided with the time I began working on this project. This book is dedicated to their memory.

Introduction

This book is a follow-up to my earlier work, *Arabic Second Language Acquisition of Morphosyntax* (2009a). The former begins where the latter ends. The main objective is to provide data-driven empirical accounts of acquisition findings on most basic and high-frequency (morphosyntactic) structures with novel typological language pairings. Thus, whereas the earlier book is based on Arabic L2 data from adult English L1, French L1, Spanish L1, and Japanese L1 speakers, the present work relies on Arabic L2 data from Chinese L1 and Russian L1 speakers. Additionally, the present work controls more closely for input exposure variables by employing twelve (cross-sectional) sets of groups comprising 105 participants. Six groups are assigned to each of the two L1 language backgrounds, with three groups belonging to three different lengths of formal exposure to Arabic as an L2 (first, second, and third year) exposed to nonintensive language instruction and six equivalent groups exposed to intensive instruction. For generalizability and replication purposes, spontaneous production data are relied on here, too, rather than other measures, such as grammaticality judgment tasks, writing completion tasks, or other similar ones. In addition, such measures are metalinguistic in nature and do not necessarily reflect the underlying often unconscious knowledge of the target forms in the learner's interlanguage. The data were collected from the participants (who were university students learning Arabic as an L2) at their home institutions in China, Taiwan, and Russia.

In addition to examining the different processes, hypotheses, and acquisition patterns or tendencies of the participants, a consistent attempt is made to relate (to the present findings) all previous relevant findings from both Arabic SLA, including those based on data from English L1, Danish L1, French L1, Spanish L1, and Japanese L1 speaking learners of Arabic as an L2, and the general SLA literature. The approach in the current work takes the following into account:

- Large data samples based on 30- to 45-minute elicitation interviews;
- The overall L2 performance of the participants as well as inclusion of snapshots of the overall raw data;
- Rule application in noncontexts and the full scope of Interlanguage rule use;

- Qualitative and quantitative analyses of the data;
- The formal input of the participants in the classroom;
- Adult Arabic learners learning Arabic as an L3, with English being their L2, and belonging to two typologically distinct L1s exhibiting structures that converge and others that diverge from those in Arabic (and English);
- Analysis of L1 transfer effects;
- Analysis of L2 transfer effects; and
- Input exposure or frequency effects on language transfer from previously known languages.

Evidently, a full account of the process of second language acquisition is contingent upon examining a whole host of internal and external acquisition variables and the presence of a comprehensive theory of acquisition as well as fully explored (and finalized) parameter-based and feature-based accounts, among others (e.g., Klein 1991; Lardiere 2009a, 2009b). However, despite such unavoidable limitations at present and in the foreseeable future, the present work is not only significant for shedding light on the production abilities and grammatical development of Arabic L2 learners with different L1s from an explanatory perspective but also for contributing to predictive issues of current theories and models of SLA, especially those related to input, cross-linguistic influence, usage-based learning, second language speech processing prerequisites, and L1 and L2 transfer accounts.

Thus, two main research objectives motivated the present work. The first is to document and explain generally how Arabic second language morphosyntactic knowledge develops over time. This includes identifying forms whose learning may be more problematic than others. This also includes explaining and identifying intermediate stages and use of certain default forms during the acquisition process. The second objective is to speculate on second language knowledge representation and internal learning and processing mechanisms. In essence, the book addresses the following questions:

- How do adult Arabic L2 learners come to know about the combinatorial properties of morphemes, words, phrases, and clauses?
- Do they develop L2 knowledge systematically or randomly?
- Can they acquire the same range of syntactic and morphological knowledge as native speakers and to what extent?
- What are the developmental paths or tendencies, if any, along which Arabic L2 learners progress?

- What is the role of L1 in learning Arabic as an L2/L3?
- What is the role of L2 in learning Arabic as an L3?
- To what extent can input exposure override or minimize the effect of L1 transfer and at what proficiency level?
- What are other factors that have a bearing on learning Arabic as a second language?

An additional aim of the present work is to make it accessible to a wide range of readers. Hence, technical and statistical jargon and details are kept to a minimum whenever possible. Furthermore, the work is organized so that the theoretical discussions are assigned to a separate chapter, but such discussions are nevertheless accessible with self-contained explanations and sufficient background information. The book is organized into eight chapters.

Chapter 1 offers a brief description of the target structures and other relevant aspects of the language related to the data reported on in chapters 3–6. Chapter 2 discusses the main issues and questions investigated and methods used in the data collection, including the participants, the typological pairings of the participants' L1s with respect to their Arabic L2, the participants' other L2s, and the participants' Arabic L2 proficiency or exposure time that they had during their formal instruction at their home institutions in their own countries. The research questions are addressed with the aim to control for L1 and L2 transfer effects, typological and structural proximity effects, and input exposure effects. Chapters 3–6 constitute the data and findings sections of the book. In these chapters, the book adopts a descriptive mode in the data analysis and reporting of the findings. In addition, an attempt is made to provide an account of the formal input that the participants received. To preserve the usability of the data (long after theories and models are superseded or modified) and to allow the reader to readily understand the nature and extent of the success of the Arabic L2 learners/participants, the data are first analyzed qualitatively (with snapshots of the raw data and ample representative examples of the participants' output production in order to provide a sufficient account of the nature of the participants' output production) and then quantitatively, while avoiding detailed interpretive discussions of factors and theoretical issues, which are addressed in chapter 7. The aim of chapter 7 is to discuss the reported observations and findings of the Arabic data in light of recent and current proposals in the SLA literature. Chapter 8 aims to provide suggested implications and practical applications of the findings to subfields of Arabic applied linguistics.

The book is particularly useful for students and experts in Arabic applied linguistics and second language acquisition, second language acquisition practitioners seeking cross-linguistic evidence, Arabic textbook writers, Arabic testing experts, teachers-in-training of Arabic as a second/foreign language, and teachers and Arabists seeking to know how Arabic is learned from the learner's perspective. The book is also useful in the contexts of foreign language learning of Arabic by Chinese, Russian, English, French, Spanish, and Japanese speakers in classrooms around the world or in the respective countries where these languages are spoken as L1s.

Abbreviations

1	first person
2	second person
3	third person
A	adjective
Acc	accusative case
AGR	grammatical agreement
ANOVA	analysis of variance
A-P	active participle
CA	Classical Arabic
CEM	cumulative enhancement model
CP	complementizer phrase
D	dual
DA	dialectal Arabic
Dem	demonstrative pronoun
Det	determiner
DIP	diptote
DP	determiner phrase
ESA	Educated Spoken Arabic
F	feminine
FP	functional projection
Gen	genitive case
H	human
IH	input hypothesis
IL	interlanguage
Impera	imperative
Imperf	imperfective
Indef	indefinite
Indic	indicative mood
Juss	jussive mood
L1	first/native language
L2	second/foreign language
L3	third language
LFG	lexical functional grammar
L2SFM	L2 status factor model

M	masculine
MSA	Modern Standard Arabic
N	noun
N-A	noun–adjective
Nom	nominative case
NP	noun phrase
OVS	object-verb-subject
P	predicate
Perf	perfective
Pl	plural
P-P	passive participle
PT	processability theory
S	singular
SLA	second language acquisition
SSA	Spoken Standard Arabic
Subjunc	subjunctive mood
S-V	subject-verb
SVO	subject-verb-object
T	time/session of data collection
TL	target language
TPM	typological primacy model
UG	universal grammar
V	verb
VP	verb phrase
VSO	verb-subject-object

Transliteration Symbols

The transcription of all Arabic texts in the body of the book follows a simplified International Phonetic Alphabet with some standard equivalents used in Arabic and Middle Eastern Studies journals. A list of all transliteration symbols used is provided. For the citation of Arabic titles and names of Arab authors in the references section, a simplified transliteration system based on standard usage in Arabic and Middle Eastern Studies journals has been adopted. The symbol ' represents the *hamza* (glottal stop) and ʿ represents the *ʿayn* (voiced pharyngeal fricative consonant). In addition, following standard practice, the definite article {ʔal-} is fully stated (without assimilating any part) in all of the Arabic examples except in cited utterances of the L2 learners, in which case transliteration follows the exact output production of the participants.

Consonants

Arabic Symbol	Transliteration Symbol	
ب	b	voiced bilabial stop
ت	t	voiceless alveolar stop
ث	θ	voiceless interdental fricative
ج	ʤ	voiced palato-alveolar affricate
ح	H	voiceless pharyngeal (epiglottal) fricative
خ	x	voiceless velar/uvular fricative
د	d	voiced alveolar stop
ذ	ð	voiced interdental fricative
ر	r	voiced alveolar tap/trill
ز	z	voiced alveolar fricative
س	s	voiceless alveolar fricative
ش	š	voiceless palato-alveolor fricative
ص	sˤ	voiceless alveolar fricative emphatic
ض	dˤ	voiced alveolar stop emphatic
ط	tˤ	voiceless alveolar stop emphatic
ظ	ðˤ	voiced interdental fricative emphatic
ع	ʕ	voiced pharyngeal (epiglottal) fricative

Arabic Symbol	Transliteration Symbol	
غ	ɣ	voiced velar/uvular fricative
ف	f	voiceless labiodental fricative
ق	q	voiceless uvular stop
ك	k	voiceless velar stop
ل	l	voiced alveolar lateral
م	m	voiced bilabial nasal
ن	n	voiced alveolar nasal
هـ	h	voiceless glottal fricative
و	w	voiced bilabial velar glide
ي	y	voiced palatal glide
ء	ʔ	(voiceless) glottal stop
يّ	yy	geminate of y
وّ	ww	geminate of w

Vowels

Arabic Symbol	Transliteration Symbol	
ـَ	a	short front/back low
ا	ā	long front/back low
ـُ	u	short high back rounded
و	ū	long high back rounded
ـِ	i	short high front unrounded
ي	ī	long high front unrounded
ـَيْ	ay	diphthong
ـَوْ	aw	diphthong

Chapter 1

Description of the Target Structures

The target forms discussed in this chapter include nominal gender agreement, verbal gender agreement, tense/aspect, and null subjects. The description provided pertains to Modern Standard Arabic (MSA), comprising the main formal classroom input of the participants as evident in their assigned textbooks (see chapters 3–6). The description is not intended to be exhaustive. Focus is on those features relevant to the data investigated. The target forms are among the high-frequency and most essential core structures to which Arabic second/ foreign learners are exposed in the first years of their learning and are characterized by a great degree of regularity.

1.1 Preliminaries

Before discussing the target forms, an overview of Arabic word structure is in order. Words in Arabic (as a Semitic language) have a unique underlying form–meaning relationship derived by combining a root and a pattern. The former (consisting of three to six consonants but most typically three) denotes the core semantic meaning while the latter (consisting of vowels and sometimes, additionally, a derivational affix/auxiliary consonant) carries some additional meaning. In other words, the complete meaning of a given word obtains only from combining both. Accordingly, a given word can have a large number of related words sharing the same root. Table 1.1 shows a list of related words derived from the root *ʔ-k-l* "that to do with eating." The derivation is carried out by different types of affixation, including prefixes, suffixes, and infixes or circumfixes. Figures 1.1 and 1.2 (following O'Grady et al. 2009) show how the pattern *-a-a-* is affixed to the root *ʔ-k-l* "that to do with eating" to form the perfective/past tense and the pattern *ya-u-* is affixed to the same root to form the imperfective/present tense, respectively (see also Alhawary 2009a, 2011).

Learners of Arabic do not usually learn Arabic words or their derivation by combining a given root with a pattern from early on. Instead, they start

Table 1.1 Lexical derivation based on root

Root	*Derived Form*	*Lexical Category*	*Gloss*
ʔ-k-l	ʔakal	V	"he ate"
	yaʔkul	V	"he eats/is eating"
	yuʔkal	V	"is eaten"
	ʔakl	N	"eating/food"
	maʔkūl	N	"eaten"
	maʔkūlāt	N	"dishes/types of food"

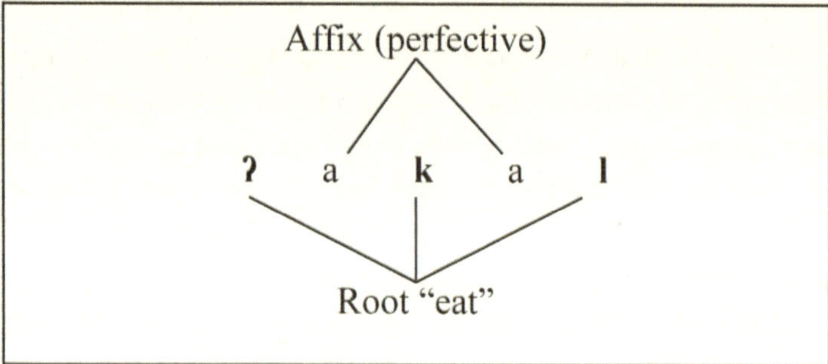

Figure 1.1 Lexical derivation based on combining root- and pattern-bound morphemes to derive the past tense verb ***ʔakal*** "he ate"

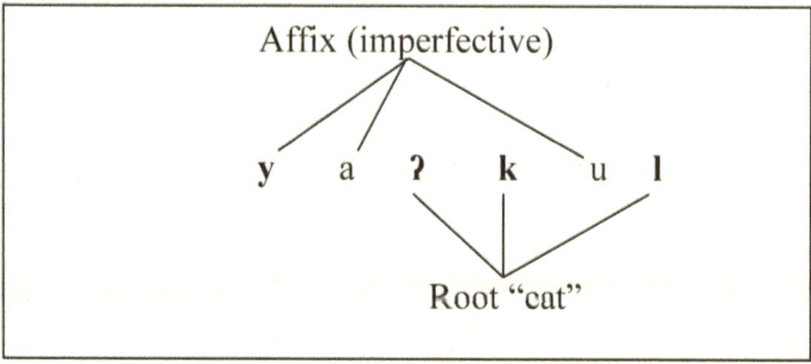

Figure 1.2 Lexical derivation based on combining root- and pattern-bound morphemes to derive the present tense verb *yaʔkul* "he eats/is eating"

Table 1.2 Lexical derivation based on word base/stem

Root	*Base & Derived Words*	*Lexical Category*	*Gender*	*Gloss*
ʔ-k-l	ʔakal	V	M (3.S)	"he ate"
	ʔakkal	V	M (3.S)	"he fed"
	ʔakla	N	F.S	"a dish/type of food"
	ʔaklatāni	N	F.D	"two dishes/types of food"
	ʔakalāt	N	F.Pl	"dishes/types of food"
	ʔākil	N/A	M.S	"eater/having eaten"
	ʔākilāni	N/A	M.D	"two eaters/having eaten"
	ʔākilūna	N/A	M.Pl	"eaters/having eaten"
	ʔākila	N/A	F.S	"eater/having eaten"
	ʔākilatāni	N/A	F.D	"two eaters/having eaten"
	ʔākilāt	N/A	F.Pl	"eaters/having eaten"
sˤ-ɣ-r	sˤaɣīr	A	M.S	"small"
	sˤaɣīrāni	A	M.D	"small"
	sˤiɣār	A	M.Pl	"small"
	sˤaɣīra	A	F.S	"small"
	sˤaɣīratāni	A	F.D	"small"
	sˤaɣīrāt	A	F.Pl	"small"

by learning words (and storing them in memory) as base forms. They learn that certain words such as perfective/past tense and imperfective/present tense verbs inflected for third person singular masculine are base forms from which other (derived) verbs as well as active and passive participles are formed. For example, from the base form *ʔakal* "he ate," another verb such as *ʔakkal* "he fed" is derived by duplicating the second root consonant to derive a causative meaning (see table 1.2). Similarly, singular nouns and singular (real) adjectives are introduced as base forms for the dual and plural of such forms (table 1.2).

Although Arabic root system may not be relevant in Arabic L2 mental lexicon (in terms of storage and recall) during the early stages of L2 development, since Arabic L2 learners learn to rely on base words for word derivation and affixation, it is worth mentioning here that many studies on Arabic L1 have provided evidence in support of the psychological reality of the root (in Arabic and Semitic languages) based on many data sources. Such sources include slips of the tongue data (e.g., Abd El-Jawad and Abu-Salim 1987; Berg and Abd El-Jawad 1996), aphasic data (e.g., Prunet, Beland, and Idrissi 2000; Idrissi, Prunet, and Beland 2008), dyslexic data (Idrissi and Kehayia 2004), hypocoristic data (e.g., Davis and Zawaydeh 2001; Frisch and Zawaydeh 2001), lexical and morphological processing (e.g., Boudelaa and Marlsen-Wilson 2001, 2004, 2011; Mahfoudhi 2005, 2007), and first language development data from

Arabic and Hebrew (e.g., Badry 2005; Berman 1985, 1999; see also McCarthy 1981).[1] In later Arabic L2 development, Arabic root and pattern systems and related word formation and affixation processes seem to become efficiently operative with more lexical/vocabulary knowledge (see Redouane 2001, 2003). Due to the scope of the data, this book does not deal with this issue, although future research should investigate the interaction between root and pattern systems (as they relate to word formation) and the different types of affixation processes more vigorously and from the outset of learning. For the purpose of the present book, it is crucial to note here that not all patterns have productive uniformity and that Arabic L2 learners are not usually introduced to the notion of root and pattern from the beginning of their exposure to the language. The derived forms illustrated in tables 1.1 and 1.2 are usually introduced as base forms for others, such as past versus present and singular versus dual and plural, with roots and patterns being introduced later mainly to develop the skill of looking up words in the dictionary or guessing their meanings (for more on the structure and derivation of Arabic verbs, nouns, and adjectives, see Alhawary 2011).

1.2 Gender Agreement

The focus of gender agreement is on three types of constructions: nominal gender agreement within the noun phrase between the attributive adjective and the head noun, nominal gender agreement between the demonstrative pronoun and the predicate noun within the equational/verbless sentence, and verbal gender agreement. Before discussing the three target structures holistically, this section discusses gender assignments of individual words, mainly nouns, adjectives, and pronouns.

Arabic nouns are marked by either natural/biological gender or grammatical gender. Natural gender refers to natural or biological assignment of gender (masculine and feminine) to words according to the biological distinction of human and animal referents, as in (1) below, whereas grammatical gender refers to the arbitrary assignment of gender (masculine or feminine) to words whose referents often do not exhibit any apparent reason for the distinction, as in (2).[2]

(1)	Natural gender:	tˁālib	"a male student"
		tˁālib-**a**	"a female student"
		ʔinsān	"a male human being"
		ʔinsān-**a**	"a female human being"

	kalb	"a male dog"
	kalb-**a**	"a female dog"
(2) Grammatical gender:	kitāb	"a book.m"
	qalam	"a pen.m"
	sayyār-**a**	"a car-f"
	mistˤar-**a**	"a ruler-f"

The examples of nouns in (1) and (2) also illustrate masculine forms marked by a zero morpheme {*-0*}, which is usually the default base form, and feminine forms marked by the suffix {*-a*}.[3] This is the case with the majority of nouns and in particular the case with derived participles (active or passive) where, for example, *tˤālib* is essentially an active participle "seeker" in Classical Arabic (CA), as in *tˤālib ʕilm* "seeker of knowledge," but it has taken on a lexicalized meaning in MSA.

However, natural/biological masculine and feminine nouns need not have apparent related forms in MSA, as in (3)—not unlike grammatical gender, as illustrated in (2).

(3)	radʒul	"a man"
	ʔimraʔ-**a**	"a woman"
	θawr	"a bull"
	baqar-**a**	"a she-cow"

The examples in (3) show feminine and masculine nouns not derived from the same root.[4] Nevertheless, such nouns exhibit the distinction between masculine and feminine forms by means of the gender suffix {*-a*}.

In addition to the feminine suffix {*-a*}, two other suffixes {*-ā*} and {*āʔ*} mark nouns for feminine, as in the words listed in (4).

(4)	ʔunθ-**ā**	"female"
	ʕasˤ-**ā**	"a stick-f"
	sˤaʜr-**āʔ**	"a desert-f"
	sam-**āʔ**	"a sky-f"[5]

Together with {*-a*}, the suffixes {*-ā*} and {*āʔ*} mark the vast majority of Arabic feminine singular nouns, with the suffix {-a} being the most frequent one (see Ṣaydāwī 1999, 297).

However, there are some exceptions (not included among the target forms) that are termed "crypto" feminine, to use Whorf's terminology, where a small subclass of words are assigned the feminine (grammatical) gender without exhibiting a feminine suffix, as in (5).

(5)	nafs	"self.f"
	ʜarb	"war.f"
	ʔardˤ	"earth.f"
	šams	"sun.f"
	kaʔs	"a glass.f"
	dār	"a house.f"[6]

In addition, there are three small subclasses of nouns, two of which are used feminine or masculine depending on the intended meaning and one where either gender use is optional. One such subclass of nouns ends with the feminine suffix {-*a*}, such as *ħayy-a* "snake," but can be used as feminine or masculine depending on the intended (natural/biological) gender of an animal. A second subclass does not end with a gender suffix, such as *faras* "horse," but can be used as feminine or masculine depending on the intended gender. A third subclass, such as those listed in (6) below, do not exhibit a feminine gender suffix and can be used as either feminine or masculine in CA—although in MSA they are mostly used as masculine as part of a simplifying trend.

(6)	tˤarīq	"road"
	sabīl	"path, road"
	sūq	"market"
	dalw	"bucket"
	sikkīn	"knife"
	xamr	"wine"

Notwithstanding the irregular cases of gender markings on nouns (especially the feminine nouns that do not end with a feminine suffix), gender use with nouns is characterized by a great deal of regularity and frequency in MSA, especially by means of the suffix {-*a*}.[7]

Use of gender with adjectives is characterized by even more regularity in MSA, exhibiting the same gender suffixes as nouns: {-*a*}, {-*ā*}, and {-*āʔ*}. Table 1.3 lists adjectives inflected for both masculine and feminine gender distinctions with the three feminine suffixes. Table 1.3 also illustrates that the choice of the suffix depends on the particular pattern of adjectives, setting aside their

Table 1.3 Inflectional derivation of gender: singular feminine suffixes

Masculine	*Feminine*	*Gloss*	*Reasons for Type of Suffix*
ʔākil	ʔākil-**a**	"eater/ having eaten"	due to pattern/derived A-P
maʔkūl	maʔkūl-**a**	"eaten"	due to pattern/derived P-P
qaliq	qaliq-**a**	"worried"	due to pattern
sˤaɣīr	sˤaɣīr-**a**	"small"	due to pattern
ɣadˤbān	ɣadˤb-ā/ɣadˤbān-**a***	"angry"	due to pattern
ʔazraq	zarqāʔ	"blue"	color adjective/due to pattern
ʔasˤlaʕ	sˤalʕāʔ	"bald"	body defects or beauties/ due to pattern

* The suffix {*-a*} is allowed in MSA instead of CA's feminine pattern *faʕ-lā*.

semantic triggers as observed by traditional Arab grammarians (for example, see Al-Ḥulwānī 1972, 270–71).

Like gender assignment on nouns, the most prevalent of all three feminine gender suffixes is the suffix{*-a*}. Given that it is permissible in MSA to supply the suffix {*-a*} where CA would require the suffix {*-ā*}, as in *ɣadˤbān* and *ɣadˤb-ā*/ *ɣadˤbān-**a*** "angry" for masculine and feminine respectively, this means that the feminine affix can in fact be restricted to two rather than three contexts (see Majmaʿ Al-Lugha Al-ʿArabiyya 1984, 126, 131–32). In other words, except when the masculine form (ending with a zero morpheme) has the pattern of *ʔafʕal* with the corresponding feminine pattern being *faʕl-āʔ*, which is specific to color and body defect/beauty adjectives, the only other option is the feminine ending {*-a*}. Hence, this makes it an easier task for the L2 learner to supply the feminine suffix on adjectives (see Alhawary 2011, 261–69).

In addition, there is a class of adjectives of certain patterns, such as *mifʕal*, *mifʕāl*, *mifʕīl*, or *faʕūl* (when they denote an active participle meaning) and *faʕīl*, *fiʕl*, or *faʕl* (when they denote a passive participle meaning), which do not require a feminine suffix in CA (that is, the masculine and feminine form are identical, ending with a zero morpheme), as in (7) below (see Al-Ghalayyīnī 2000, 100–101).

(7)	radʒul dʒarīʜ	ʔimraʔa dʒarīʜ
	man wounded.s	woman wounded.s
	"a wounded man"	"a wounded woman"[8]

However, the simplification tendency in MSA has been to mark the adjective with the feminine referent by means of the {*-a*} suffix as acknowledged by the

Egyptian Arabic Language Academy to be grammatically correct (see Majmaʿ Al-Lugha Al-ʿArabiyya 1984). The CA examples in (7) are rewritten in (8) as sanctioned MSA use and dialectal use as well.

(8)	radʒul dʒarīħ		ʔimraʔa	dʒarīħ-**a**
	man	wounded.s	woman	wounded-s.f
	"a wounded man"		"a wounded woman"	

Finally, there are words in CA that do not exhibit a feminine ending, as they refer to an exclusively female quality, such as *ħāmil* "pregnant," *ħāʔidˤ* "menstruating," and *θayyib* "a female who is not virgin." Such words follow the regular rule in MSA, exhibiting the feminine suffix {*-a*}. Thus, it is grammatically correct in MSA to have *ħāmil-a* "pregnant," *ħāʔidˤ-a* "menstruating," and *θayyib-a* "a female who is not virgin" (Majmaʿ Al-Lugha Al-ʿArabiyya 1984, 126, 131–33).

The above thus far illustrates that gender assignment on adjectives, similar to nouns, is quite regular in MSA. It is also worth mentioning here that current Arabic L2 textbooks follow the simplification tendencies and rules of MSA. Furthermore, the highly regular feminine gender suffix {*-a*} in nouns and adjectives is the most prevalent of the three suffixes and almost exclusively used during the first year of Arabic L2 instruction.

In addition to nouns and adjectives, pronouns, including demonstratives, are also marked for gender. Demonstrative pronouns are realized as free morphemes. In addition to gender, demonstrative pronouns are inflected for number, distance, humanness, and (the ones marking the dual) for case. Table 1.4 lists the basic demonstrative pronouns in MSA (see Alhawary 2011, 108–111).

Not all of the demonstrative pronouns listed in table 1.4 are available in the input, especially during most of the first year of instruction. In addition, four of the pronouns are rarely used in MSA (i.e., those marked by an asterisk).

Table 1.4 Arabic (MSA) demonstrative pronouns

Demonstrative	*Gloss*	*Demonstrative*	*Gloss*
hāðā	"this.S.M"	ðālika	"that.S.M"
hāðihi	"this.S.F"	tilka	"that.S.F"
hāðāni	"these.D.M.Nom"	ðānika*	"those.D.M.Nom"
hāðayni	"these.D.M.Acc/Gen"	ðaynika*	"those.D.M.Acc/Gen"
hātāni	"these.D.F.Nom"	tānika*	"those.D.F.Nom"
hātayni	"these.D.F.Acc/Gen"	taynika*	"those.D.F.Acc/Gen"
hāʔulāʔi	"these.Pl.H.M/F"	ʔulāʔika	"those.Pl.H.M/F"
hāðihi	"these.Pl.None-H"	tilka	"those.Pl.None-H"

* = infrequent in MSA

Focus here is on the singular masculine and singular feminine pronouns *hāðā* "this.s.m" and *hāðihi* "this.s.f," respectively.

1.2.1 Nominal Gender Agreement within the Arabic Noun Phrase

In Arabic, a noun phrase (NP) consisting of a head noun and an attributive (modifying) adjective agree in gender (masculine or feminine), number (singular, dual, or plural), definiteness, and case (nominative, accusative, or genitive). Examples (9)–(12) illustrate the Arabic agreement phenomenon between the head noun and the attributive adjective with respect to number (singular), gender (singular masculine and singular feminine), and case (nominative, accusative, and genitive) features.

9(a) tˤālib-(u-n) ʤadīd-(u-n)
student.s.m-(Nom-Indef) new.s.m-(Nom-Indef)
"a new male student"

9(b) tˤālib-(a-n) ʤadīd-(a-n)
student.s.m-(Acc-Indef) new.s.m-(Acc-Indef)
"a new male student"

9(c) tˤālib-(i-n) ʤadīd-(i-n)
student.s.m-(Gen-Indef) new.s.m-(Gen-Indef)
"a new male student"

10(a) tˤālib-a[t]-(u-n) ʤadīd-a[t]-(u-n)
student-s.f-(Nom-Indef) new-s.f-(Nom-Indef)
"a new female student"

10(b) tˤālib-a[t]-(a-n) ʤadīd-a[t]-(a-n)
student-s.f-(Acc-Indef) new-s.f-(Acc-Indef)
"a new female student"

10(c) tˤālib-a[t]-(i-n) ʤadīd-a[t]-(i-n)
student-s.f-(Gen-Indef) new-s.f-(Gen-Indef)
"a new female student"

11(a) (ʔal)-qalam-(u) (ʔal)-ʤadīd-(u)
(the)-pen.s.m-(Nom) (the)-new.s.m-(Nom)
"the new pen"

11(b) (ʔal)-qalam-(a) (ʔal)-ʤadīd-(a)
(the)-pen.s.m-(Acc) (the)-new.s.m-(Acc)
"the new pen"

11(c) (ʔal)-qalam-(i) (ʔal)-ʤadīd-(i)
(the)-pen.s.m-(Gen) (the)-new.s.m-(Gen)
"the new pen"

12(a)	(ʔal)-sayyār-a[t]-(u)	(ʔal)-ʤadīd-a[t]-(u)
	(the)-car-s.f-(Nom)	(the)-new-s.f-(Nom)
	"the new car"	
12(b)	(ʔal)-sayyār-a[t]-(a)	(ʔal)-ʤadīd-a[t]-(a)
	(the)-car-s.f-(Acc)	(the)-new-s.f-(Acc)
	"the new car"	
12(c)	(ʔal)-sayyār-a[t]-(i)	(ʔal)-ʤadīd-a[t]-(i)
	(the)-car-s.f-(Gen)	(the)-new-s.f-(Gen)
	"the new car"	

Examples (9)–(10) show that the indefinite (in the singular) feature is signaled by *nunation* {-*n*}. In pause form, indefiniteness corresponds to the bare form of the word (i.e., as a zero morpheme). In addition and as explained above, when case is produced on words inflected for singular feminine {-*a*} in full MSA/CA form, the feminine ending is realized as {-*at*} with [t] surfacing, as in (10) and (12). However, in pause form (i.e., without producing case endings), the consonant [t] is not required.[9] Focus here is on the gender distinction between singular masculine and singular feminine irrespective of case and definiteness. Hence, case and definiteness features are provided in parentheses in (9)–(12). Essentially, the bare target forms with respect to gender agreement within Arabic NPs are provided in (13)–(16).

(13)	tˤālib	ʤadīd
	student.s.m	new.s.m
	"a new male student"	
(14)	tˤālib-a	ʤadīd-a
	student.s-f	new-s.f
	"a new female student"	
(15)	qalam	ʤadīd
	pen.s.m	new.s.m
	"a new pen"	
(16)	sayyār-a	ʤadīd-a
	car-s.f	new-s.f
	"a new car"	

1.2.2 Nominal Gender Agreement Involving Demonstratives

Focus of nominal gender agreement involving demonstrative pronouns is on the distinction between the singular masculine demonstrative *hāðā* "this.s.m" and singular feminine demonstrative *hāðihi* "this.s.f" and agreement with a corresponding (singular masculine or singular feminine) predicate noun in nominal/verbless construction. Accordingly, agreement between a demonstrative and a predicate noun (within a nominal/verbless sentence) involves gender (masculine versus feminine) and number (singular), as in (17)–(20).

(17) hāðā tˁālib-(u-n)
this.s.m student.s.m-(Nom-Indef)
"This is a male student."

(18) hāðihi tˁālib-a[t]-(u-n)
this.s.f student-s.f-(Nom-Indef)
"This is a female student."

(19) hāðā qalam-(u-n)
this.s.m pen.s.m-(Nom-Indef)
"This is a pen."

(20) hāðihi sayyār-a[t]-(u-n)
this.s.f car-s.f-(Nom-Indef)
"This is a car."

Case suffixes with nouns following a demonstrative pronoun are included within parentheses to indicate their use in full form, resulting in the surfacing of [t] with singular feminine nouns that exhibit the gender suffix {*-a*}. However, as stated above, case is not a target feature. L2 learners can produce the nominal/verbless constructions in pause form and the constructions would still be intact grammatically.

1.2.3 Verbal Gender Agreement

Any given Arabic verb is inflected for the features tense/aspect (past/perfective or present/imperfective), person, number, and gender.[10] An Arabic verb agrees either with an implied subject in the discourse (Arabic being a null-subject language as discussed further below), an explicit NP, or explicit pronoun subject. Sentences (21)–(22) illustrate the target verbal agreement inflectional features in the present tense: third person singular masculine and third person singular feminine.

(21) ʔal-tˁālib-(u) **ya**-ʔkul-(u)
the-student.s.m-(Nom) 3.s.m-eat-(Indic)
"The male student eats/is eating."

(22) ʔal-tˁālib-a[t]-(u) **ta**-ʔkul-(u)
the-student-s.f-(Nom) 3.s.f-eat-(Indic)
"The female student eats/is eating."

Examples (21)–(22) illustrate the verbs *ya-ʔkul* "he eats/is eating" and *ta-ʔkul* "she eats/is eating" inflected for third person singular masculine and feminine agreement features to agree with a singular masculine and singular feminine subject through use of the prefixes {*ya*-} and {*ta*-}, respectively. In addition, in full form, present tense verbs are inflected for mood (indicative, subjunctive, and jussive). Past tense forms are not inflected for mood. In (21)–(22), mood suffixes are included in parentheses since they are optional and, like case, have no consequences to the target forms of the current study and are not included in the target forms of the study.

Similar agreement holds between the subject and the verb in the past form but through suffixes. A verb in the past tense is inflected for third person singular masculine through its unique zero morpheme (and one that represents the shortest form of Arabic verbal paradigm) and for third person singular feminine through the suffix {-*t*}. Sentences (23)–(24) illustrate the target verbal agreement inflectional features in the past tense.

(23) ʔal-tˁālib-(u) ʔakala
the-student.s.m-(Nom) ate.3.s.m
"The male student ate."

(24) ʔal-tˁālib-a[t]-(u) ʔakala-t
the-student-s.f-(Nom) ate-3.s.f
"The female student ate."

Finally, Arabic verbal agreement involves asymmetrical agreement in a VSO word order as opposed to an SVO one. In the former, the verb agrees with a following (postverbal) subject in gender only, whereas in the latter the verb agrees with a preceding (preverbal) subject in all respects: person, number, and gender. However, since the focus of the present study is on third person singular masculine and feminine agreement, word order has no consequences here. Sentences (21)–(24) are restated as (25)–(28) in a VSO order.

(25) **ya**-ʔkul-(u) ʔal-tˁālib-(u)
3.s.m-eat-(Indic) the-student.s.m-(Nom)
"The male student eats/is eating."

(26) **ta**-ʔkul-(u) ʔal-tˤālib-a[t]-(u)
3.s.f-eat-(Indic) the-student-s.f-(Nom)
"The female student eats/is eating."

(27) ʔakala ʔal-tˤālib-(u)
ate.3.s.m the-student.s.m-(Nom)
"The male student ate."

(28) ʔakala-t ʔal-tˤālib-a[t]-(u)
ate-3.s.f the-student-s.f-(Nom)
"The female student ate."

Examples (25)–(28) are identical to sentences (21)–(24) with respect to the target verbal agreement forms: third person singular masculine and third person singular feminine, exhibiting the same prefixes and suffixes. In summary, what is important here is that in each case, whether for preverbal or postverbal agreement and whether for past or present tense agreement, the verb is distinctly marked for third person singular masculine versus third person singular feminine. In other words, and in terms of the target forms and the purpose of the present study, agreement features contained in the prefix include person, number, and gender information just as agreement features contained in the suffix indicate person, number and gender information.[11]

1.3 Tense/Aspect

As discussed above, the distinction between past/perfective and present/imperfective is readily established by the presence of a prefix or suffix. Present/imperfective is marked with a prefix and past/perfective is marked with a suffix. Focus here is on third person singular masculine and third person singular feminine regardless of word order (i.e., with both SVO and VSO word orders being included). Hence, examples that illustrate the target present/imperfective forms are identical to sentences (21)–(22) and (25)–(26) and examples that illustrate the target past/perfective forms are identical to sentences (23)–(24) and (27)–(28) stated above.

1.4 Null Subjects

Arabic is a pro-drop/null-subject language.[12] This means a verb with a pronoun suffix attached to it can stand alone (in the matrix clause) without an explicit NP or overt pronominal subject. This is applicable to both present and past tenses, as in (29)–(32).

(29) ya-ʔkul-(u)
3.s.m-eat-(Indic)
"He eats/is eating."

(30) ta-ʔkul-(u)
3.s.f-eat-(Indic)
"She eats/is eating."

(31) ʔakala
ate.3.s.m
"He ate."

(32) ʔakala-t
ate-3.s.f
"She ate."

Like the other target forms, mood marking in the present tense/aspect, which is produced in full form in MSA, is stated in parentheses and is not the focus of the present study.

However, there are contexts in Arabic where use of an overt pronoun or explicit NP is obligatory. One such context is when a verb occurs in a lower or embedded clause following the complementizers *ʔinna* "that" and *ʔanna* "that" or any of their sisters *lākinna* "but," *kaʔanna* "it seems that/as though," *layta* "would that," and *laʕalla* "hope that." The six particles and verbs comprise a small class known as *ʔinna* and its sisters. Sentences (33)–(35) illustrate non-null-subject contexts.[13]

(33)	ʔa-ðˤunn-(u)		ʔanna-**hu**	ʔakala
	1.s-think-(Indic)		that-**he**	ate.3.s.m
	"I think that he ate."			
(34)	ʔana	dʒawʕān-(u)	lākinna-**hā**	ʔakala-t
	I	hungry-(Nom)	but-**she**	ate-3.s.f
	"I am hungry, but she ate."			
(35)	ya-bdū		kaʔanna-**hu**	ya-ʔkul-(u)
	3.s.m-seem		as though-**he**	3.s.m-eat-(Indic)
	"It/he seems as though he is eating."			

Thus, while Arabic can be characterized as a null-subject language, where use of an explicit subject or overt pronoun subject is optional syntactically, there are contexts where optionality of subject use is blocked,, such as occurrence after *ʔinna* and any of its sisters.[14] The present study attempts to mainly investigate null subjects whether or not subjects are dropped in optional syntactic contexts. Non-null-subject use is also discussed (in chapter 6) in the production and instructional input of the participants of the present study.

1.5 Summary

The foregoing account is a basic though sufficiently detailed description of the target forms of the current study, which include

- nominal gender agreement,
- verbal gender agreement,
- tense/aspect, and
- null subjects.

These target morphosyntactic forms are among the most basic and regular features to which Arabic L2 learners are exposed in their first years of learning. Explanation of Arabic root and pattern morphemes and word derivation—quite relevant to the target structures—is also offered in order to underscore the full scope of what is entailed in acquiring and producing the inflectional morphological and syntactic features focused on here. This is important since the findings and conclusions take into account the learning task involved, which is one of the most important L2 learning factors. In subsequent chapters (3–6), the presence and absence of the target structures in the participants' L1s and L2s are also discussed, and analyses are given of the distribution of the target forms and their frequency in the instructional input that the participants received.

Notes

1. Others have claimed that the processes of derivation in Arabic rely on the word as a base form rather than the root (e.g., Ratcliffe 1997, 1998; Benmamoun 1999).

2. Arabic does not exhibit neutral gender.

3. The corresponding feminine suffix in pause form in CA is {*-ah*}. When an additional suffix is added (in both MSA and CA), such as that for case or the dual, a final consonant {*-t*} surfaces, as in *tˤālib-a-t-āni* "two female students." Of course, this does not apply to the masculine form, as in *tˤālib-āni* "two male students."

4. It is to be noted here that *ʔimraʔ-a* and its variant *marʔ-a*, as in *ʔal-marʔ-a* "the woman," in MSA and CA have a corresponding masculine noun *ʔimruʔ/ʔimraʔ/ʔimriʔ* "a man" in CA but is no longer commonly used in MSA, although the variant *ʔal-marʔ* "the man/person" is still used in MSA.

5. Note words ending in {*-āʔ*} such as *māʔ* "water" and *dāʔ* "disease" are masculine because the two segment sounds {*-āʔ*} are part of their triliteral roots and only one consonant would be left of the word if dropped.

6. Note that other equivalent and synonymous terms *kūb* "cup" and *bayt* "house" are treated as masculine. Although no apparent reason for the feminine gender assignment of such nouns can be found, often entities denoting some kind of a source are feminine (e.g., *šams* "sun," *biʔr* "water well," *ʔardˤ* "Earth," etc.).

7. Some body parts do not exhibit a feminine ending, yet they are treated as feminine. The general rule is that a body part that is part of a pair is treated as feminine. For example, *yad* "hand," *qadam* "foot," *sinn* "tooth," and *ʕayn* "eye" all behave as feminine words, since each consists of two identical body parts versus *raʔs* "head," *lisān* "tongue," *ðˤahr* "back," and *batˤn* "abdomen," all of which behave as masculine (see also Barakāt 1988). There are a few exceptions, such as *sāʕid* "forearm" and *xadd* "cheek." What is important here is that body parts (as well as color adjectives) are usually either presented late in the curriculum (for example, Brustad, Al-Batal, and Al-Tonsi 1995, 334, 339) or, if presented earlier in the curriculum, the gender marking and the underlying rule are not presented. For this reason, the gender of body parts (and color adjectives) is not included among the target gender agreement forms.

8. It should be noted that in CA when adjectives belonging to such patterns are used as nouns and when the gender of the referent is not possible to ascertain from context, then the rule is to supply the feminine {*-a*} suffix as in: *raʔaytu ʤarīħ-a* "I saw a wounded female" (Al-Ghalayyīnī 2000, 101).

9. However, it is quite possible for L2 learners of Arabic to produce [t] in pause form as attested in the output production of some of the participants of this study, such as the example (a) below (see also Alhawary 2009a for similar output by other Arabic L2 learners):

(a)	sayyār-at	sˤaɣīr-at
	car-s.f	small-s.f
	"a small car"	

10. It is not the intention here to force a strict tense versus aspect analysis of the Arabic verb. Fassi Fehri argues that a proper characterization of Arabic is one that takes both into account with Arabic exhibiting "a dual tense-aspect" verbal inflectional system (1993, 146). For the purpose of the current study, reference is primarily made to tense, but this should not necessarily preclude an aspectual component.

11. In terms of the full verbal agreement paradigm and in the case of present/imperfective verb forms inflected for plural masculine or plural feminine, agreement features for person, number, and gender are shared by both a prefix and a suffix.

12. Evidently, null-subject use follows pragmatic and discourse rules and use of overt subject pronouns is a marked rather than the default use. This is further discussed in chapter 6 together with the output production of the participants.

13. This is so since the two complementizers and any of their sisters subcategorize for a nominal sentence whose predicate can be a noun, an adjective, or a verb.

14. For other uses of pronominal subjects, see chapter 6.

Chapter 2

Methods

This chapter discusses the main research questions investigated, methods used in the data collection, the participants, the typological constellations or pairings of the participants' L1s with respect to their Arabic L2, the participants' other L2s, and the participants' Arabic L2 proficiency or exposure time that they had during their formal instruction at their home institutions in their own countries. The research questions are formulated with the aim to control for L1 and L2 transfer effects, typological and structural proximity effects, and input exposure effects.

2.1 Research Questions

The present research addresses Arabic L2 grammatical development with two distinct L2 and L1 pairings: Arabic L2 acquisition by Chinese L1 and Russian L1 speakers. To date, such pairings have been woefully underinvestigated despite the significant findings that can be yielded from investigating them. In addition, all participants had previously learned English as an L2. The following questions are examined:

- What types of L2 knowledge and use with respect to the target structure, including nominal gender agreement, verbal agreement, tense/aspect, and null subjects (see chapter 1), do Russian L1 and Chinese L1 learners of Arabic exhibit?
- What is the role of L1 transfer given the two distinct L1 and L2 pairings: an L2 such as Mandarin Chinese with an impoverished morphological system where, for example, verb forms are uniformly uninflected and where nominal gender agreement is not exhibited (typologically unlike Arabic) and an L2 such as Russian with a rich morphological system where verb forms are uniformly inflected and where nominal gender agreement is exhibited (typologically like Arabic)?

- To what extent can input exposure override or minimize the effect of L1 transfer and at what proficiency level?
- Can adult L2 learners of Arabic acquire the same range of syntactic and morphological knowledge as native speakers and to what extent?
- What is the role of L2 transfer (with respect to the target structures) from a language such as English (and other possible L2s) in acquiring Arabic as an L3?
- What developmental paths or tendencies, if any, do such Arabic L2 learners progress when acquiring the target forms?
- What other factors have a bearing on learning Arabic as a foreign language?

Crucial to addressing the above questions is controlling for a number of factors, which include the participants' L1 and L2 language backgrounds, the types of instructional input to which the participants were exposed, and lengths or time settings (e.g., intensive versus nonintensive) in which the participants received their classroom instruction of Arabic. The above questions are addressed in light of recent crosslinguistic influence, usage-based learning, L1 transfer, L2 transfer, and speech processing prerequisites accounts.

2.2 Participants

Twelve groups of Arabic L2 learners at the university level participated in the study in their home institutions in their respective countries in Russia, China, and Taiwan. Table 2.1 displays the demographic data of the participants. The participants belonged to four sets of pairings. One set of Chinese L1 speakers (referred to here as Chinese L1-A) had intensive exposure to Arabic and belong to three groups according to their enrollment in Arabic (1st year, 2nd year, and 3rd year) and were at the time of the study receiving 14 hours of instruction per year. Another set of Chinese L1 speakers (referred to here as Chinese L1-B) had nonintensive exposure to Arabic and belong to three groups according to their year of enrollment in Arabic (1st year, 2nd year, and 3rd year) and were receiving about half as much time in Arabic instruction (6, 8, and 8 hours, respectively) as their Chinese L1-A counterparts. A third set of Russian L1 speakers (referred to here as Russian L1-A) had intensive exposure to Arabic and belong to three groups according to their year of enrollment in Arabic (1st year, 2nd year, and 3rd year) and were at the time of the study receiving 12, 10, and 10 hours of instruction per year, respectively. A fourth set of Russian L1 speakers (referred to here as Russian L1-B) had nonintensive exposure to

Table 2.1 Participants

Groups	*Length of Exposure*	*Credit Hours Enrolled in*	*Males/ Females*	*Age Range*	*Age Means*
Chinese L1-A					
Group1 (n = 10)	Year 1	14	5/5	18–19	18.5
Group2 (n = 10)	Year 2	14	5/5	19–20	19.9
Group3 (n = 10)	Year 3	14	6/4	20–22	20.9
Chinese L1-B					
Group1 (n = 9)	Year 1	6	3/6	18–20	18.55
Group2 (n = 10)	Year 2	8	4/6	18–20	19.5
Group3 (n = 10)	Year 3	8	3/7	20-21	20.3
Russian L1-A					
Group1 (n = 9)	Year 1	12	4/5	17–19	17.77
Group2 (n = 9)	Year 2	10	3/6	18–19	18.44
Group3 (n = 9)	Year 3	10	3/6	19–21	19.55
Russian L1-B					
Group1 (n = 5)	Year 1	6	3/2	17–18	17.6
Group2 (n = 6)	Year 2	6	3/3	18–19	18.5
Group3 (n = 8)	Year 3	4.5	4/4	19–20	19.62

Arabic and belong to three groups according to their year of enrollment in Arabic (1st year, 2nd year, and 3rd year) and were at the time receiving half as much time in Arabic instruction (6, 6, and 4.5 hours of instruction per year, respectively) as their Russian L1-A counterparts.

In other words, the participants essentially make up four sets of groups (two intensive sets and two nonintensive sets) along three different proficiency levels belonging to (1) two different L1s (in order to control for structural and typological effects) and (2) two sets of groups, one set having double (intensive) the amount of L2 exposure than the other (nonintensive) one.[1] The latter is intended to examine the extent to which L1 effect can be overridden or minimized by controlling for the amount of (Arabic) L2 input exposure.

To control for any earlier (Arabic) exposure effects, the participants had no background in Arabic prior to their enrollment in Arabic courses in their home institutions and were not heritage speakers. In other words, all participants had zero exposure to Arabic prior to joining their academic institution. In addition, none of the participants in Group 1 of all four sets had made any trip to an Arabic-speaking country. Neither had any of the Chinese L1-A and Chinese L1-B Groups 2 and 3 except for two participants (one in Chinese L1-A Group 3 and another in Chinese L1-B Group 3), who had done so for one week. Similarly, Russian participants in Groups 2 and 3 (of both sets) had not made trips to Arabic-speaking countries with a significant stay or study beyond one to two weeks except for one Russian L1-A participant in Group 3 who had studied Arabic in Egypt for one month, one in Russian L1-B in Group 2 who had studied for one month in Syria, three in Russian L1-B in Group 3 who had made two separate trips to Egypt and studied Arabic for a month in each, and a fourth in the last group who studied in Egypt for three weeks.[2] At the time of the study, participants were in the middle of their school year.

In addition, and in order to establish a baseline against which the production of null subjects (one of the target structures) can be measured, a group of native speakers of Arabic were invited (in a previous study) to participate as a control group. The control group consists of six native educated speakers of Arabic. The demographic information for the control participants is displayed in table 2.2. The native speakers were from different Arab countries (including Egypt, Jordan, Palestine, Syria, and Tunisia) with a mean age of thirty-two. They were all graduate students pursuing different graduate programs at a university in the United States.

Table 2.2 Control participants

Controls Arabic L1	*Country of Origin*	*Graduate Major*	*Gender*	*Ages*
1	Egypt	Geology	M	32
2	Jordan	Industrial engineering	M	33
3	Palestine	Education	M	37
4	Palestine	Mathematics	M	33
5	Syria	Biochemistry	M	32
6	Tunisia	Computer engineering	M	25

2.3 Typological Pairings: Participants' L1s and L2s

To control for L1 and L2 transfer effects, language background biographical data were collected from participants through a short survey and a follow-up interview to clarify supplied information in the completed form (see appendix A for the survey form that was used). Table 2.3 lists the self-reported proficiency levels after averaging out their rankings of the four language skills (speaking, listening, reading, and writing). As table 2.3 shows, all participants reported knowledge of English as an L2, with the vast majority of self-reported proficiency ranging from "fair" to "good," except for one participant (in the Russian L1-A Group 1), who reported "weak" knowledge, and ten participants

Table 2.3 Participants' L1s and L2s

	Other L1s	*L2*	*L2*	*L2*	*L2*
Chinese L1-A Mandarin					
Group1 (n = 10)	—	10 = English 5 = G; 5 = F	—	—	—
Group2 (n = 10)	—	10 = English 6 = G; 4 = F	1 = Japanese 1 = F	—	—
Group3 (n = 10)	1 = C	10 = English 4 = G; 6 = F	—	—	—
Chinese L1-B Mandarin					
Group1 (n = 9)	3 = C	9 = English 4 = G; 5 = F	—	—	—
Group2 (n = 10)	1 = C 8 = T	10 = English 7 = G; 3 = F	1 = German 1 = F	1 = Spanish 1 = F	2 = Japanese 2 = F
Group3 (n = 10)	6 = T	10 = English 6 = G; 3 = F; 1 = N	1 = Polish 1 = F	1 = Korean 1 = F	1 = Japanese 1 = F
Russian L1-A					
Group1 (n = 9)	—	9 = English 6 = N; 2 = G; 1 = W	2 = French[a] 2 = F	1 = Spanish[a] 1 = F	1 = Hindi 1 = G
Group2 (n = 9)	—	9 = English 5 = N; 4 = G	2 = French[a] 2 = F	3 = German[a] 2 = G; 1 = F	1 = Spanish 1 = G
Group3 (n = 9)	—	9 = English 3 = N; 5 = G; 1 = F	2 = French[a] 1 = G; 1 = F	2 = German[a] 1 = G; 1 = F	1 = Spanish 1 = G
Russian L1-B					
Group1 (n = 5)	—	5 = English 4 = G; 1 = F	2 = French 1 = N; 1 = F	—	—
Group2 (n = 6)	1 = D	6 = English 3 = G; 3 = F	—	—	—
Group3 (n = 8)	—	8 = English 6 = G; 1 = N; 1 = F	3 = French 1 = G; 2 = F	—	—

[a] One participant reported more than one L2.
C = Cantonese; T = Taiwanese; D = Daghestani. N = Near-native; G = Good; F = Fair; W = Weak.

(in the Russian L1-A Groups 1-2 and Russian L1-B Group 3) reported as "near native." Based on the language background survey and follow-up interview, participants rated their proficiency in English consistently higher than that of Arabic, indicating that, for almost all participants, English was a stronger/earlier L2 and Arabic was an L3.[3]

Whereas the Russian language is known to exhibit a rich morphological system (where, for example, verb forms are uniformly inflected and where nominal gender agreement is exhibited) like Arabic, Mandarin Chinese has an impoverished morphological system (where, for example, verb forms are uniformly uninflected and where nominal gender agreement is not exhibited) unlike Arabic. Accordingly, together with the input setting, the general typological pairings in (1)–(4) are yielded.[4]

(1) Chinese Mandarin L1 participants who are speakers of a language with a [-rich] morphological system, receiving input in a [+intensive] setting in L2/L3 Arabic [+rich], and with previous knowledge of L2 English [±rich].[5]
(2) Chinese Mandarin L1 participants who are speakers of a language with a [-rich] morphological system, receiving input in a [-intensive] setting in L2/L3 Arabic [+rich], and with previous knowledge of L2 English [±rich].
(3) Russian L1 participants who are speakers of a language with a [+rich] morphological system, receiving input in a [+intensive] setting in L2/L3 Arabic [+rich], and with previous knowledge of L2 English [±rich].
(4) Russian L1 participants who are speakers of a language with a [+rich] morphological system, receiving input in a [-intensive] setting in L2/L3 Arabic [+rich], and with previous knowledge of L2 English [±rich].

Additionally, the four languages (Chinese, Russian, Arabic, and English) converge and diverge on two of the target structures. All four languages share structural proximity by exhibiting a distinction between past versus present tense. However, the four languages diverge in different respects on null-subject use. Whereas Arabic and Chinese exhibit null subjects, English disallows null subjects, and Russian seems to exhibit a "mixed" null-subject system (Franks 1995; see also Lakshmanan 1994; Ayoun 2003).

In addition to the typological pairings mentioned above, some of the Chinese participants also reported being bilingual native speakers of Mandarin and Cantonese, and others reported being bilinguals of Mandarin and Taiwanese. However, both Cantonese and Taiwanese exhibit similar morphological systems (and target structures) to that of Mandarin. As for the Russian participants, only one reported to be a bilingual of Russian and Daghestani.[6]

In addition, as table 2.3 shows, participants reported knowledge (beyond a mere little or weak knowledge) of other L2s—with the Chinese participants reporting fewer L2s than their Russian counterparts. One Chinese L1-A participant (Group 2) reported knowledge of another L2 (Japanese), three Chinese

L1-B participants (Groups 2 and 3) reported knowledge of one additional L2 (German, Spanish, or Polish), three reported knowledge of Japanese L2, and one reported knowledge of Korean. Apart from Japanese and Korean, which exhibit a similar (uniformly impoverished) morphological system (and target structures) to that of Mandarin, this means that only three participants of all the Chinese participants (all of whom are in the Chinese L1-B Groups 2 and 3) reported knowledge of an L2 (German, Polish, or Spanish), which exhibits a rich morphological system that differs from both their L1 and English L2 but is similar to their Arabic L2, although whereas Polish and Spanish allow null subjects, German, like English, does not (see also Lakshmanan 1994). L2 effects of these L2s on the participants' performance are examined and further discussed in chapter 7.

As for the Russian L1 groups, twelve Russian L1-A participants reported L2 knowledge of additional languages: three in Group 1 (one reported knowledge of French, one of Hindi, and one of both French and Spanish), five in Group 2 (one of French, one of Spanish, two of German, and one of both French and German), and four in Group 3 (one of French, one of Spanish, one of German, and one of both French and German). Five of the Russian L1-B participants reported L2 knowledge of French L2: two in Group 1 and three in Group 3. Accordingly, this means that, of all Russian participants, a total of eight had knowledge of an L2 (French) similar to their L1 and Arabic L2 (in exhibiting nominal gender agreement), similar to their other English L2 in not allowing null subjects, and partly similar to their other English L2 in exhibiting a mixed verbal paradigm; a total of six had knowledge of an L2 (Hindi, German, or Spanish) similar to their L1 and Arabic L2 but dissimilar to their other English L2 in exhibiting a uniformly rich verbal paradigm (although only German, similarly to English, does not allow null subjects); and a total of three had knowledge of two different languages (two of French and Spanish and one of French and German) with opposite (i.e., mixed versus uniformly rich) verbal paradigmatic features, although only Spanish in such pairings allows null subjects. Of all the above participants who reported L2 knowledge of languages other than English, all rated their proficiency in English higher than other L2s, except for three participants who reported similar proficiency ratings (one in the Russian L1-A Group 3 with L2 Spanish and L2 English, one in each of the Russian L1-B Group 1 and Group 3 with L2 French and L2 English). Accordingly, for almost all participants English L2 was a stronger/earlier L2 and other languages were L3s similar to Arabic. Effects of these L2s (or L3s) on the participants' performance are examined and further discussed in chapter 7.

2.4 Instructional Input of the Participants

Expectedly, the participants used different textbooks and instructional materials in their respective home institutions and countries. The Chinese L1-A participants relied on *al-Jadīd fī al-Lugha al-'Arabiyya* textbook series (Guo and Zhou 2002; Guo and Jiang 2002; Guo et al. 2004; Guo et al. 2006) and covered the entire first volume (Guo and Zhou 2002) in the first year of instruction. The Chinese L1-B participants used four booklets—two for teaching the Arabic script (*al-Kitāba al-'Arabiyya* and *Kurrāsat Tadrībāt al-Khaṭṭ*) and two for reading (*Kitāb al-Qirā'a* and *Mudhakkira 'Iḍāfiyya li-l-Mustawā al-'Awwal*)—developed by the Commissioned Saudi Teaching Delegates, in addition to half of the first volume of *al-'Arbiyya bayna Yadayk* series (Al-Fawzān, Hussein, and Faḍl 2003). The Russian L1-A participants used Khanna (2006), Franka (2007), and Jushmanov (1999) as main texts for the first year. As for the Russian L1-B participants, they used a series of two volumes by Semyonova and Lukyanova (2004) and Semyonova and colleagues (2005).[7] Subsequent chapters provide detailed analyses of the frequency of the target structures in the instructional materials of all four sets of groups of participants in their first year of their formal instruction. The textbooks used are similar in that they focus on the development of the four language skills (speaking, listening, reading, and writing) as well as on all grammatical forms (of MSA) from early on.[8]

2.5 Data Collection

Participants attended one-on-one interview sessions (about thirty to forty-five minutes each) with a total of about eighty hours of audio recording. Data collection during the interview aimed at eliciting spontaneous production data of the target forms in order to attempt to tap the participants' actual L2 knowledge of Arabic rather than their conscious or metalinguistic knowledge of the rules through conscious tasks or through tasks that would allow participants to invoke consciously learned rules or their metalinguistic awareness of rule application. The techniques elicited obligatory contexts of the target structures. Elicitation techniques were of two types: purely picture-based (picture description, picture differences, and picture sequences) and narrative-based tasks. Each task included random distractor items and the tasks themselves were arranged as distractors for each other so that the elicitation materials did not prompt participants to think of any of the target forms, including agreement or tense.

In addition, caution was taken against affecting any gender bias or stereotypes through elicitation materials or prompting the participants to know any

Figure 2.1 A Sample Picture Description Task

of the target forms, as explained above. For tasks designed to elicit, for example, tokens such as "Arab woman," "Arab man," stereotypical pictures such as "tall man" and "short woman," etc. were avoided. For the purely picture-based tasks, the participants were simply asked to describe each picture presented in as many words as they could. Samples of picture-based elicitation tasks appear in figure 2.1.

As for the narrative tasks, a total of four tasks were used: two in the past tense and two in the present tense divided equally between a female and a male character. The narratives in the past tense were each about a female character and a male character. Participants were requested to narrate day by day the vacation activities (on a calendar) carried out by each character during his or her vacation (which each character took the previous month for a period of ten days). As a distracter, the participants were asked to figure out and to comment on whether or not the male and female characters were compatible based on what they did during their vacations. The two narratives in the present tense were also about a female and a male character. The participants were requested to describe the daily activities of each of the characters at different times of the day. As a distracter, the participants were asked to figure out where the

Figure 2.2 A sample (past tense) narrative elicitation task with a male character. The vacation went from the 17th to the 26th of last month. Adapted from *Going Places*, Burton and Maharg 1995, 141, 159.

character was from based on his/her routine activities. The two sets of narratives (past versus present) were not presented sequentially. Rather, the past set was presented toward the middle of the interview and the present toward the end, with tasks of other (target and nontarget) structures used in the beginning of the first and second halves of the interview, serving as additional distracters. Sample narrative elicitation tasks appear in figures 2.2 and 2.3.

The materials were piloted and used in earlier studies (see Alhawary 2009a). The elicitation tasks were held constant and were consistently used across all

Figure 2.3 A sample (past tense) narrative task with a female character. The vacation went from the 17th to the 26th of last month. Adapted from *Going Places*, Burton and Maharg 1995, 141, 159.

the participants. All interviews were audio-recorded. The data were transcribed and coded using the MAXQDA software program for data analysis (MAXQDA 2010). Each data sample was at least triple-checked for accuracy after each step. To preserve the data from contamination from elicitation errors, the elicitation statements were used consistently across participants, kept general and short, and at times even given in English or the participant's native language to ensure participants understood the tasks. Certain tokens were not coded. These were hesitations and self-corrections except the last attempt in each case. In coding verbal agreement tokens, agreement was determined by considering the verbal form and whether it was inflected properly, not by identifying first the subject and then the verb it agreed with. This is crucial since the verb may agree with a discourse referent subject and the participants may be mindlessly producing the wrong subject, especially when the subjects used are the pronouns *hiya* "she" and *huwa* "he," which are close in their pronunciation (see also Poeppel and Wexler 1993; Prévost and White 2000; cf. Meisel 1991).

2.6 Summary

The different methodological aspects of the present study take into account effects related to L1 transfer, L2 transfer, prior exposure to Arabic as an L2 as well as other L2s, quantity of input of the instructional materials, and duration or intensity of input exposure. The primary aim is to control for all potential variables that may have a bearing on L1 transfer, intensifying it, or mitigating it and insofar as the findings are applicable to Chinese L1 as well as Russian L1 speakers learning Arabic as an L2/L3 who also had had exposure to English as an L2. Data relevant to those individual participants who reported knowledge of other L2s are further discussed (in chapter 7) together with the data findings of the target structures in subsequent chapters (3–6). Taken together, the typological pairings as well as the structural proximity and dissimilarities between the four languages (Chinese, Russian, Arabic, and English) provide ideal testing grounds for investigating input exposure effects, L1 and L2 transfer effects, and typological and structural proximity effects.

Notes

1. Proficiency levels, the terms for which are used somewhat loosely here, correspond to beginner, intermediate, and advanced and are based on the number of years of study (first through third year), reflecting the accumulated years of study and exposure to Arabic L2. Although there was no independent measure for proficiency, based on the elicitation interviews (thirty to forty-five minutes), participants in their different years of enrollment did signal noticeable differences in L2 development (e.g., in terms of quantity, quality, and speed of their output production). In addition, the terms "beginner," "intermediate," and "advanced" were also designated to the years of study (first through third year) by the home institutions of the participants. Notwithstanding the lack of a proficiency measure here, use of general proficiency tests would have limited value, since such tests do not necessarily test the participants' knowledge of the target forms.

2. In other words, none of the participants had any exposure to Arabic prior to joining their Arabic program nor had any additional significant exposure during their program of study.

3. In addition, the educational systems to which the participants belong (i.e., China, Russia, and Taiwan) normally provide English-language instruction to students before college, whereas for a language like Arabic, the only such opportunity is provided at the college level.

4. More specific feature-based pairings are provided in subsequent chapters 3–6.

5. English is analyzed as a language with a nonuniformly, impoverished morphological system since, among other things, it exhibits a "mixed" verbal paradigm, hence the notation [±] representing its mixed system (e.g., Lakshmanan 1994).

6. Daghestani languages (such as Lezgian) do not exhibit nominal gender agreement (although they exhibit number agreement like English), verbal gender agreement (although the verb is inflected for case), a tense distinction, or null subjects (Ramazan Mamedshahov, personal communication). Importantly here, the performance of the bilingual Russian and Daghestani participant was within range on all target structures except that he dropped slightly (and insignificantly) more subjects (in his use of null subjects) than other participants within his group.

7. For subsequent years (i.e., year 2 and beyond), the Chinese L1-A participants continue to use the rest of the volumes (2–4) of *al-Jadīd fī al-Lugha al-ʿArabiyya* series (Guo and Jiang 2002; Guo et al. 2004; Guo et al. 2006) for the remainder of the (four-year) program with a volume in each year, respectively. The Chinese L1-B participants complete the second half of the first volume of *al-ʿArbiyya bayna Yadayk* series (Al-Fawzān et al. 2003) as well as half of the second volume in their second year. They cover the rest of the second volume of Al-Fawzān's series in the third year and use additionally *al-Qawāʿid al-ʿArabiyya al-Muyassara* (Sīnī, Al-Sayyid, and Al-Shaykh 1990), the dialogues in *al-Jadīd fī al-Lugha al-ʿArabiyya*, vol. 3 (Guo et al. 2004), and authentic supplementary materials. The Russian L1-A participants use authentic materials, depending on the subject matter and supplementary readings, as well as optional references such as Chernov (1995) in addition to Jushmanov (1999), which is also used during the entire (six-year) program. The Russian L1-B participants use a special series of two volumes by Semyonova and Lukyanova (2003) in their second year and two different texts in their third year, one on literary texts by Semyonova and Lukyanova (2008) and another on media Arabic by Maiburov (2010), in addition to supplementary materials on Arabic grammar.

8. Analysis of the instructional input of subsequent years is not provided. Given the high-frequency and basic nature of the target forms and judging from the contents of the actual instructional materials used in those years, the presence of the target structures is prevalent in the lessons, drills, and activities throughout. It is deemed necessary here to provide input analysis for the first year in order to examine, among other things, whether or not input in the first year differ significantly across groups and to determine their presence and distribution since such information is directly relevant to the participants' early outset of L2 exposure and L1 and L2 transfer.

Chapter 3

The Acquisition of Nominal Gender Agreement

This chapter discusses the acquisition of nominal gender agreement based on the collected cross-sectional data from all of the Chinese L1 and Russian L1 groups. As discussed in chapter 1, the target structures focused on here include gender agreement between the head noun and attributive adjective within the noun phrase, as in (9)–(16) in chapter 1 restated below as (1)–(4), and gender agreement involving a subject demonstrative pronoun and a predicate noun within the equational/verbless sentence, as in (17)–(20) in chapter 1 restated below as (5)–(8).

(1)	tˤālib	ʤadīd
	student.s.m	new.s.m
	"a new male student"	
(2)	tˤālib-a	ʤadīd-a
	student-s.f	new-s.f
	"a new female student"	
(3)	qalam	ʤadīd
	pen.s.m	new.s.m
	"a new pen"	
(4)	sayyār-a	ʤadīd-a
	car-s.f	new-s.f
	"a new car"	
(5)	hāðā	tˤālib
	this.s.m	student.s.m
	"This is a male student."	
(6)	hāðihi	tˤālib-a
	this.s.f	student-s.f
	"This is a female student."	
(7)	hāðā	qalam
	this.s.m	pen.s.m
	"This is a pen."	

(8) hāðihi sayyār-a
this.s.f car-s.f
"This is a car."

As explained in chapter 1, investigation of the above target forms has been carried out irrespective of the participants' production of case and definiteness. In other words, gender agreement features are the focus alone and regardless as to whether the participants produced case and definiteness appropriately, avoided producing them partially or wholly, or did not produce them at all.

3.1 Typological Pairings

With respect to gender agreement within the NP, two opposite typological pairings are yielded based on the participants' L1s. On one hand, like Arabic underlyingly, Russian exhibits gender agreement (between the head noun and attributive adjective); in addition to the distinction it makes between masculine and feminine in the singular, it exhibits a neuter feature, as in (9)–(13).

(9) nov-yi studyent
new-s.m student.s.m
"a new male student"

(10) nov-əya studyent-kə
new-s.f student-s.f
"a new female student"

(11) nov-əya ruč-kə
new-s.f pen-s.f
"a new pen"

(12) nov-əya məšin-ə
new-s.f car-s.f
"a new car"

(13) nov-əye əkn-o
new-s.neuter window-s.neuter
"a new window"

The surface gender correspondence between Arabic and Russian is not one-to-one since individual words are annotated differently in the two languages, as in (11)–(13) and (3)–(4), where the word for "pen" in Arabic is masculine but feminine in Russian, the word for "car" is feminine in both, and the word for "window" is neuter in Russian but feminine (as in *nāfiða*) or masculine (as in *šubbāk*) in Arabic. However, the underlying abstract gender agreement features are similar (i.e., with both exhibiting a gender feature) although Russian additionally exhibits the neuter feature. On the other hand, Chinese, unlike Arabic, does not exhibit nominal gender agreement (between the head noun and attributive adjective) as illustrated in (14)–(17) where, for example, the adjective for "new" in Chinese is not inflected for gender.[1]

(14)	yi ge	xin de	nan	xue	sheng
	one Q.	new	male	study	apprentice
	"a new male student"				
(15)	yi ge	xin de	nu	xue	sheng
	one Q.	new	female	study	apprentice
	"a new female student"				
(16)	yi zhi	xin de	qian bi		
	one Q.	new	lead pen		
	"a new pencil"				
(17)	yi tai	xin de	che		
	one Q.	new	car		
	"a new car"				

Accordingly, the typological pairings (a) and (b) are yielded.

(a) Russian participants who are speakers of a [+gender] and [+strong] L1, learning L2 Arabic [+gender] and [+strong], with previous knowledge of L2 English [-gender] and [-strong]

(b) Chinese participants who are speakers of a [-gender] and [-strong] L1, learning L2 Arabic [+gender] and [+ strong], with previous knowledge of L2 English [-gender] and [-strong][2]

However, a different set of pairings is yielded for gender agreement involving a demonstrative pronoun and a predicate noun where, unlike Arabic, neither Russian nor Chinese exhibits distinct demonstrative pronouns for singular masculine versus singular feminine. This is illustrated for Russian in sentences (18)–(22) and for Chinese in sentences (23)–(26).

(18)	etə	studyent
	this	student.s.m
	"This is a male student."	

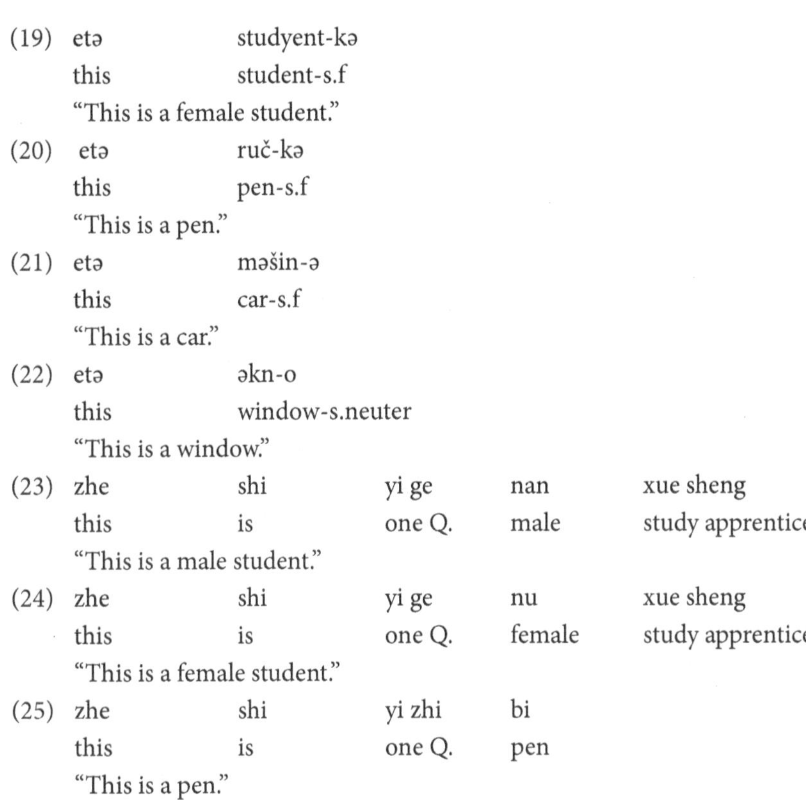

(19)	etə	studyent-kə			
	this	student-s.f			
	"This is a female student."				
(20)	etə	ruč-kə			
	this	pen-s.f			
	"This is a pen."				
(21)	etə	məšin-ə			
	this	car-s.f			
	"This is a car."				
(22)	etə	əkn-o			
	this	window-s.neuter			
	"This is a window."				
(23)	zhe	shi	yi ge	nan	xue sheng
	this	is	one Q.	male	study apprentice
	"This is a male student."				
(24)	zhe	shi	yi ge	nu	xue sheng
	this	is	one Q.	female	study apprentice
	"This is a female student."				
(25)	zhe	shi	yi zhi	bi	
	this	is	one Q.	pen	
	"This is a pen."				
(26)	zhe	shi	yi tai	liang che	
	this	is	one Q.	car	
	"This is a car."				

Accordingly, the typological/structural pairings (c) and (d) are yielded.

(c) Russian participants who are speakers of a [-gender] and [-strong] L1, learning L2 Arabic [+gender] and [+strong], with previous knowledge of L2 English [-gender] and [-strong]

(d) Chinese participants who are speakers of a [-gender] and [-strong] L1, learning L2 Arabic [+gender] and [+strong], with previous knowledge of L2 English [-gender] and [-strong]

The surface form of the demonstrative pronoun "this" is the same for singular feminine and masculine in both Russian and Chinese. This means that, with respect to nominal gender agreement involving demonstratives, Russian and

Chinese (as well as English) are structurally similar to one another, on one hand, and are all dissimilar to Arabic, on the other.

3.2 Previous Findings

Previous findings on similar target forms (in particular, nominal gender agreement within the NP between a head noun and an attributive adjective and nominal sentential agreement between a demonstrative pronoun and a predicate noun/adjective by Arabic L2 learners who are speakers of English, French, and Japanese as L1s) reveal:

- L2 learners of Arabic across groups exhibited higher accuracy on masculine gender than feminine gender agreement within nominal agreement constructions, due likely to use of the singular masculine as the default form by participants across groups (Alhawary 2009a, 95–100; see also Alhawary 2009b, 382–83; for a similar finding of use of the masculine as the default form in Spanish L2, see White et al. 2004).
- English L1 and Japanese L1 learners of Arabic significantly undersupplied the productive feminine suffix {*-a*} more so than their French L1 counterparts, even though feminine head nouns produced by the participants were almost all inflected for the correct feminine suffix and yet participants failed to inflect the adjective similarly for the feminine gender feature (Alhawary 2009a, 95–100).
- English L1 learners of Arabic (in particular the beginner and advanced groups, corresponding to Groups 1 and 3, respectively) exhibited far more errors in feminine demonstrative agreement than their French L1 and Japanese L1 counterparts.
- French L1 and Japanese L1 learners of Arabic performed comparably on demonstrative agreement (including feminine demonstrative agreement), but both significantly outperformed their English counterparts on the same target form.
- The above findings were yielded when, in particular, the French L1 (and English L1 groups) had half as much input exposure as their Japanese L1 counterparts; hence, the performance of the Japanese participants on (feminine) demonstrative agreement offers a preliminary finding that input may play a role in mitigating or reducing L1 transfer effects (Alhawary 2009a, 95–98; see also Alhawary 2009b, 382–83).

Since English and Japanese do not exhibit a distinction in nominal gender agreement whereas French does, in particular with respect to agreement between the head noun and attributive adjective within Arabic NPs, it has been argued that the findings provide strong evidence of L1 transfer.

In addition, Nielsen (1997) reported a similar finding based on production data from two Danish L1 learners of Arabic where neither of the two participants exhibited emergence of demonstrative gender agreement during the entire fifteen-month period of the longitudinal observation. This finding is also significant since Danish (like English and Japanese) does not display a distinction in demonstrative pronoun use between singular masculine and singular feminine.

Finally, relevant to the present investigation is Al-Hamad's (2003) study, which reported on a cross-sectional study of intermediate and advanced groups of Chinese L1 and Russian L1 learners of Arabic as an L2. The study investigated the production of a set of morphosyntactic structures including noun–adjective agreement in gender and number.[3] Although the study analyzed gender for both the singular and plural collapsed together, the findings are relevant for the present study. The findings reported high rates of accurate suppliance of gender markings on nouns across groups. As for suppliance of gender markings on adjectives, both Russian groups achieved higher accuracy than their Chinese counterparts (Al-Hamad 2003, 85, 89). These findings are in accordance with the conclusion of previous studies in support of L1 transfer and are relevant to the current investigation.[4]

In other words, the preponderance of evidence thus far indicates that absence or presence of a feature in L1 seems to play a role in L2 grammatical development (Alhawary 2009a, 156, 153 ff.). The typological constellations of the present study—with participants who are Russian L1 and Chinese L1 speakers—is significant to further verify the conclusion reached above (i.e., absence or presence of a feature in L1 plays a role in L2 acquisition). Furthermore, the different groups and their exposure settings (i.e., with two sets of groups receiving double the amount of instruction than their two counterpart sets) is significant to examine the extent of such a role and whether it can be overridden or minimized by input frequency.

3.3 Results

3.3.1 Results of Nominal (Noun-Adjective) Gender Agreement

The majority of nominal agreement tokens that the participants produced comprise NPs (i.e., consisting of a head noun modified by an attributive adjective) such as those in (1)–(4) above. In addition, the participants produced a small number of tokens where a noun occurs as a subject followed by an adjective predicate within nominal/verbless constructions such as (27)–(30).

(27)	IL:	ʔal-marʔ-a	mabsūtˤ-a	
		the-person-s.f	happy-s.f	
	TL:	ʔal-marʔ-a	mabsūtˤ-a	
		the-person-s.f	happy-s.f	
		"The woman is happy."		
		(Chinese L1-A: Group 3)		
(28)	IL:	*lākin	ʔal-bint-u	ʔasˤsˤaɣīr
		but	the-girl-Nom	the-small.s.m
	TL:	lākin	ʔal-bint-u	ˤsaɣīr-a
		but	the-girl-Nom	small-s.f
		"But the girl is young."		
		(Chinese L1-A: Group 3)[5]		
(29)	IL:	*ʔal-marʔ-a	waʜīd	
		the-person-s.f	lonely.s.m	
	IL:	ʔal-marʔ-a	waʜīd-a	
		the-person-s.f	lonely-s.f	
		"The woman is lonely."		
		(Chinese L1-A: Group 2)		
(30)	IL:	wa-tˤtˤaqs	barīd	
		and-the-weather.s.m	cold.s.m	
	IL:	wa-tˤ-tˤaqs	bārid	
		and-the-weather.s.m	cold.s.m	
		"And the weather is cold."		
		(Russian L1-A: Group 2)		

These tokens have a similar gender agreement distribution and were collapsed with the nominal agreement tokens within NPs to allow for better effects for sample size of the data for running statistical tests.

The data for nominal gender agreement—mainly singular feminine and singular masculine agreement—yielded three main findings (table 3.1 provides a snapshot of the data; see also figure 3.1). First, the participants of Group 1 of all L1 backgrounds, except for the Chinese L1-A group, seem to have used the singular masculine as the default form as evident in their high accuracy levels on masculine agreement and low accuracy on feminine agreement, especially in the latter, where the low accuracy levels are due to nonsuppliance of the

Table 3.1 Production of nominal (noun–adjective) gender agreement

L2 Arabic	*N-A Feminine Agreement Correct/Total*	*% Correct*	*N-A Masculine Agreement Correct/Total*	*% Correct*
Chinese L1-A				
Group1 (n = 10)	160/189	85	91/108	84
Group2 (n = 10)	312/379	82	176/228	77
Group3 (n = 10)	273/348	78	244/290	84
Chinese L1-B				
Group1 (n = 9)	19/87	22	60/68	88
Group2 (n = 10)	160/212	75	108/144	75
Group3 (n = 10)	245/319	77	190/233	82
Russian L1-A				
Group1 (n = 9)	106/174	61	146/150	97
Group2 (n = 9)	159/178	89	106/126	84
Group3 (n = 9)	175/189	93	105/116	91
Russian L1-B				
Group1 (n = 5)	25/88	28	34/40	85
Group2 (n = 6)	102/131	78	67/99	68
Group3 (n = 8)	127/157	81	100/120	83

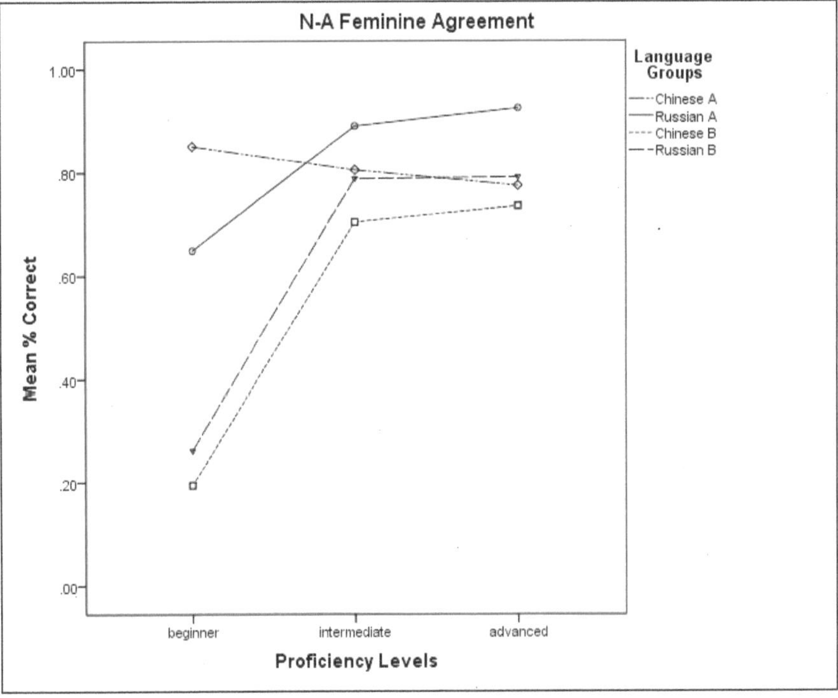

Figure 3.1 Interaction Plot of Mean % Correct for the Participants' Performance on N-A Feminine Agreement by Language Group and Proficiency Level

feminine suffix on adjectives following feminine nouns.[6] Second, the performance on feminine agreement of all except the Chinese L1-A groups seem to have improved over time. Although participants in the Chinese L1-A Group 1 exhibited a high accuracy rate of rule application (i.e., in terms of correct supplance of the feminine suffix) at 85%, Groups 2 and 3 backslid slightly with their 82% and 78%, respectively. Third, participants in Group 1 of both the Russian L1-A and Chinese L1-A outperformed their Russian L1-B and Chinese L1-B counterparts on feminine agreement, and whereas participants in the Chinese L1-A Group 1 had a higher accuracy rate (85%) of correct rule application than their Russian counterparts (61%), the reverse is true for Groups 2–3 where participants in the Russian L1-A groups had a higher rate (89% and 93%) than their Chinese counterparts (82% and 78%).

A full factorial two-way ANOVA showed the following findings: a main effect for L1 backgrounds on feminine agreement ($F(3, 93) = 14.709$, $p < 0.001$, partial $\eta^2 = 0.322$), a main effect for proficiency on feminine agreement ($F(2,93) = 28.894$, $p < 0.001$, partial $\eta^2 = 0.383$), and a main interaction effect between L1 backgrounds and proficiency on feminine agreement ($F(6,93) = 6.407$, $p < 0.001$, partial $\eta^2 = 0.292$). Post hoc analyses using Tukey tests of all possible pairwise comparisons revealed that the Chinese L1-A groups differed significantly overall from their Chinese L1-B ($p < 0.001$) and Russian L1-B ($p = 0.027$) counterparts; so did the Russian L1-A groups from their Chinese L1-B ($p < 0.001$) and Russian L1-B ($p = 0.019$) counterparts. In particular, the difference is mainly due to performance of the beginner groups, with the Chinese L1-A Group 1 differing significantly from its Chinese L1-B and Russian L1-B ($p < 0.001$) counterparts and the Russian L1-A Group 1 differing significantly from its Chinese L1-B ($p < 0.001$) and Russian L1-B ($p = 0.021$) counterparts. As for the Chinese L1-A and Russian L1-A groups, they did not differ significantly from each other. With respect to proficiency within each individual language, post hoc analyses using Tukey tests revealed that the Chinese L1-B Groups 1and 2 and Groups 1 and 3 differed significantly ($p < 0.001$) and the Russian L1-B Groups 1 and 2 and Groups 1 and 3 differed significantly ($p = 0.001$ and $p < 0.001$, respectively). Post hoc analyses within groups also revealed that the Russian L1-A Groups 1 and 2 differed significantly ($p = 0.035$) as did Groups 1 and 3 ($p = 0.015$), but none of the Chinese L1-A groups did (see also figure 3.1).[7]

In other words, although the participants in the Chinese L1-A and Russian L1-A beginner groups outperformed their Chinese L1-B and Russian L1-B counterparts, there was no statistical difference between the performance of the participants in the Chinese L1-A and that of the participants in the Russian L1-A Groups 1–3 (or beginner through advanced, respectively). However, the Russian L1-A Groups 2 and 3 maintained an advantage (though not statistically significant) over their Chinese L1-A counterparts in both feminine and masculine agreement; so did the Russian L1-B Groups 1–3, with a slighter advantage, over their Chinese L1-B counterparts as well as the Chinese L1-A Group 3 in feminine agreement (table 3.1). In addition, the performance of all L1 groups improved significantly over time except that of the Chinese L1-A groups. In fact, rather than exhibiting improvement over time, the performance of the participants in the Chinese L1-A Groups 1–3 showed a somewhat steady decline (especially between Groups 1 and 2) as shown in table 3.1 and figure 3.1.

3.3.1.1 Results of Natural versus Grammatical Gender Agreement

The data of nominal (noun–adjective) gender agreement were further analyzed to determine if there was a difference in the participants' performance on correct natural/biological versus grammatical gender agreement markings since Arabic exhibits both types of gender, as discussed in chapter 1 (section 1.2). Tables 3.2 and 3.3 provide snapshots of the data (see also figure 3.2). The findings of the participants' performance on nominal gender (singular masculine and singular feminine) overall seem to reflect their production of grammatical and natural gender agreement, but more so in grammatical than natural agreement.

A full factorial two-way ANOVA showed the following findings with respect to natural gender (noun–adjective) agreement: a main effect for L1 backgrounds on natural feminine agreement ($F(3, 86) = 5.440$, $p = 0.002$, partial $\eta^2 = 0.159$), a main effect for proficiency on natural feminine agreement ($F(2,86) = 22.735$, $p < 0.001$, partial $\eta^2 = 0.346$), and a main interaction effect between L1 backgrounds and proficiency on natural feminine agreement ($F(6,86) = 2.740$, $p = 0.017$, partial $\eta^2 = 0.160$). Post hoc analyses using Tukey tests revealed that the Chinese L1-A Group 1 differed significantly from its Chinese L1-B ($p = 0.002$) and Russian L1-B ($p = 0.004$) counterparts, but the Chinese L1-A Group 1 and the Russian L1-A Group 1 did not differ significantly from each other.[8] With respect to proficiency within each individual language, post hoc analyses using Tukey tests revealed that the Chinese L1-B Groups 1 and 2 and Groups 1 and 3 differed significantly ($p = 0.003$), that the Russian L1-B Groups 1 and 2 differed significantly ($p = 0.013$) and Groups 1 and 3 differed significantly ($p = 0.002$), that the Russian L1-A Groups 1 and 2 differed significantly ($p =$

0.040), as did (though marginally so) Groups 1 and 3 ($p = 0.085$), but none of the Chinese L1-A groups did.[9]

Similarly, a full factorial two-way ANOVA showed the following findings with respect to grammatical gender (noun–adjective) agreement: a main effect for L1 backgrounds on grammatical feminine agreement ($F(3, 93) = 14.041$, $p < 0.001$, partial $\eta^2 = 0.312$), a main effect for proficiency on grammatical feminine agreement ($F(2,93) = 22.142$, $p < 0.001$, partial $\eta^2 = 0.323$), and a main interaction effect between L1 backgrounds and proficiency on grammatical feminine agreement ($F(6,93) = 5.842$, $p < 0.001$, partial $\eta^2 = 0.274$). Post hoc analyses using Tukey tests revealed that the Chinese L1-A Group 1 differed significantly from the Chinese L1-B and Russian L1-B counterparts ($p < 0.001$) and the Russian L1-A Group 1 differed significantly from its Chinese L1-B counterpart ($p < 0.001$) and nearly so from its Russian L1-B ($p = 0.056$) counterpart, but the Chinese L1-A and Russian L1-A Groups 1 did not. With respect to proficiency within each individual language, post hoc analyses tests revealed that the Chinese L1-B Groups 1 and 2 and Groups 1 and 3 differed significantly ($p < 0.001$), and the Russian L1-B Groups 1 and 2 and Groups 1 and 3 differed significantly ($p = 0.006$ and $p = 0.004$, respectively).[10]

In other words, the data of natural and grammatical (noun–adjective)

Table 3.2 Production of natural (noun–adjective) gender agreement

L2 Arabic	*Natural Feminine Correct/Total*	*% Correct*	*Natural Masculine Correct/Total*	*% Correct*
Chinese L1-A				
Group1 (n = 10)	28/37	76	32/35	91
Group2 (n = 10)	54/65	83	61/74	82
Group3 (n = 10)	51/66	77	63/66	95
Chinese L1-B				
Group1 (n = 9)	13/53	25	30/34	88
Group2 (n = 10)	39/49	80	54/65	83
Group3 (n = 10)	48/60	80	76/87	87
Russian L1-A				
Group1 (n = 9)	31/68	46	70/71	99
Group2 (n = 9)	30/33	91	33/38	87
Group3 (n = 9)	30/33	91	39/40	98
Russian L1-B				
Group1 (n = 5)	7/35	20	18/22	82
Group2 (n = 6)	33/45	73	40/56	71
Group3 (n = 8)	26/32	81	38/42	90

Table 3.3 Production of grammatical (noun–adjective) gender agreement

L2 Arabic	*Grammatical Feminine Correct/Total*	*% Correct*	*Grammatical Masculine Correct/Total*	*% Correct*
Chinese L1-A				
Group1 (n = 10)	132/152	87	59/73	81
Group2 (n = 10)	258/314	82	115/154	75
Group3 (n = 10)	222/282	79	181/224	81
Chinese L1-B				
Group1 (n = 9)	6/34	18	30/34	88
Group2 (n = 10)	121/163	74	54/79	68
Group3 (n = 10)	197/259	76	114/146	78
Russian L1-A				
Group1 (n = 9)	75/106	71	76/79	96
Group2 (n = 9)	129/145	89	73/88	83
Group3 (n = 9)	145/156	93	66/76	87
Russian L1-B				
Group1 (n = 5)	18/53	34	16/18	89
Group2 (n = 6)	69/86	80	27/43	63
Group3 (n = 8)	101/125	81	62/78	79

agreement yielded three main findings. First, although the participants in the Chinese L1-A and Russian L1-A beginner groups outperformed their Chinese L1-B and Russian L1-B counterparts (especially based on grammatical gender agreement), their performance did not differ significantly from each other. Second, the Russian L1-A Groups 2 and 3 maintained a lead (though not statistically significant) over their Chinese L1-A counterparts in both feminine and masculine agreement; so did the Russian L1-B Group 3, with a slighter lead, over its Chinese L1-B as well as Chinese L1-A counterparts in feminine agreement (table 3.2). Third, the performance of all L1 groups improved significantly over time except that of the Chinese L1-A groups. The performance of the participants in the Chinese L1-A Groups 1–3 showed a somewhat steady decline. Additionally, the high correct percentages in masculine agreement (compared to those for the feminine) exhibited by the beginner participants (in Group 1) across all L1 groups (except the Chinese L1-A group) indicate use of the masculine as the default form.

3.3.1.2 Rule Application of Nominal Gender Agreement in Noncontexts

Examining rule application in productive or noncontexts may help us understand the extent to which the participants are aware (whether consciously or

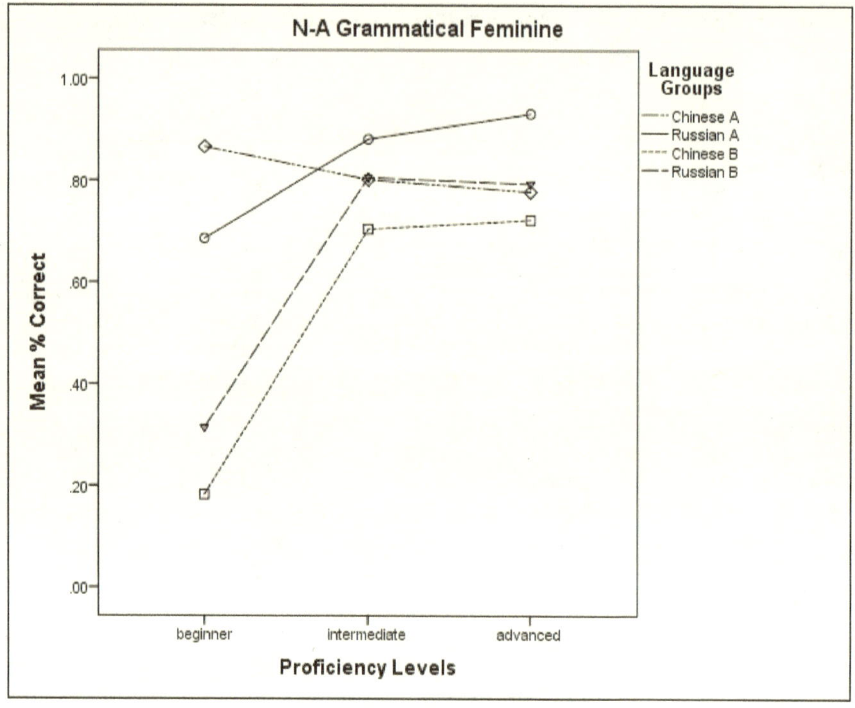

Figure 3.2 Interaction Plot of Mean % Correct for the Participants' Performance on N-A Grammatical Feminine Agreement by Language Group and Proficiency Level

unconsciously) of the rules involving the target forms.[11] A small number of productive interlanguage (IL) utterances or rule application of singular feminine and singular masculine agreement in noncontexts were found in the data sets: eighteen produced by the Chinese L1-A groups, eight by the Chinese L1-B groups, thirty-six by the Russian L1-A groups, and six by the Russian L1-B groups (see table 3.4). These tokens included (1) feminine nouns produced correctly as feminine nouns but followed by (feminine) adjectives exhibiting oversuppliance of the most common feminine suffix {*a*} rather than use of the appropriate feminine suffix; (2) invariant, comparative forms inflected in Arabic for the default masculine gender but produced by the participants with the feminine gender marking agreeing with a preceding feminine noun; (3) masculine nouns produced as feminine nouns followed by agreeing feminine adjectives; and (4) feminine nouns produced as masculine nouns followed by agreeing masculine adjectives. Type 3 and 4 tokens were produced by the individual groups as follows: ten by the Chinese L1-A groups (four feminine and

Table 3.4 Total of nominal (noun–adjective) gender agreement tokens in productive/ noncontexts

L2 Arabic	*N-A Feminine Agreement Productive Tokens/Total*	*% Correct*	*N-A Masculine Agreement Productive Tokens/Total*	*% Correct*
Chinese L1-A				
Group1 (n = 10)	2/189	1.1	2/108	1.9
Group2 (n = 10)	7/379	1.8	2/228	0.9
Group3 (n = 10)	3/348	0.9	2/290	0.7
Chinese L1-B				
Group1 (n = 9)	1/87	1.1	0/68	0.0
Group2 (n = 10)	5/212	2.4	0/144	0.0
Group3 (n = 10)	1/319	0.3	1/233	0.4
Russian L1-A				
Group1 (n = 9)	2/174	1.1	15/150	10.0
Group2 (n = 9)	4/178	2.2	1/126	0.8
Group3 (n = 9)	6/189	3.2	8/116	6.9
Russian L1-B				
Group1 (n = 5)	1/88	1.1	0/40	0.0
Group2 (n = 6)	2/131	1.5	1/99	1.0
Group3 (n = 8)	0/157	0.0	2/120	1.7

six masculine), four by the Chinese L1-B groups (three feminine and one masculine), twenty-six by the Russian L1-A groups (three feminine and twenty-three masculine), and six by the Russian L1-B groups (three feminine and three masculine). Examples of nominal gender agreement in noncontexts, extracted from the participants' data samples, are illustrated in sentences (31)–(40).

(31) IL: sayyār-**a** ʔaʜmar-**a**
car-**s.f** red-**s.f**
TL: sayyār-**a** ʜamr-āʔ
car-**s.f** red-**s.f**
"a red car"
(Russian L1-A: Group 1; also Group 2)

(32) IL: ʔas-sayyār-**a** ʔal-ʔabyadˁ-**a**
car-**s.f** white-**s.f**
TL: ʔas-sayyār-**a** ʔal-byadˁ-āʔ
car-**s.f** white-**s.f**
"the white car"
(Russian L1-A: Group 3)

(33)	IL:	sayyār-**a**	ʔasˤɣar-**a**		
		car-**s.f**	smaller-**s.f**		
	TL:	sayyār-**a**	ʔasˤɣar		
		car-**s.f**	smaller		
		"a smaller car"			
		(Chinese L1-B: Group 2)			
(34)	IL:	ʔal-fatāt	ʔakbar-**a**	min	ʔal-fatā
		the-girl	older-**s.f**	from	the-boy
	TL:	ʔal-fatāt	ʔakbar	min	ʔal-fatā
		the-girl	older	from	the-boy
		"The girl is older than the boy."			
		(Chinese L1-A: Group 2)			
(35)	IL:	kitāb-**a**	kabīr-**a**		
		book-**s.f**	big-**s.f**		
	TL:	kitāb	kabīr		
		book.**s.m**	big.**s.m**		
		"a big book"			
		(Chinese L1-B: Group 2; also Russian L1-B: Group 2)			
(36)	IL:	kursiyy-**a**	muxtalif-**a**		
		chair-**s.f**	different-**s.f**		
	TL:	kursiyy	muxtalif		
		chair.**s.m**	different.**s.m**		
		"a different chair"			
		(Russian L1-B: Group 1)			
(37)	IL:	makān-**a**	ʔal-ʤamīl-**a**		
		place-**s.f**	the-beautiful-**s.f**		
	TL:	makān	ʤamīl		
		place.**s.m**	beautiful.**s.m**		
		"a beautiful place"			
		(Russian L1-B: Group 2)			
(38)	IL:	sayyār-un	ʤadīd-un		
		car.**s.m**-Nom	new.**s.m**-Nom		
	TL:	sayyār-**at**-un	ʤadīd-**at**-un		
		car-**s.f**-Nom	new-**s.f**-Nom		
		"a new car"			
		(Chinese L1-A: Group 1)			
(39)	IL:	madīn	sˤaɣīr		
		city.**s.m**	small.**s.m**		

	TL:	madīn-**a**	sˁaγīr-**a**	
		city-**s.f**	small-**s.f**	
		"a small city"		
		(Russian L1-A: Group 1)		
(40)	IL:	ʕalā	sˁūr	sāni
		on	picture.**s.m**	second.**s.m**
	TL:	fi	sˁ- sˁūr-a	θ-θāniy-a
		in	the-picture-**s.f**	the-second-**s.f**
		"in the second picture"		
		(Russian L1-A: Group 1)		

Although the number of rule of application tokens in noncontexts is not significant compared with that in obligatory contexts, the distribution of such tokens across groups is noticeable. The Russian L1-A groups exhibit by far the highest number of such tokens of any of the groups. This indicates that they were more aware (consciously or unconsciously) of the rule application of nominal gender agreement (i.e., gender assignment on adjectives) than their other counterpart groups. In addition, only a small subset of the (3) and (4) types of errors were made by the participants, which indicates that the participants overall do not seem to have a noticeable problem with gender assignment on nouns.

3.3.1.3 Word Order of Nominal Gender Agreement

As for maintaining the noun–adjective word order sequence in Arabic, the participants produced NPs with mostly correct noun–adjective word order (i.e., with postnominal adjectives). The Russian L1-A groups produced a very small number of tokens with incorrect prenominal adjectives (a total of three tokens); so did their Chinese L1-A counterparts (a total of eight tokens). The Russian L1-B groups produced a larger number of tokens (a total of twenty-five tokens), and the Chinese L1-B groups produced the largest number (a total of fifty-one) of all the groups. Table 3.5 lists all the correct and incorrect noun–adjective word placement tokens in all the data sets.

Examples of incorrect noun–adjective placement, extracted from the data samples of the participants, are illustrated in sentences (41)–(51). Among these tokens, there are instances that also exhibit feminine gender agreement mismatches (i.e., with the feminine noun being followed by a masculine adjective). In fact, the majority of the tokens (thirty-six out of the total of forty-five tokens) with word order misplacement that involved feminine gender

Table 3.5 Noun–adjective word order

L2 Arabic	*N–A Word Order Total Correct*	**A–N Word Order Total/Total all Word Order*	*% Correct*
Chinese L1-A			
Group1 (n = 10)	295	2/297	0.07
Group2 (n = 10)	607	3/610	0.05
Group3 (n = 10)	635	3/638	0.05
Chinese L1-B			
Group1 (n = 9)	108	47/155	0.30
Group2 (n = 10)	354	2/356	0.06
Group3 (n = 10)	550	2/552	0.04
Russian L1-A			
Group1 (n = 9)	321	3/324	0.09
Group2 (n = 9)	304	0/304	0.0
Group3 (n = 9)	305	0/305	0.0
Russian L1-B			
Group1 (n = 5)	107	21/128	0.16
Group2 (n = 6)	228	2/230	0.09
Group3 (n = 8)	275	2/277	0.07

* = ungrammatical

agreement also exhibited gender agreement mismatches, although only two tokens that involved masculine gender agreement exhibited gender agreement mismatches. The significant observation here is that the Chinese L1-B Group 1 exhibited the greatest number of noun–adjective word order misplacement tokens and about half the number of such instances by its counterpart group: Russian L1-B Group 1. Both the Chinese L1-A and Russian L1-A groups exhibited a very small number of noun–adjective word order misplacement tokens compared to those with accurate word order placement.[12]

(41)	IL:	*ʔal-ʔuxr-ā	ʔal-kitāb
		the-other-**s.f**	the-book.**s.m**
	TL:	ʔal-kitāb	ʔal-ʔāxar
		the-book.**s.m**	the-other.**s.m**
		"the other book"	
		(Chinese L1-A: Group 2)	
(42)	IL:	*ʔāxar	bin-**t**-un
		other.**s.m**	girl-**s.f**-Nom

	TL:	bin-**t**-un	ʔuxr-ā
		girl-**s.f**-Nom	other-**s.f**
		"another girl"	
		(Chinese L1-A: Group 2)	
(43)	IL:	*mumtāz	šayʔ
		excellent.**s.m**	thing.**sm**
	TL:	šayʔ	mumtāz
		thing.**s.m**	excellent.**s.m**
		"an excellent thing"	
		(Chinese L1-A: Group 2)	
(44)	IL:	*tˤaw īl	tˤālib
		tall.**s.m**	student.**s.m**
	TL:	tˤālib	tˤawīl
		student.**s.m**	tall.**s.m**
		"a tall male student"	
		(Chinese L1-B: Group 1)	
(45)	IL:	*kabīl	sayyāl-**a**
		big.**s.m**	car-**s.f**
	TL:	sayyār-**a**	kabīr-**a**
		car-**s.f**	big-**s.f**
		"a big car"	
		(Chinese L1-B: Group 1)	
(46)	IL:	*ʤamīl-**a**	ʔumm
		beautiful-**s.f**	mother.**s.f**
	TL:	ʔumm	ʤamīl-**a**
		mother.**s.f**	beautiful-**s.f**
		"a beautiful mother"	
		(Chinese L1-B: Group 1)	
(47)	IL:	*kabīr	ʔusr-**a**
		big.**s.m**	family-**s.f**
	TL:	ʔusr-**a**	kabīr-**a**
		family-**s.f**	big-**s.f**
		"a big family"	
		(Russian L1-B: Group 1)	
(48)	IL:	*sˤaxīr-**at**-un	ɣurf-**a**
		small-**s.f**-Nom	room-**s.f**

	TL:	ɣurf-**at**-un room-**s.f**-Nom "a small room" (Russian L1-B: Group 1)	s^{ʕ}aɣīr-**at**-un small-**s.f**-Nom
(49)	IL:	*saʕīd happy.**s.m**	ʔusr-**a** family-**s.f**
	TL:	ʔusr-**a** family-**s.f** "a happy family" (Russian L1-B: Group 2)	saʕīd-**a** happy-**s.f**
(50)	IL:	*ʔal-ʔuxr-ā the-other-**s.f**	ɣurf-**at**-un room-**s.f**-Nom
	TL:	ʔal-ɣurf-**at**-u the-room-**s.f**-Nom "the other room" (Russian L1-A: Group 1)	ʔal-ʔuxr-ā the-other-**s.f**
(51)	IL:	*sūriyy-un Syrian.**s.m**-Nom	bādiy-**a** desert-**s.f**
	TL:	ʔal-bādiy-**at**-u the-Syrian-**s.f**-Nom "the Syrian desert" (Russian L1-A: Group 1)	ʔas-sūriyy-**at**-u the-desert-**s.f**-Nom

3.3.1.4 Input Frequency of Nominal Gender Agreement

The above findings were obtained despite the presentation of nominal (noun–adjective) gender agreement construction in the input, which the participants received. Tables 3.6–3.9 display how often and when noun–adjective agreement patterns were presented in the textbooks of Group 1 of the Chinese L1-A, Chinese L1-B, Russian L1-A, and Russian L1-B participants. Although nominal (noun–adjective) gender agreement is a high-frequency structure, input information is provided only for Group 1 (corresponding to the first year of exposure) due to the variation in the introduction and presentation of the structure in first year Arabic curricula and due to introduction of Arabic letters and sounds.

Table 3.6 shows that noun–adjective agreement patterns (including those of singular masculine and singular feminine) were formally introduced in the instructional input of Chinese L1-A Group 1 in Lesson 6 (after Arabic sounds and letters were introduced in the preceding lessons). Input containing noun–adjective agreement was maintained consistently throughout until Lesson 24,

Table 3.6 Frequency of noun–adjective agreement occurrence in the textbook of the Chinese L1-A Group 1

	Noun–Adjective Agreement				
Unit[a]	*s.m*	*s.f*	*p.m.h*	*p.f.h*	*p.non-h*
1					
2					
3					
4					
5	(X)	(X)			
6	X	X			X
7	(X)	(X)			
8	(/)				
9		(/)			(X)
10	(X)	(X)			(/)
11	(X)	(X)	X	X	
12	(X)	(/)	(/)		
13	(X)	(X)	(X)	(X)	(/)
14	(X)	(X)	(X)	(X)	(X)
15	(X)	(X)			(X)
16	(X)	(X)	(/)		(/)
17	(X)	(X)			(/)
18	(X)	(X)	(X)		(X)
19	(X)	(X)	(X)		(X)
20	X	X	X	X	X
21	(X)	(X)			(X)
22	(X)	(X)	(X)		(X)
23	(X)	(X)	(/)		(X)
24	(X)	(X)	(X)	(X)	(X)

[a] The text used is *al-Jadīd fī al-Lugha al-ʿArabiyya*, vol. 1 (Guo and Zhou 2002).

X = focused attempt to teach the structure; (X) = structure is not the focus of instruction but occurs in the lesson and drills 4 or more times; (/) = structure is not the focus of instruction and occurs less than four times.

which is the concluding lesson of the first volume of the textbook series assigned for first year instruction.

Table 3.7 shows that noun–adjective agreement was present sporadically in the instructional input of the Chinese L1-B Group 1 for a rather extended period of time first in the two booklets teaching Arabic letters and sounds (left half of table 3.7), but it was later maintained consistently in the main textbook (right half of table 3.7) when it was formally introduced in Lesson 9 and maintained consistently thereafter throughout. Note here that the data from the Chinese L1-B participants were collected when the participants in Group 1 were completing instruction of the Arabic letters and sounds and basic parts

Table 3.7 Frequency of noun–adjective agreement in the textbooks of the Chinese L1-B Group 1

Unit/ Lesson[a]	Noun–Adjective Agreement					Unit/ Lesson[b]	Noun–Adjective Agreement				
	s.m	s.f	p.m.h	p.f.h	p.non-h		s.m	s.f	p.m.h	p.f.h	p.non-h
1–40						1					
1						2	(/)				
2		(/)			(/)	3	(X)	(X)			
3						4	(X)	(X)			
4	(/)					5		(/)			
5	(/)				(/)	6	(X)	(/)			(/)
6						7	(X)	(X)			(X)
7	(/)	(/)			(/)	8	(/)	(X)			
8						9	X	X			X
9	(/)	(/)			(/)	10	(/)	(/)			
10	(/)	(/)				11	(X)	(X)			
11	(/)					12	X	X			(X)
12						13	(X)	(X)			X
13	(/)					14	(X)	(X)			
14						15	(X)	(X)			
15	(/)					16	(X)	(X)			
1											
2	(/)										
3											
4											
5		(X)			(/)						
6											
7											

[a] The textbook for the left half of the table: *Kitāb al-Qirāʾa* & *Mudhakkira ʾIḍāfiyya li-l-Mustawā al-ʾAwwal* (Saudi Teaching Delegates, n.d.).

[b] The textbook for the right half of the table: *al-ʿArbiyya bayna Yadayk*, vol. 1 (Al-Fawzān Hussein, and Faḍl 2003).

X = focused attempt to teach the structure; (X) = structure is not the focus of instruction but occurs in the lesson and drills 4 or more times; (/) = structure is not the focus of instruction and occurs less than 4 times; shaded area = skipped in *Kitāb al-Qirāʾa* and *Mudhakkira* (below the shaded area) was covered instead.

of speech (left half of table 3.7). This may have contributed to the low accuracy levels of feminine singular agreement in Chinese L1-B Group 1.

Table 3.8 shows that noun–adjective agreement was present in the instructional input of the Russian L1-A Group 1 quite consistently throughout. It is not clear when it was formally introduced, but it is likely that it was introduced while teaching the Arabic letters and sounds informally (i.e., without use of specific texts for Arabic letters and sounds) or in the grammar reference book (Jushmanov 1999) in Lesson 4.

Table 3.9 shows that noun–adjective agreement was maintained consistently

Table 3.8 Frequency of noun–adjective agreement in the textbooks of the Russian L1-A Group 1

Unit/ Lesson[a]	*Noun–Adjective Agreement*					*Unit/ Lesson*[b]	*Noun–Adjective Agreement*				
	s.m	*s.f*	*p.m.h*	*p.f.h*	*p.non-h*		*s.m*	*s.f*	*p.m.h*	*p.f.h*	*p.non-h*
1–10	(X)	(X)			(/)	1–2	(/)	(X)			(X)
11–20	(X)	(X)			(/)	3–4	(/)	(X)			(/)
21–30	(X)	(X)			(X)	5–6	(/)	(X)			(/)
31–40	(X)	(X)			(X)	7–8	(X)	(X)			(X)
41–50	(/)	(/)			(X)	9–10	(X)	(/)			(/)
51–60	(X)	(X)			(X)	11–12	(/)	(/)	(/)		(X)
61–70	(X)	(X)			(X)	13–14	(X)	(X)	(/)		(X)
71–80	(X)	(X)		(/)	(X)	15–16	(/)	(X)			(/)
81–90	(X)	(X)			(X)	17–18	(X)	(X)			(X)
91–100	(X)	(X)			(X)	19–20	(X)	(X)			(X)
101–10	(X)	(X)			(X)	21–22	(/)	(X)			(/)
111–20	(X)	(X)			(X)	23–24	(X)	(/)			(X)
121–30	(X)	(X)			(/)	25–26	(X)	(X)	(/)		(X)
131–40	(X)	(X)			(X)	27–28	(X)	(X)	(/)		(X)
141–50	(X)	(X)			(X)	29–30	(X)	(X)			(X)
						31–32	(X)	(X)			(X)
						33–34	(X)	(X)	(/)		(X)
						35–36	(X)	(X)	(X)		(X)

[a] The textbook for the left half of the table: *Povsednevnyarabskijjazyk* (Franka 2007).
[b] The textbook for the right half of the table: *Literaturnyarabskyjazyk* (Khanna 2006).

X = focused attempt to teach the structure; (X) = structure is not the focus of instruction but occurs in the lesson and drills 4 or more times; (/) = structure is not the focus of instruction and occurs less than 4 times.

once presented in the input of the Russian L1-B Group 1. It was informally introduced in Lesson 6 in the book, which focuses on Arabic phonology and orthography (left half of table 3.9), and consistently maintained. Later, it was introduced formally in Lesson 8 and was maintained consistently thereafter in the main textbook (see right half of table 3.9). Despite this constant presence of the form in the input, the Russian L1-B participants in Group 1 exhibited low levels of accuracy in their interlanguage production of feminine agreement (see tables 3.1 and 3.2 above).

The foregoing description of the input frequency of N-A agreement patterns in the Group 1 of all the participants reflect variations due to the need to introduce Arabic phonology and orthography. However, in subsequent input for subsequent years 2 and 3 (corresponding to Groups 2 and 3), the variation becomes minimal, as in table 3.6 and the left half of tables 3.7–3.9, due to the high frequency of the structure.[13] However, two observations can be made here. First, although the input frequency of N-A agreement patterns is

Table 3.9 Frequency of noun–adjective agreement occurrence in the textbooks of the Russian L1-B Group 1

Unit/	*Noun-Adjective Agreement*					*Unit/*	*Noun-Adjective Agreement*				
Lesson[a]	*s.m*	*s.f*	*p.m.h*	*p.f.h*	*p.non-h*	*Lesson*[b]	*s.m*	*s.f*	*p.m.h*	*p.f.h*	*p.non-h*
1						1	(X)	(X)	(X)	(/)	(X)
2						2	(X)	(X)	(/)		(X)
3						3	(X)	(X)			(X)
4						4	(X)	(X)	(X)	(X)	(X)
5						5	(X)	(x)	(X)		(X)
6	(X)	(X)				6	(X)	(X)	(/)		(X)
7	(X)	(X)				7	(X)	(X)	(/)	(X)	(X)
8	X	X				8	(X)	(X)	(/)		(X)
9	(X)	(X)				9	(X)	(X)	(/)		(X)
10	(X)	(X)				10	(X)	(X)	(/)		(X)
11	(X)	(X)				11	(X)	(X)	(/)		(X)
						12	(X)	(X)			(X)

[a] The textbook for the left half of the table is *Vvodno Foneticheskii Koors Arabskovo Yezika* (Semyonova and Lukyanova 2004).

[b] The textbook for the right half of the table is *Oochebna-Metodicheskoye Possobiye Po Arabskomu Yaziku* (Semyonova et al. 2005).

X = focused attempt to teach the structure; (X) = structure is not the focus of instruction but occurs in the lesson and drills 4 or more times; (/) = structure is not the focus of instruction and occurs less than 4 times.

a little more sporadic for the Chinese L1-B group than its Russian L1-B counterpart, both groups exhibited low accuracy in feminine agreement (see tables 3.1–3.3). Recall, both groups received instruction time about less than half compared to their Chinese L-A and Russian L1-A counterparts. Second, despite the high frequency of N-A agreement in the input in Groups 2 and 3, not all participants showed improvement. In particular, the Chinese L1-A Groups 2 and 3 exhibited slight steady decline despite the intensive amount of instruction time (see table 2.1, chapter 2).

3.3.2 Results of Demonstrative Gender Agreement

As explained above, nominal gender agreement involving demonstrative agreement here focuses on agreement between the demonstrative pronoun and a predicate noun (within a nominal/verbless sentence) in gender (masculine versus feminine) and number (singular). The majority of demonstrative agreement tokens that the participants produced consist of a demonstrative pronoun followed by a predicate noun within nominal/verbless constructions such as those in (5)–(8) above. In addition, the participants produced a small number of tokens where a demonstrative modifies a following head noun within a determiner phrase (DP) such as (51) and (52).

(51)	IL:	hāðihi	l-marʔ-a	miθl-ī
		this.s.f	the-person-s.f	like-me
	TL:	hāðihi	l-marʔ-a	miθl-ī
		this.s.f	the-person-s.f	like-me
		"This woman is like me."		
		(Chinese L1-A: Group 2)		
(52)	IL:	*ʔammā	hāðā	ʔal-ʔimraʔ-at
		as for	this.s.m	the-person-s.f
	TL:	ʔammā	hāðihi	ʔal-marʔ-a
		as for	this.s.f	the-person-s.f
		"As for this woman . . . "		
		(Chinese L1-A: Group 3)		

These tokens have a similar gender agreement distribution and were collapsed with the rest of the demonstrative agreement tokens within nominal/verbless constructions to allow for better effects for sample size of the data for running statistical tests.

The produced demonstrative gender agreement tokens with demonstrative pronouns occurring as a subject of the nominal/verbless sentence followed by a predicate noun include instances where the definite article is oversupplied on the predicate noun across groups as in examples (53) and (54).

(53)	IL:	*hāðihi	l-marʔ-a
		this.s.f	the-person-s.f
	TL:	hāðihi	ʔimraʔ-a
		this.s.f	person-s.f
		"This is a woman."	
		(Russian L1-A: Group 2; Russian L1-B: Group 3; Chinese L1-A: Group 2; Chinese L1-B: Group 3)	
(54)	IL:	*hāðā	r-raʤul
		this.s.m	the-man.s.m
	TL:	hāðā	raʤul
		this.s.m	man.s.m
		"This is a man."	
		(Russian L1-A: Group 2; Russian L1-B: Group 3; Chinese L1-A: Group 2; Chinese L1-B: Group 3)	

The oversuppliance of the definite article in this context indicates developmental issues in the acquisition of the definite article by the participants. However, due to the focus of the present study, the definite article feature is not among the target forms here.

Unlike their performance on nominal (noun–adjective) gender agreement, the participants exhibited a different acquisition pattern in their performance on nominal gender agreement involving demonstratives. Although the data snapshot in table 3.10 shows that the Chinese L1-B and Russian L1-A groups seem to have improved their accuracy on demonstrative feminine agreement along proficiency, no statistical difference was found in the performance of the participants between and within groups. A full factorial two-way ANOVA test detected no effects. Performance of the participants exhibits a great deal of variation between and within groups as displayed in the boxplot of figure 3.3 where the quartiles are quite spread out.

A similar finding is yielded with respect to the participants' performance on demonstrative masculine agreement (see table 3.10 and figure 3.4). A full factorial two-way ANOVA revealed no main effects. The general observation here is that all groups (1–3) seem to have used the singular masculine demonstrative pronoun *hāðā* as the default form except for the Russian L1-A Group 3. This is evident in the high accuracy levels in masculine agreement in comparison with those of feminine agreement listed in table 3.10.

Table 3.10 Production of demonstrative gender agreement

L2 Arabic	*Feminine Dem. Agreement Correct/Total*	*% Correct*	*Masculine Dem. Agreement Correct/Total*	*% Correct*
Chinese L1-A				
Group1 (n = 10)	78/104	75	75/90	83
Group2 (n = 10)	127/205	62	143/154	92
Group3 (n = 10)	116/221	52	171/178	96
Chinese L1-B				
Group1 (n = 9)	1/16	6	12/13	92
Group2 (n = 10)	10/35	29	17/19	89
Group3 (n = 10)	88/13	68	70/74	95
Russian L1-A				
Group1 (n = 9)	52/102	51	98/111	88
Group2 (n = 9)	134/180	74	103/113	91
Group3 (n = 9)	95/114	83	43/57	75
Russian L1-B				
Group1 (n = 5)	8/20	40	16/16	100
Group2 (n = 6)	58/101	57	44/55	80
Group3 (n = 8)	97/173	56	170/174	98

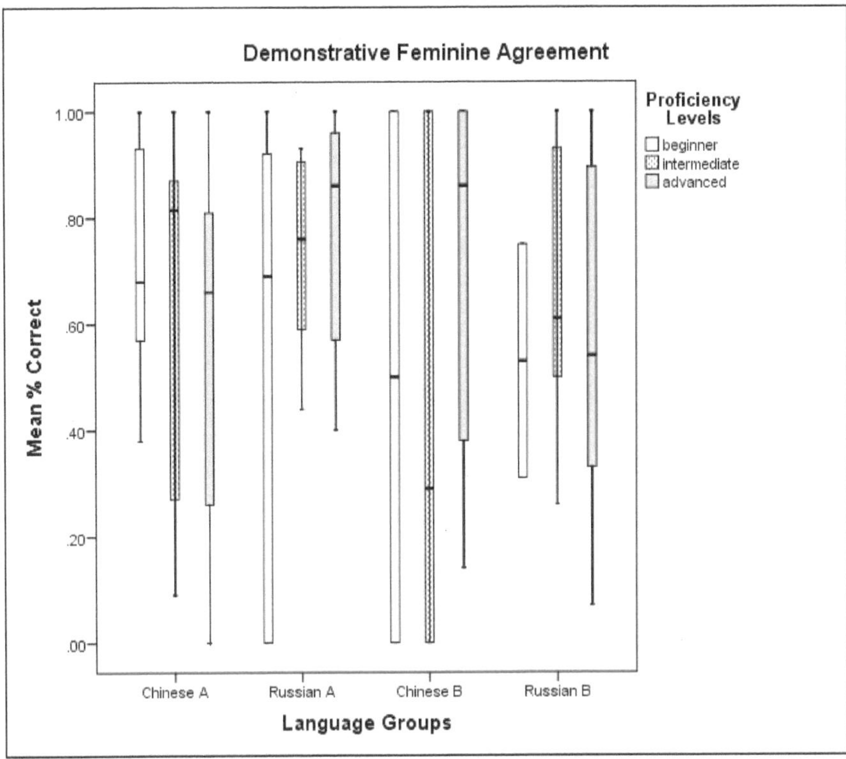

Figure 3.3 Boxplot of Mean % Correct for the Participants' Performance on Demonstrative Feminine Agreement by Language Group and Proficiency Level

The main observation overall, with respect to gender agreement involving demonstratives, is that the Russian L1-A Groups 2–3 (the intermediate and advanced groups) seem to maintain a lead (though not statistically significant) over other counterpart groups (in particular, the Chinese L1-A Groups 2–3, the Chinese L1-B Groups 1–3, and Russian L1-B Groups 1 and 3) in feminine agreement alone. However, the Russian L1-B Groups 2 and 3 do not seem to maintain such an advantage over the Chinese L1-A or Chinese L1-B groups (see table 3.10).

3.3.2.1 Results of Natural versus Grammatical Demonstrative Gender Agreement

The data were further analyzed for the distinction between natural/biological gender (masculine versus feminine) and grammatical gender (masculine versus feminine) where in the former the demonstrative pronoun is followed by a noun exhibiting natural gender as in sentences (5) and (6) above and in the latter the demonstrative pronoun is followed by a noun exhibiting grammatical gender as in sentences (7) and (8). With respect to natural feminine

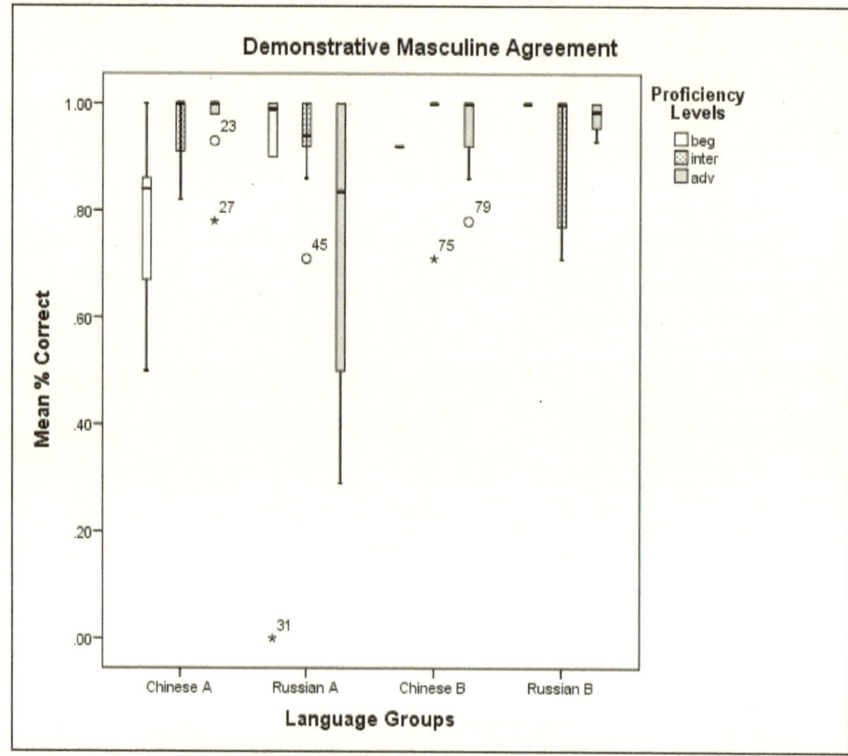

Figure 3.4 Boxplot of Mean % Correct for the Participants' Performance on Demonstrative Masculine Agreement by Language Group and Proficiency Level

and masculine agreement—other than use of the masculine as the default form by all except for the Russian L1-A Group 3—a full factorial two-way ANOVA revealed no effects (see table 3.11). The same finding was yielded from the demonstrative agreement data involving grammatical feminine agreement where a full factorial two-way ANOVA test revealed no main effects (see table 3.12). The findings of demonstrative agreement involving grammatical masculine agreement is similar to that of natural masculine agreement where the tendency by all participants (except those in the Russian L1-A Group 3) to use the masculine as the default form is evident in the high accuracy percentages of masculine versus feminine agreement (table 3.12). The general observation is that the difference in performance displayed in table 3.12 can be due to the Chinese L1-A participants (in Group 3) continuing to use the masculine as the default form (with 97% accuracy rate of masculine versus only 50% of feminine agreement) and the Russian L1-A participants no longer using the masculine as the default form (with 71% accuracy rate of masculine versus 82% of feminine agreement).

Table 3.11 Production of natural demonstrative gender agreement

L2 Arabic	*Natural Feminine Correct/Total*	*% Correct*	*Natural Masculine Correct/Total*	*% Correct*
Chinese L1-A				
Group1 (n = 10)	8/13	62	27/33	82
Group2 (n = 10)	54/74	73	104/110	95
Group3 (n = 10)	42/73	58	98/103	95
Chinese L1-B				
Group1 (n = 9)	0/1	0	6/6	100
Group2 (n = 10)	3/7	43	7/8	88
Group3 (n = 10)	15/23	65	30/31	97
Russian L1-A				
Group1 (n = 9)	16/43	37	40/46	87
Group2 (n = 9)	41/55	75	63/70	90
Group3 (n = 9)	24/27	89	28/36	78
Russian L1-B				
Group1 (n = 5)	3/7	43	13/13	100
Group2 (n = 6)	30/54	56	40/45	89
Group3 (n = 8)	52/72	72	116/116	100

Table 3.12 Production of grammatical demonstrative gender agreement

L2 Arabic	*Grammatical Feminine Correct/Total*	*% Correct*	*Grammatical Masculine Correct/Total*	*% Correct*
Chinese L1-A				
Group1 (n = 10)	70/91	77	48/57	84
Group2 (n = 10)	73/131	56	39/44	89
Group3 (n = 10)	74/148	50	73/75	97
Chinese L1-B				
Group1 (n = 9)	1/15	6.7	6/7	86
Group2 (n = 10)	7/28	25	10/11	91
Group3 (n = 10)	73/107	68	40/43	93
Russian L1-A				
Group1 (n = 9)	36/59	61	58/65	89
Group2 (n = 9)	93/125	74	40/43	93
Group3 (n = 9)	71/87	82	15/21	71
Russian L1-B				
Group1 (n = 5)	5/13	38	3/3	100
Group2 (n = 6)	28/47	60	8/10	80
Group3 (n = 8)	45/101	45	54/58	93

Thus, the big picture that emerges here is that the participants overall seem to use the masculine demonstrative pronoun *hāðā* as the default form as they tend to use the masculine form for a following noun whether feminine or masculine, hence contributing to the high accuracy percentages of masculine agreement. The only minor exception is the Russian L1-A Group 3 where the participants in both natural and grammatical masculine agreement seem to stop using the masculine as the default form and instead they tend to oversupply the feminine form with two consequences: (1) higher accuracy on feminine natural and grammatical agreement, and (2) comparatively lower accuracy on masculine natural and grammatical agreement. In addition, similar to the overall results of demonstrative gender agreement, the Russian L1-A Groups 2 and 3 seem to maintain a lead (though not statistically significant) over other counterpart groups (in particular, the Chinese L1-A Groups 2 and 3, the Chinese L1-B Groups 1–3, and the Russian L1-B Groups 1 and 3) in feminine grammatical agreement. The Russian L1-B Groups 2 and 3 do not seem to maintain such an advantage (in feminine grammatical gender) over the Chinese L1-A or the Chinese L1-B groups (table 3.12).

3.3.2.2 Rule Application of Demonstrative Gender Agreement in Noncontexts

A total of fifty-three IL instances of rule application of singular masculine and singular feminine demonstrative gender agreement in productive/noncontexts were found in all the data sets. The Russian L1-A Group 1 produced the majority of these instances (a total of thirty-nine tokens) followed by the Chinese L1-A Groups 1–3 who produced eleven tokens. Apart from two tokens, all were produced with a noun in the masculine form following the singular masculine demonstrative *hāðā* (see table 3.13). Sentences (55)–(60) are examples of rule application by the participants where nouns are used in the masculine or feminine form (in noncontext) preceded by an agreeing (singular masculine or singular feminine) demonstrative pronoun.

(55) IL: *hāzā sayyār-un
this.**s.m** car.**s.m**-Nom
TL: hāðihi sayyār-**at**-un
this.**s.f** car-**s.f**-Nom
"This is a car."
(Russian L1-A: Group 1)

(56) IL: *hāðā ʕāʔil
this.**s.m** family.**s.m**

	TL:	hāðihi	ʕāʔil-a	
		this.**s.f**	family-**s.f**	
		"This is a family."		
		(Russian L1-A: Group 1)		
(57)	IL:	*hāðā	madīn-un	saɣīr-un
		this.**s.m**	city.**s.m**-Nom	small.**s.m**-Nom
	TL:	hāðihi	madīn-**at**-un	sˁaɣīr-**at**-un
		this.**s.f**	city-**s.f**-Nom	small-**s.f**-Nom
		"This is a small city."		
		(Russian L1-A: Group 1)		
(58)	IL:	*hāðā	sˁūr	
		this.**s.m**	picture.**s.m**	
	TL:	hāðihi	sˁūr-a	
		this.**s.f**	picture-**s.f**	
		"This is a picture."		
		(Russian L1-A: Group 1)		
(59)	IL:	*hāðā	sˁuwar	
		this.**s.m**	picture.**pl**	
	TL:	hāðihi	sˁūr-a	
		this.**s.f**	picture-**s.f**	
		"This is a picture."		
		(Chinese L1-A: Group 3)		
(60)	IL:	*hāðihi	tˁabaq-a	
		this.**s.f**	dish-**s.f**	
	TL:	hāðā	tˁabaq	
		this.**s.m**	dish.**s.m**	
		"This is a dish."		
		(Chinese L1-A: Group 2 by two different participants)		

Whereas the vast majority of tokens of demonstrative agreement in non-context were produced by the Russian L1-A and Chinese L-A groups, the Russian L1-A (in particular Group 1) produced almost four times the number of tokens that the Chinese L1-A groups did. However, it turns out only three of the Russian L1-A participants in Group 1 were responsible for producing all thirty-nine tokens. Thus, the observation here is that of all groups, only the Russian L1-A and Chinese L1-A participants seem to show awareness of (and application of) demonstrative masculine agreement with the former doing more so than the latter. The production of demonstrative agreement in

Table 3.13 Total of demonstrative agreement tokens in noncontexts

L2 Arabic	*Dem. Feminine Agreement Productive Tokens/Total*	*% Correct*	*Dem. Masculine Agreement Productive Tokens/Total*	*% Correct*
Chinese L1-A				
Group1 (n = 10)	0/104	0.0	3/90	3.3
Group2 (n = 10)	2/205	0.98	2/154	1.3
Group3 (n = 10)	0/221	0.0	4/178	2.2
Russian L1-A				
Group1 (n = 9)	0/102	0.0	39/111	35.0
Group2 (n = 10)	0/180	0.0	1/113	0.9
Group3 (n = 10)	0/114	0.0	1/57	1.8
Russian L1-B				
Group3 (n = 9)	0/173	0.0	1/174	0.6

noncontext may also be due to individual variation where only a few individual participants at the beginning stage are encountering a difficulty with gender assignment on nouns and have not yet learned the gender assignment of such nouns and instead tend to use the masculine forms of both the demonstratives and predicate nouns as a default strategy to deal with gender assignment on nouns. Nevertheless, this indicates such learners (more so the Russian than the Chinese) seem to be more sensitive or attuned to the gender feature on nouns, which, in turn, seems to trigger agreement with a demonstrative.

3.3.2.3 Input Frequency of Demonstrative Gender Agreement

These findings were obtained in spite of the presentation of demonstrative gender agreement in the instructional input that the participants received. Tables 3.14–3.17 display how often and when demonstrative pronouns (both in predicative and attributive contexts) were presented in the textbooks of the Chinese L1-A, Chinese L1-B, Russian L1-A, and Russian L1-B participants. Instructional input information is provided for Group 1 (corresponding to the first year of exposure) due to the variation in the introduction and presentation of the structure in first year Arabic curricula and due to introduction of Arabic letters and sounds (for a detailed explanation of the instructional input that the other groups received, see chapter 2, section 2.4).

Table 3.14 shows that the target structure was formally introduced in the input (textbook) of the Chinese L1-A participants (Group 1) toward the end

Table 3.14 Frequency of demonstrative gender agreement occurrence in the textbook of the Chinese L1-A Group 1

	Demonstrative Agreement				
Unit[a]	*s.m*	*s.f*	*p.m.h*	*p.f.h*	*p.non-h*
1					
2					
3					
4					
5	X	X	XL	XL	XL
6	X	X			X
7	(X)	(/)			
8	(X)	(/)			
9					
10		(/)			
11		(/)	X	X	
12		(/)			
13	(X)	(X)	(/)	(/)	(/)
14	(/)	(/)	(X)	(/)	
15	(/)	(X)			(/)
16	(X)	(X)			
17	(X)	(X)			(/)
18	(/)	(/)			
19	(X)	(/)			(/)
20	(X)	(X)	(/)		(/)
21	(X)	(/)	(/)		
22	(X)	(X)			(/)
23	(/)	(X)			(/)
24	(X)	(/)			(/)

[a] The text used is *al-Jadīd fī al-Lugha al-'Arabiyya*, vol. 1 (Guo and Zhou 2002).

X = focused attempt to teach the structure; XL = focused attempt to teach the structure without examples; (X) = structure is not the focus of instruction but occurs in the lesson and drills 4 or more times; (/) = structure is not the focus of instruction and occurs less than 4 times.

of the lessons focusing on Arabic letters and sounds (i.e., Lessons 5 and 6) and was maintained and recycled somewhat consistently thereafter. Table 3.15 shows that the target structure was introduced as soon as Arabic orthography and phonology was covered in the instructional input of the Chinese L1-B Group 1 (i.e., in the right half of table 3.15) and was maintained in the input consistently thereafter. Table 3.16 does not show when the target structure was formally introduced in the instructional input of the Russian L1-A Group 1, but it is somewhat densely present in the dialogue textbook (the left half of table 3.16) and sporadically so in the reading textbook (the right half of table

Table 3.15 Frequency of demonstrative gender agreement in the textbook of the Chinese L1-B Group 1[a]

Unit/ Lesson[a]	*Demonstrative Agreement*					*Unit/ Lesson*[b]	*Demonstrative Agreement*				
	s.m	*s.f*	*p.m.h*	*p.f.h*	*p.non-h*		*s.m*	*s.f*	*p.m.h*	*p.f.h*	*p.non-h*
1–40						1	X	X			
1						2	X	X			
2						3		(/)			
3						4					
4						5	(X)	(/)			
5						6	(X)	(X)			
6						7	(/)	(/)			
7						8		(/)			
8	(X)	(X)				9	X	X			(/)
9			(X)	(X)		10	(X)	(/)			(/)
10	X	X	X	X		11	(/)	(/)			
11						12	(X)	(X)			(X)
12						13	(/)	(X)			X
13	(/)	(/)	(/)	(/)		14		(/)			(/)
14						15	(/)				
15	(/)	(/)	(/)			16					
1											
2											
3											
4											
5											
6											
7	XL	XL	XL	XL							

[a] The textbooks used for the left half of the table are *Kitāb al-Qirā'a* and *Mudhakkira 'Iḍāfiyya li-l-Mustawā al-'Awwal* (Commissioned Saudi Teaching Delegates, n.d.).

[b] The textbook used for the right half of the table is *al-'Arbiyya bayna Yadayk*, vol. 1 (Al-Fawzān, Hussein, and Faḍl 2003).

X = focused attempt to teach the structure; XL = focused attempt to teach the structure without examples; (X) = structure is not the focus of instruction but occurs in the lesson and drills 4 or more times; (/) = structure is not the focus of instruction and occurs less than 4 times; shaded area = skipped in *Kitāb al-Qirā'a* and *Mudhakkira* (below the shaded area) was covered instead.

3.16). The adopted grammar reference book introduces demonstrative use in Lesson 3 (Jushmanov 1999). Finally, table 3.17 shows the target structure was introduced in the Russian L1-B participants' instructional input from early on during the presentation of Arabic phonology and orthography as the textbook attempts to teach the letters and sounds in context at the sentence level (the left half of table 3.17) and was maintained somewhat densely throughout but less so in the reading texts and dialogues (the right half of table 3.17).

Based on the analysis of the input that the participants received, the overall

Table 3.16 Frequency of demonstrative gender agreement in the textbook of the Russian L1-A Group 1

Unit/ Lesson[a]	*Demonstrative Agreement*					*Unit/ Lesson*[b]	*Demonstrative Agreement*				
	s.m	*s.f*	*p.m.h*	*p.f.h*	*p.non-h*		*s.m*	*s.f*	*p.m.h*	*p.f.h*	*p.non-h*
1–10	(X)	(X)				1–2	(X)				
11–20	(X)	(X)				3–4					
21–30	(X)	(/)				5–6					
31–40	(X)	(/)				7–8					
41–50	(X)	(/)				9–10					
51–60	(X)					11–12					
61–70	(X)	(/)			(/)	13–14	(/)	(/)			(/)
71–80	(X)	(/)			(/)	15–16					
81–90	(X)	(/)			(/)	17–18		(/)			
91–100	(X)	(X)				19–20					
101–10	(X)	(X)			(/)	21–22		(/)	(/)		(/)
111–20	(X)	(/)			(/)	23–24					
121–30	(/)	(/)				25–26		(/)			
131–40	(/)	(/)			(/)	27–28	(/)	(/)			
141–50	(/)	(X)			(/)	29–30	(/)	(/)			
						31–32		(/)			
						33–34	(/)				
						35–36	(X)	(X)			

[a] The text used for the left half of the table is *Povsednevnyarabskijjazyk* (Franka 2007).

[b] The text used for the right half of the table is *Literaturnyarabskyjazyk* (Khanna 2006).

X = focused attempt to teach the structure; (X) = structure is not the focus of instruction but occurs in the lesson and drills 4 or more times; (/) = structure is not the focus of instruction and occurs less than 4 times.

observation here is that participants across groups received a somewhat sustained amount of exposure to agreement patterns involving demonstrative pronouns. This is more evident in the target (i.e., singular masculine and singular feminine) than in other forms. In addition, recall that both the Chinese L1-A and Russian L1-A groups received double the time of input exposure than their Chinese L1-B and Russian L1-B counterparts, respectively. Yet, despite the difference in time and intensity of exposure, the findings did not reveal any statistical significance between and within groups except where the Russian L1-A Group 3 tended to underperform compared to the other groups in their performance on singular masculine. This is likely due either to less reliance on the use of the masculine as the default form or oversuppliance of the feminine form. By the same token, the Russian L1-A Groups 2–3 seem to maintain a lead (though not statistically significant) over other counterpart groups (in particular, the Chinese L1-A Groups 2 and 3, the Chinese L1-B Groups 1–3, and

Table 3.17 Frequency of demonstrative gender agreement occurrence in the textbook of the Russian L1-B Group 1

Unit/ Lesson[a]	*Demonstrative Agreement*					*Unit/ Lesson*[b]	*Demonstrative Agreement*				
	s.m	*s.f*	*p.m.h*	*p.f.h*	*p.non-h*		*s.m*	*s.f*	*p.m.h*	*p.f.h*	*p.non-h*
1						1					(/)
2						2	(/)	(/)			
3						3	(/)				
4	X	X				4			(X)	(X)	
5	(X)	(X)				5		(/)	(/)		
6	(X)	(X)				6	(/)	(/)			
7	(/)	(X)				7	(X)				(/)
8	X	X				8	(/)		(/)		
9	(X)	(/)				9	(/)	(/)	(/)		(/)
10	(/)	(/)				10	(/)	(/)			
11	(/)	(/)				11	(/)				
						12		(/)			(/)

[a] The text used for the left half of the table is *Vvodno Foneticheskii Koors Arabskovo Yezika* (Semyonova and Lukyanova 2004).

[b] The text used for the right half of the table is *Oochebna-Metodicheskoye Possobiye Po Arabskomu Yaziku* (Semyonova et al. 2005).

X = focused attempt to teach the structure; (X) = structure is not the focus of instruction but occurs in the lesson and drills 4 or more times; (/) = structure is not the focus of instruction and occurs less than 4 times.

the Russian L1-B Groups 1 and 3) in feminine grammatical agreement alone. However, the Russian L1-B Groups 2 and 3 do not seem to maintain such an advantage over the Chinese L1-A or the Chinese L1-B groups (table 3.12).

3.4 Summary

Based on the nominal gender agreement data from the participants (Chinese L1-A, Chinese, L1-B, Russian L1-A, and Russian L1-B), the main observation found is that all participants in their early stage of Arabic L2 acquisition corresponding to Group 1 (except for the Chinese L1-A Group 1) exhibit a tendency to use the masculine zero morpheme form as the default form for nominal (noun–adjective) gender agreement, and all participants in Groups 1–3 (except for the Russian L1-A Group 3) tend to use the masculine demonstrative pronoun *hāðā* as the default form preceding a predicate noun whether feminine or masculine. In addition, four main findings are yielded.

First, there was no statistical difference with respect to nominal (noun–adjective) gender agreement between the performance of the participants in the

Chinese L1-A Group 1 and their Russian L1-A counterparts, but both groups outperformed their Chinese L1-B and Russian L1-B counterparts. This finding would be expected if the role of input is taken into account. Recall, both the Chinese L1-A and Russian L1-A groups received double the exposure time than their Chinese L1-B and Russian L1-B counterparts, and by far the Chinese L1-A groups received the most exposure time (see table 2.1, chapter 2). However, when considering the performance of the participants over time along proficiency levels (i.e., Group 1 through Group 3), the data revealed the performance of all L1 groups improved significantly over time except for the Chinese L1-A groups. In fact, rather than exhibiting improvement over time, the performance of the participants in the Chinese L1-A Groups 1–3 plateaued and even showed a somewhat steady decline. In other words, although the Chinese L1-A participants (in Group 1) had an initial advantage over all other participants at the beginning stage of Arabic L2 development (with the highest degree of accuracy that they exhibited), due likely to the increase in input exposure, such an advantage was not maintained in subsequent groups/levels. By contrast, the Russian L1-A Groups 2 and 3 maintained an advantage over their Chinese L1-A and Chinese L1-B counterparts in both feminine and masculine agreement (though not statistically significant in all cases); so did the Russian L1-B groups 1–3, with a slighter advantage, over their Chinese L1-B counterparts as well as the Chinese L1-A Group 3 in feminine agreement. This finding is congruent with that reported in Al-Hamad's (2003) study, which showed the Russian L1 participants were more accurate in their suppliance of gender markings on nouns and adjectives than their Chinese L1 counterparts.

Second, due likely to the role of the amount of input exposure, of all the groups, only the beginner Chinese L1-B and Russian L1-B Group 1 exhibited a high percentage of tokens with the wrong noun–adjective word order where the adjective is placed prenominally rather than postnominally (30% and 16%, respectively). Recall, the beginner Chinese L1-B and Russian L1-B Group 1 received half as much input exposure as their Chinese L1-A and Russian L1-A counterparts.

Third, with respect to the demonstrative gender agreement data, the findings reveal no statistically significant differences between and within groups. Here, too, participants seem to use the singular masculine demonstrative as the default form. Recall, the findings obtained despite the different intensity of input exposure of the different groups of the study. However, despite lack of (significant) group difference, the Russian L1-A Groups 2 and 3 seem to maintain a lead (though not statistically significant) over other counterpart groups (in particular, the Chinese L1-A Groups 2 and 3, the Chinese L1-B Groups 1–3, and the Russian L1-B Groups 1 and 3) in feminine grammatical agreement alone, though the Russian L1-B Groups 2 and 3 do not seem to maintain such an advantage over the Chinese L1-A or the Chinese L1-B groups.

Fourth, apart from the small number of tokens with the wrong gender assignment on nouns as well as the (three) individual cases where participants tend to use singular masculine gender assignment with feminine nouns with an agreeing masculine demonstrative, almost all participants seem to have no difficulty with gender assignment on nouns. The main learning problem posed by nominal gender agreement is gender assignment on adjectives (uniformly more so by the Chinese than the Russian participants) as well as on demonstrative pronouns.

Evidently, there is a number of acquisition factors at play here, the most prominent of which is the role of input exposure and L1 transfer. The latter seems to relate in particular to presence or absence of a feature in L1. A detailed discussion of the acquisition factors involved as well as theoretical and applied implications of the observations and findings mentioned above is provided in chapters 7 and 8.

Notes

1. The adjective marker *de* is a formal marker and can be dropped in colloquial Chinese.

2. In attributing parametric variation to strength of functional features, standard minimalist assumption is adopted here. On this account, due to rich nominal agreement features, both Arabic and Russian are analyzed with the functional feature strength set to [+strong] while functional feature strength in Chinese and English is set to [-strong].

3. The study elicited production data from forty Russian L1 and Chinese L1 learners (assigned to two intermediate and two advanced groups with ten participants in each group) during "guided conversations"/interviews for an average of ten minutes each. The interviews were about general topics to do with the participant's family, country, previous and current studies, plans for the future, and social life in their native country and in Saudi Arabia. The study investigated definiteness, gender, number, tense, and verbal agreement. It collapsed the singular and plural together (for both number and gender) and eliminated the dual feature from the investigation. Although the data of the study are useful and relevant, analyzing features separately rather than in clusters would have yielded more relevant findings to the target structures here (Al-Hamad 2003, 74–75).

4. It is not clear how the data were analyzed in addition to the limitation in note 3, above. For example, the total obligatory contexts (TOC) of suppliance of the feminine markings on adjectives in the Chinese intermediate group (which is 62) does not match the total of TOC of omission of feminine markings on adjectives in the same group (which is 90) unless (most likely) "addition of feminine marking to adjectives" and "omission of feminine marking from adjectives" refer to feminine and masculine adjectives, respectively. The same is true for the advanced Chinese group as well as the intermediate and advanced Russian groups, where the TOC for suppliance and omission in each group are not the same (Al-Hamad 2003, 89).

5. The asterisk "*" indicates the utterance is ungrammatical. Hence, "IL" stands for "Interlanguage" utterance and "TL" stands for Target-like" utterance.

6. This is expected and is in line with previous findings (e.g., Alhawary 2009a) since the masculine form is the derivational default form and the feminine form is derived by affixing the feminine suffix (for a similar finding of use of the masculine as the default form in Spanish L2, see White et al. 2004). Hence, participants' performance on gender agreement is likely to be more readily captured by their performance on feminine rather than masculine forms.

7. As for the participants' performance on masculine N-A agreement, a full factorial two-way ANOVA showed a marginal effect for L1 backgrounds ($F(3, 93) = 2.410$, $p = 0.072$, partial $\eta^2 = 0.072$), a near effect for proficiency ($F(2,93) = 2.885$, $p = 0.061$, partial $\eta^2 = 0.058$), and no interaction effect between language backgrounds and proficiency.

8. Since all participants can process natural gender intuitively, their performance on grammatical gender agreement is more likely to be reflective of L1 group difference, an observation in accordance with previous findings (see Alhawary 2009a, 81). Accordingly, the findings on grammatical rather than natural gender is more identical in accordance with feminine gender agreement overall.

9. As for the participants' performance on natural masculine (noun–adjective) agreement, a full factorial two-way ANOVA showed a near effect for L1 backgrounds only: $F(3, 89) = 2.580$, $p = 0.059$, partial $\eta^2 = 0.080$.

10. As for the participants' performance on grammatical masculine (noun–adjective) agreement, a full factorial two-way ANOVA showed no effects.

11. Of course, examining rule application of the target forms in noncontexts is equally significant in order to avoid the pitfalls of the comparative fallacy (see Bley-Vroman 1983). Although such use is not necessarily target-like, it sheds light on the underlying L2 representation of the IL systems of the participants, including hypotheses that the participants make about the target forms.

12. For a similar finding on L2 German by Turkish, Korean, and Romance speakers, see Parodi and colleagues (2004), where many of the Romance speakers (in whose L1s the adjective is placed prenominally, unlike in Turkish and Korean where it occurs postnominally, similar to German) produced a large number of tokens with the wrong order of the adjective occurring in postnominal position at the earliest stage of their German L2 acquisition. However, previous findings on Arabic L2 based on data from English L1, Japanese L1, and French L1 participants

(where the Arabic noun–adjective word order is only exhibited similarly in French participants' L1) did not reveal the same observation. There, all groups, including the beginner groups, produced a small number of tokens with the adjective occurring in prenominal position (Alhawary 2009a, 85).

13. This is also verified by examining the instructional input of the participants as was done in tables 3.6–3.9.

Chapter 4

The Acquisition of Verbal Gender Agreement

This chapter discusses the acquisition of verbal gender agreement based on the collected cross-sectional data from all of the Chinese L1 and Russian L1 groups. As discussed in chapter 1, the focus of verbal gender agreement here is on third person singular masculine and third person singular feminine between the subject and the verb in the past and present tense regardless of whether the subject occurs preverbally or postverbally, as in (21)–(28) in chapter 1, restated below as (1)–(8).

(1) ʔal-tˁālib-(u) ʔakala
the-student.s.m-(Nom) ate.3.s.m
"The male student ate."

(2) ʔal-tˁālib-a[t]-(u) ʔakala-t
the-student-s.f-(Nom) ate-3.s.f
"The female student ate."

(3) ʔal-tˁālib-(u) ya-ʔkul-(u)
the-student.s.m-(Nom) 3.s.m-eat-(Indic)
"The male student eats/is eating."

(4) ʔal-tˁālib-a[t]-(u) ta-ʔkul-(u)
the-student-s.f-(Nom) 3.s.f-eat-(Indic)
"The female student eats/is eating."

(5) ʔakala ʔal-tˁālib-(u)
ate.3.s.m the-student.s.m-(Nom)
"The male student ate."

(6) ʔakala-t ʔal-tˁālib-a[t]-(u)
ate-3.s.f the-student-s.f-(Nom)
"The female student ate."

(7) ya-ʔkul-(u) ʔal-tˁālib-(u)
3.s.m-eat-(Indic) the-student.s.m-(Nom)
"The male student eats/is eating."

(8) ta-ʔkul-(u) ʔal-tˤālib-a[t]-(u)
3.s.f-eat-(Indic) the-student-s.f-(Nom)
"The female student eats/is eating."

As explained in chapter 1, investigation of the above target forms has been carried out irrespective of the participants' production of mood endings. In other words, gender agreement features are the focus alone and regardless as to whether or not the participants produced verbal mood endings appropriately, avoided producing them partially or wholly, or did not produce them at all.

4.1 Typological Pairings

Focus on verbal gender agreement (third person singular masculine versus third person singular feminine) features results in two opposite typological pairings based on the participants' L1s. On one hand, Russian, like Arabic, exhibits a distinction in gender (but not person) between singular masculine and singular feminine verbal agreement in the past tense (i.e., it exhibits gender and number), as in (9) and (10), but it does not exhibit gender in nonpast/present tense (i.e., it exhibits person and number), as in (11) and (12).

(9) studyent yel
student.s.m ate.s.m
"The (male) student ate."

(10) studyent-kə yel-a
student-s.f ate-s.f
"The (female) student ate."

(11) studyent yest
student.s.m eat.3.s
"The (male) student eats/is eating."

(12) studyent-kə yest
student-s.f eats.3.s
"The (female) student eats/is eating."

On the other hand, Chinese, unlike Arabic, does not exhibit verbal gender agreement, neither in the past tense nor in the present tense, as illustrated in (13)–(16).[1]

(13) nan xue sheng chi le
male study apprentice eat past
"The male student ate."

(14) nu xue sheng chi le
female study apprentice eat past
"The female student ate."

(15) nan xue sheng (zai) chi
male study apprentice (is) eat
"The male student eats (is eating)."

(16) nu xue sheng (zai) chi
female study apprentice (is) eat
"The female student eats (is eating)."

Accordingly, the typological constellations (a) and (b) are yielded, in particular with respect to past tense verbal agreement features.

(a) Russian participants who are speakers of a [+gender] and [+strong] L1, learning L2 Arabic [+gender] and [+strong], with previous knowledge of L2 English [-gender] and [-strong]
(b) Chinese participants who are speakers of a [-gender] and [-strong] L1, learning L2 Arabic [+gender] and [+ strong], with previous knowledge of L2 English [-gender] and [-strong][2]

However, with respect to present tense verbal agreement features, a different pairing (c) and (d) is yielded.

(c) Russian participants who are speakers of a [-gender] and [+strong] L1, learning L2 Arabic [+gender] and [+strong], with previous knowledge of L2 English [-gender] and [-strong]
(d) Chinese participants who are speakers of a [-gender] and [-strong] L1, Learning L2 Arabic [+gender] and [+ strong], with previous knowledge of L2 English [-gender] and [-strong]

Here the verb is not inflected for singular feminine versus singular masculine in both Russian and Chinese, although Russian overall exhibits a uniformly rich morphological paradigm and Chinese uniformly lacks one.[3]

4.2 Previous Findings

Data from previous studies that investigated acquisition of verbal gender agreement (third person singular masculine and third person singular feminine) features by Arabic L2 learners who are speakers of English, French, and Japanese as L1s yielded the following findings:

- Arabic L2 learners of different L1 backgrounds and across all groups showed higher accuracy on masculine gender than feminine gender agreement, likely due to use of the masculine as the default form by participants across groups (Alhawary 2005, 299; 2009a, 77–78; 2009b, 379–82).
- French L1 learners somewhat outperformed English L1 and Japanese L1 learners of Arabic in producing the appropriate verbal agreement features for third person singular masculine and third person singular feminine in all groups (except for first year French L1 participants, who slightly underperformed their English and Japanese L1 counterparts on singular feminine agreement) although such differences were not found to be statistically significant (Alhawary 2009a, 77–78).
- English L1 learners of Arabic slightly outperformed their Japanese L1 counterparts on third person singular feminine (in particular those at the beginner and advanced level) and on third person singular masculine (in particular, those at the advanced level). Conversely, Japanese L1 learners slightly outperformed their English L1 counterparts on third person singular feminine (in particular, those at the intermediate level) and on third person singular masculine (in particular, those at the beginner and intermediate level). However, such differences were not found to be statistically significant (Alhawary 2009a, 77–78; see also 112).

Since no statistically significant effect was found in the performance of all three participants of the three L1 backgrounds (French, English, and Japanese) and since none of the three L1s exhibits a distinction in verbal gender agreement between third person singular masculine and third person singular feminine, it has been suggested that the findings of verbal agreement do not necessarily provide evidence for L1 transfer (see Alhawary 2009a, 153–57).

Nielsen (1997) reported mixed results based on production data from two Danish L1 learners of Arabic. Whereas verbal gender (third person singular masculine and third person singular feminine) agreement was found to emerge in one of the two participants (in recording 4), the other participant did not exhibit emergence of verbal gender agreement during the entire fifteen-month period of the longitudinal observation. This finding is relevant, since Danish (like English, French, and Japanese) does not display a gender distinction in third person singular verbal agreement paradigm.

Al-Hamad's (2003) reported findings on a cross-sectional study of intermediate and advanced groups of Chinese L1 and Russian L1 learners of Arabic as an L2 are most relevant here. The study investigated the production of a set of morphosyntactic structures including verbal gender agreement.[4] The findings reveal that the Russian intermediate group was more successful acquiring verbal gender agreement than its Chinese counterpart and that both Russian and Chinese groups were generally less accurate on gender than other (number and tense) features (Al-Hamad 2003, 103–8).[5] The production data of verbal gender agreement by the intermediate groups is potentially relevant to examining L1 transfer effects, but since the verbal agreement data of past and present tense are collapsed together in Al-Hamad's (2003) study, this precludes drawing any clear conclusion or finding about L1 transfer. Recall, whereas Russian exhibits a gender feature in past tense and does not do so in the present tense, Chinese does not exhibit a gender feature in any tense.

The typological pairings of the present study—with participants who are Russian L1 and Chinese L1 speakers—are significant to examining L1 transfer effects while taking into account the separation (in the analysis) between verbal gender agreement data in the past tense and verbal gender agreement in the present tense. Furthermore, employment of the different groups and their exposure settings (i.e., with two sets of groups receiving double the amount of instruction than their two counterpart sets) is significant in order to examine the extent according to which L1 transfer plays a role in L2 acquisition and whether or not it can be overridden or minimized by input exposure.

4.3 Results

The four narrative tasks (discussed in chapter 2) elicited descriptions of the activities of a female and a male character, containing mainly tokens of verbal gender agreement for third person singular masculine and third person singular feminine in the past and present tense. Examples of correct rule application of third person singular masculine and third person singular feminine are illustrated in sentences (17)–(24), extracted from the respective participants' data samples.

(17)	IL:	hāðihi	ʔal-marʔ-a	qad	ðahaba-t	ʔilā	nafs	ʔal-makān
		this.s.f	the-person-s.f	indeed	went-3.s.f	to	same	the-place
	TL:	hāðihi	ʔal-marʔ-a	qad	ðahaba-t	ʔilā	nafs	ʔal-ʔamākin
		this.s.f	the-person-s.f	indeed	went-3.s.f	to	same	the-places

"This woman had gone to the same places."
(Chinese L1-A: Group 3)

(18)	IL:	wa	hiya	ðahaba-t	ʔilā	xāliʤ
		and	she	went-3.s.f	to	outside
	TL:	wa	hiya	ðahaba-t	ʔilā	ʔal-xāriʤ
		and	she	went-3.s.f	to	the-outside

"And she went abroad."
(Chinese L1-B: Group 2)

(19)	IL:	ðahaba-t	hiya	ʔilā	Hadīq-i	ʔal-Hayawān
		went-3.s.f	she	to	park-Gen	the-animal
	TL:	ðahaba-t	ʔilā		Hadīq-at-i	ʔal-Hayawān
		went-3.s.f	to		park-s.f-Gen	the-animal

"She went to the zoo."
(Russian L1-A: Group 3)

(20)	IL:	wasˤala-t	ʔilā	ʔamrīka
		arrived-3.s.f	to	America

"She arrived in America."
(Russian L1-B: Group 2)

(21)	IL:	ya-lʕab-u	ʔal-kur-a	ʔal-qadam
		3.s.m-play-Indic	the-ball-s.f	the-foot.s.f
	TL:	ya-lʕab-u	kur-at	ʔal-qadam
		3.s.m-play-Indic	ball-s.f	the-foot.s.f

"He plays football."
(Chinese L1-A: Group 2)

(22)	IL:	wa	huwa	ya-qraʔ-u	l-qurʔān
		and	he	3.s.m-read-Indic	the-Qur' ān

"And he reads the Qur'ān."
(Chinese L1-B: Group 2)

(23)	IL:	ya-stayqiðˤ-u	hāðā	r-raʤul
		3.s.m-wakes-Indic	this.s.m	the-man

"This man wakes up."
(Russian L1-A: Group 3)

(24)	IL:	ya-ktub-u	shayʔan
		3.s.m-writes-Indic	thing.s.m

"He writes something."
(Russian L1-B: Group 3)

As illustrated in examples (17)–(24), the produced tokens contain preverbal subjects, as in (17), (18), and (22); postverbal subjects, as in (19) and (23); and null subjects, where no explicit pronoun or subject NP is used, as in (20), (21), and (24).[6] Tokens of incorrect use of rule applications of third person singular masculine and third person singular feminine occurred with similar subject types, as illustrated in examples (25)–(32) from the respective participants' data samples.

(25) IL: *sˤadīq-at-i-hā qad ʔandʒaba ʔal-mawlūd
friend-s.f-Gen-her indeed birthed.3.s.m the-baby
TL: sˤadīq-at-u-hā qad ʔandʒaba-t ʔal-mawlūd
friend-s.f-Nom-her indeed birthed-3.s.f the-baby
"Her female friend had given birth to the baby."
(Chinese L1-A: Group 3)

(26) IL: *ʔal-ʔimraʔ-a ðahab-tu ʔilay-hu
the-person-s.f went-1.s to-him
TL: ʔal-marʔ-a ðahaba-t ʔilay-hi
the-person-s.f went-3.s.f to-him
"The woman went to him."
(Chinese L1-B: Group 2)

(27) IL: *hiya dʒāʔa fi l-ʜadīq-a
she came.3.s.m in the-park
TL: hiya dʒāʔa-t ʔila l-ʜadīq-a
she came-3.s.f to the-park
"She came to the park."
(Russian L1-A: Group 2)

(28) IL: *wasˤala ʔal-fatā-t ʔal-bank
arrived.3.s.m the-young-s.f the-bank
TL: wasˤala-t ʔal-fatā-t ʔilā ʔal-bank
arrived-3.s.f the-young-s.f to the-bank
"The girl arrived at the bank."
(Russian L1-B: Group 2)

(29) IL: *ta-qūm-u bi-r-riyādˤ-at-i l-badaniyy-a
3.s.f-perform-Indic with-the-sport-s.f-Gen the-physical-s.f
TL: ya-qūm-u bi-r-riyādˤ-at-i l-badaniyy-a
3.s.m-perform-Indic with-the-sport-s.f-Gen the-physical-s.f
"He does physical exercise."
(Chinese L1-A: Group 3)

(30) IL: *wa huwa ta-shrab-u qahw-a
and he 3.s.f-drink-Indic coffee-s.f
TL: wa huwa ya-shrab-u qahw-a
and he 3.s.m-drink-Indic coffee-s.f
"And he drinks coffee."
(Chinese L1-B: Group 2)

(31) IL: *wa ʔa-qraʔ kitāb-in
and 1.s-read book-Gen
TL: wa ya-qraʔ kitāb-an
and 3.s.m-read book-Acc
"And he reads a book."
(Russian L1-A: Group 1)

(32) IL: *wa ta-dras-a
and 3.s.f-study-Subjunc
TL: wa ya-drus-u
and 3.s.m-study-Indic
"And he studies."
(Russian L1-B: Group 3)

Although some of the errors are due to use of different person and gender agreement features inflected on the verbs, such as first person singular or second person singular masculine or feminine, as in (26) and (31), the majority of errors are due to use of third person singular masculine instead of third person singular feminine, as in (25), (27), and (28), or conversely due to use of third person singular feminine instead of third person singular masculine, as in (29), (30), and (32). Correct agreement was determined by considering the verbal form and whether it was inflected properly for the intended referent rather than identifying first the subject and then the verb it agreed with. This is significant since the verb may agree with a discourse referent subject and the participants may be mindlessly producing the wrong subject, especially when the subjects used are the pronouns *hiya* "she" and *huwa* "he," which are close in their pronunciation (see also Poeppel and Wexler 1993; Prévost and White 2000; cf. Meisel 1991).

4.3.1 Verbal Agreement in the Past Tense

A snapshot of the participants' production data of verbal gender agreement for third person singular masculine and feminine in the past tense is provided in table 4.1 (see also figure 4.1, illustrating the production trends of all participants across all groups). At a glance, the aggregate data generally show that the participants of all L1 backgrounds seem to have used third person singular masculine as the default form as evident in their high 90%–100% accuracy on third person singular masculine agreement in comparison with their lower accuracy levels of third person singular feminine agreement. Third person singular masculine form of the verb is usually the same form provided when new vocabulary items/verbs are introduced in a given lesson. However, the Chinese

Table 4.1 Production of verbal gender agreement in the past tense

L2 Arabic	*Verbal F. Agreement (Past) Correct/Total*	*% Correct*	*Verbal M. Agreement (Past) Correct/Total*	*% Correct*
Chinese L1-A				
Group1 (n = 10)	36/69	52	58/74	78
Group2 (n = 10)	75/87	86	101/105	96
Group3 (n = 10)	98/114	86	140/141	99
Chinese L1-B				
Group1 (n = 9)	0/6	0	9/9	100
Group2 (n = 10)	33/40	83	37/41	90
Group3 (n = 10)	77/95	81	98/101	97
Russian L1-A				
Group1 (n = 9)	30/81	37	64/77	83
Group2 (n = 9)	95/116	82	102/105	97
Group3 (n = 9)	84/97	87	106/106	100
Russian L1-B				
Group1 (n = 5)	0/11	0	13/13	100
Group2 (n = 6)	32/53	60	52/56	93
Group3 (n = 8)	66/81	81	99/101	98

L1-A and Russian L1-A participants in Group 1 seem to be using third person singular masculine as a default to a much lesser extent, with their 78% and 83% accuracy percentages, respectively. Group 1 of both the Chinese L1-A and Russian L1-A seem to be aware of the gender distinction noticeably more so than their other counterpart groups due likely to the intensity of their received instructional input at the outset of their Arabic L2 learning (see chapter 2, table 2.1).

Full factorial two-way ANOVA tests showed a main effect for L1 backgrounds on third person singular feminine agreement in the past tense ($F(3, 76) = 4.041$, $p = 0.010$, partial $\eta^2 = 0.138$) and a main effect for proficiency on singular feminine agreement ($F(2,76) = 22.843$, $p < 0.001$, partial $\eta^2 = 0.375$). No interaction effect between L1 backgrounds and proficiency was found. Post hoc analyses using Bonferroni tests for between and within group effects revealed that the Chinese L1-A groups differed significantly overall from their Russian L1-B counterparts ($p = 0.011$), and particularly between participants in Group 1 of the two language backgrounds ($p = 0.039$), the Russian L1-A groups differed marginally from their Russian L1-B counterparts ($p = 0.096$), but no other significant L1 background differences at this level were found.[7] With respect to proficiency within each individual L1 group, post hoc analyses

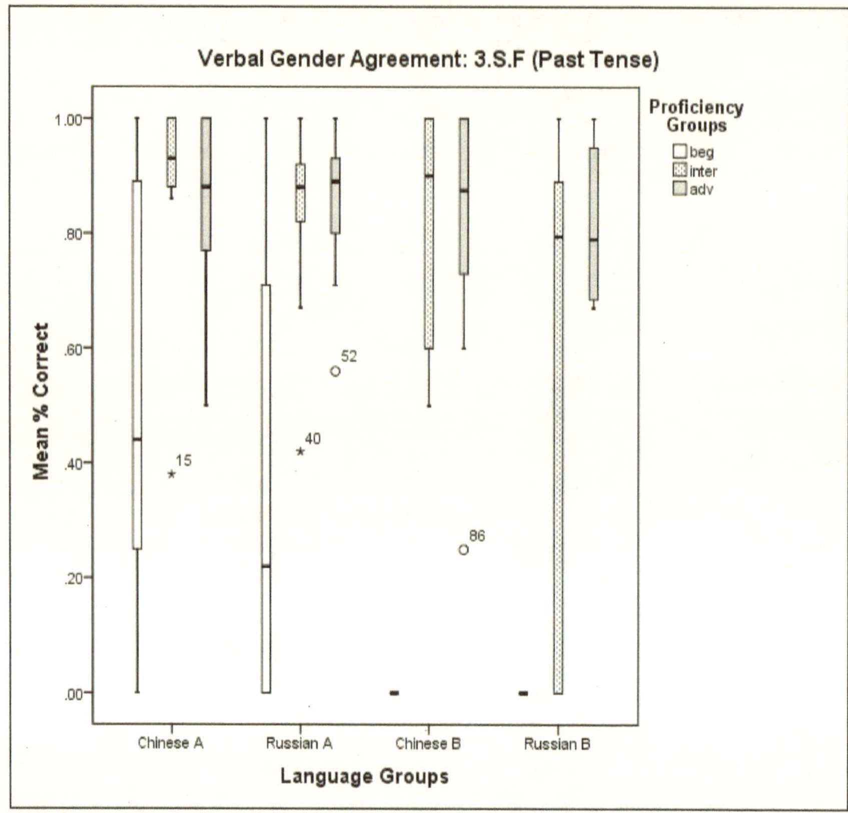

Figure 4.1 Boxplot of Mean % Correct for the Participants' Performance on Verbal Gender Agreement (3rd Person Singular Feminine in Past Tense) by Language Group and Proficiency Level

revealed that, within each of the four L1 background groups (Chinese L1-A, Chinese L1-B, Russian L1-A, and Russian L1-B), Group 1 differed from Group 2 significantly ($p = 0.007$, $p=0.022$, $p = 0.001$, and $p = 0.008$, respectively) and so did Group 1 from Group 3 ($p = 0.013$, $p = 0.015$, $p = 0.000$, and $p < 0.001$, respectively). As for participants' performance on third person singular masculine agreement in the past tense, no main effects were found.

In other words, two main findings emerge here with respect to third person singular feminine (verbal) agreement (in the past tense). First, while the Russian L1-B participants, especially those in Group 1, seem to have underperformed their counterparts in other groups, no other significant differences were found between groups. Second, participants of all L1 backgrounds exhibited improvement over time between the beginner level (Group 1) and intermediate level (Group 2) as well as beginner (Group 1) and advanced (Group 3) levels.

4.3.2 Verbal Agreement in the Present Tense

The aggregate data of verbal agreement in the present tense show a somewhat different pattern than verbal agreement in the past tense. Table 4.2 provides a snapshot of verbal agreement in the present tense (see also figure 4.2).[8] Overall, on one hand, all except the beginner participants (i.e., Group 1) of all groups as well as the advanced participants (Group 3) of the Chinese L1-B participants exhibited high agreement accuracy, ranging from 90% to 100%, in their use of third person singular masculine. On the other hand, Group 1 of the Russian L1-A and Russian L1-B participants exhibited low accuracy, 17% and 57%, respectively. Similarly, participants in Groups 2 and 3 of all L1 backgrounds achieved a higher degree of accuracy on third person singular feminine agreement than their counterparts in Group 1: the Chinese L1-A (76%), the Chinese L1-B (65%), the Russian L1-A (56%), and the Russian L1-B (40%) groups.

Full factorial two-way ANOVA tests showed only a main effect for proficiency on third person singular feminine agreement in the present tense ($F(2, 72) = 13.881, p < 0.001$, partial $\eta^2 = 0.278$). Post hoc analyses using Tukey tests of all possible pairwise comparisons revealed no particular group as a whole differed from other groups. In addition, tests showed the Chinese L1-B Group 1 differed significantly from the Chinese L1-B Group 2 ($p = 0.004$) as well as

Table 4.2 Production of verbal gender agreement in the present tense

L2 Arabic	*Verbal F. Agreement (Present) Correct/Total*	*% Correct*	*Verbal M. Agreement (Present) Correct/Total*	*% Correct*
Chinese L1-A				
Group1 (n = 10)	19/25	76	15/18	83
Group2 (n = 10)	64/77	83	77/79	97
Group3 (n = 10)	66/77	86	89/92	97
Chinese L1-B				
Group1 (n = 9)	11/17	65	20/23	87
Group2 (n = 10)	82/87	94	92/102	90
Group3 (n = 10)	66/68	97	48/61	79
Russian L1-A				
Group1 (n = 9)	9/16	56	1/6	17
Group2 (n = 9)	68/75	91	67/69	97
Group3 (n = 9)	58/68	85	92/93	99
Russian L1-B				
Group1 (n = 5)	2/5	40	4/7	57
Group2 (n = 6)	10/10	100	16/16	100
Group3 (n = 8)	24/27	89	26/27	96

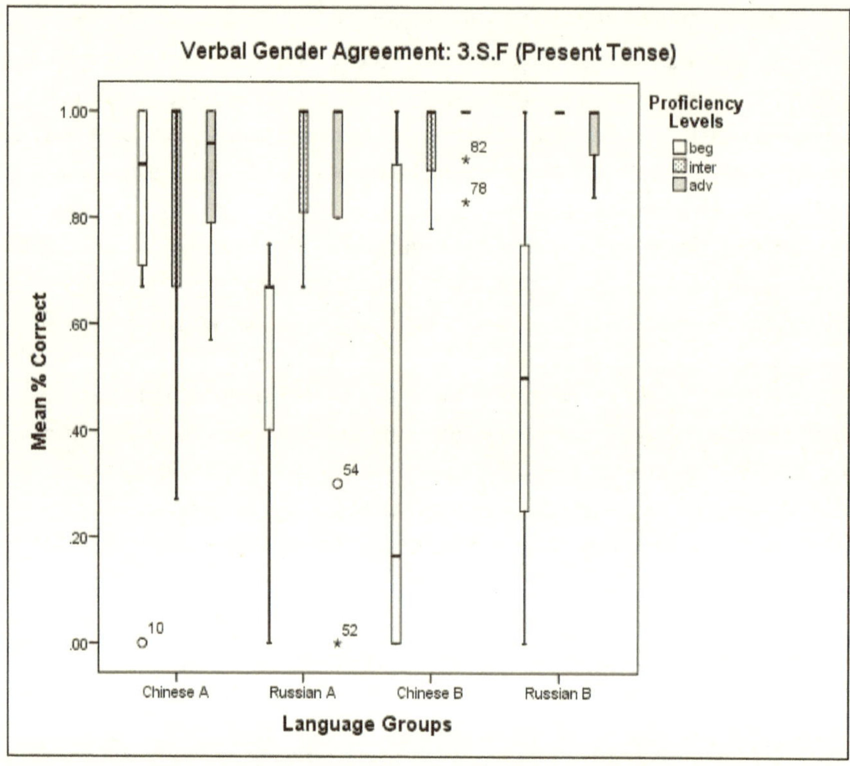

Figure 4.2 Boxplot of Mean % Correct for the Participants' Performance on Verbal Gender Agreement (3rd Person Singular Feminine in Present Tense) by Language Group and Proficiency Level

the Chinese L1-B Group 3 ($p = 0.002$) with the latter two groups significantly outperforming the former group. As for third person singular masculine (in the present tense), full factorial two-way ANOVA tests showed a main effect for proficiency ($F(2, 72) = 9.390$, $p < 0.001$, partial $\eta^2 = 0.207$) and a main interaction effect between L1 backgrounds and proficiency ($F(6, 72) = 3.849$, $p = 0.002$, partial $\eta^2 = 0.243$). Post hoc analyses using Tukey tests of all possible pairwise comparisons showed the Chinese L1-A Group 1 differed nearly significantly from its Russian L1-A counterpart ($p = 0.058$), and the Chinese L1-B Group 1 differed significantly from its Russian L1-A counterpart ($p = 0.001$). However, the Russian L1-A Group 1 differed significantly from the Russian L1-A Group 2 ($p < 0.001$) as well as the Russian L1-A Group 3 ($p < 0.001$). In other words, although participants in the Russian L1-A Group 1 underperformed their Chinese L1-A and Chinese L1-B counterparts on third person singular masculine verbal agreement in the present tense, no other significant differences at this level between groups were found. Despite their underperformance, the Russian L1-A Group 1 showed significant improvement over time.

To sum up the findings in the two preceding sections, while participants in the Russian L1-B beginner group underperformed their counterparts in the Chinese L1-A and Russian L1-A beginner groups on singular feminine verbal agreement in the past tense, participants in the Russian L1-A beginner group underperformed their counterparts in the Chinese L1-A and Chinese L1-B beginner groups on singular masculine verbal agreement in the present tense. The main difference seems to be in the performance of beginner groups with the Chinese L1-A beginner group starting off with an advantage over the Russian L1-B beginner groups in verbal feminine agreement in past tense and over the Russian L1-A beginner group in verbal masculine agreement in present tense. In addition, while the Russian L1-B beginner group underperformed the Chinese L1-A (and Russian L1-A) beginner group in verbal feminine agreement in past tense, the Chinse L1-B beginner group outperformed the Russian L1-A beginner group in verbal masculine agreement in present tense.

4.3.3 Verbal Agreement in the Random Present Tense Task

In anticipation of an artifact to do with the nature of the narrative tasks where some participants may misunderstand the tasks and use the past tense in present tense narratives or the present tense in past tense narratives, participants' performance on a random present tense task was examined to provide additional evidence (see chapter 3).[9] Table 4.3 summarizes the performance of all participants of all L1 groups on the correct production of verbal gender (third person singular masculine versus third person singular feminine) agreement (see also figures 4.3 and 4.4, illustrating the distribution and variation of the data by all groups). The data show that, overall, participants of all groups (except for Group 1 of the Chinese L1-B and Russian L1-A) achieved high agreement accuracy (ranging from 88% to 100%) in their use of third person singular masculine in comparison with third person singular feminine.[10] In addition, only Group 1 of the Chinese L1-A participants seem to start off with a high 91% accuracy in their use of third person singular feminine, although later in the intermediate and advanced levels (i.e., Groups 2 and 3) they exhibit backsliding (with 78% and 77% accuracy, respectively). Similarly, the Chinese L1-B and Russian L1-B exhibit backsliding from Group 2 (87% and 93%, respectively) to Group 3 (78% and 73%, respectively). Among all L1 groups, the Russian L1-A Groups 1–3 are the only ones that exhibit steady gains in their accuracy of rule application on third person singular feminine (46%, 77%, and 89%) across all three levels.

Table 4.3 Production of verbal gender agreement in the present tense random task

L2 Arabic	*Verbal F. Agreement (Random) Correct/Total*	*% Correct*	*Verbal M. Agreement (Random) Correct/Total*	*% Correct*
Chinese L1-A				
Group1 (n = 10)	20/22	91	35/40	88
Group2 (n = 10)	72/92	78	187/198	94
Group3 (n = 10)	143/186	77	208/218	95
Chinese L1-B				
Group1 (n = 9)	1/2	50	5/7	71
Group2 (n = 10)	59/68	87	105/117	90
Group3 (n = 10)	79/101	78	128/143	90
Russian L1-A				
Group1 (n = 9)	6/13	46	11/14	79
Group2 (n = 9)	66/86	77	111/126	88
Group3 (n = 9)	58/65	89	113/118	96
Russian L1-B				
Group1 (n = 5)	4/6	67	4/4	100
Group2 (n = 6)	13/14	93	16/18	89
Group3 (n = 8)	48/66	73	84/90	93

Full factorial two-way ANOVA tests showed a main interaction effect between L1 background and proficiency on third person singular feminine agreement (in the random present tense task): $F(6, 73) = 2.278$, $p = 0.045$, partial $\eta^2 = 0.158$. Post hoc analyses using Bonferroni tests for between and within group effects revealed a marginal difference between the Chinese L1-A beginner group and its counterpart Russian L1-A group ($p = 0.084$) and a near significant difference between Group 1 and Group 3 of the Russian L1-A participants ($p = 0.058$).[11] As for third person masculine agreement, a near main effect for proficiency ($F(2, 80) = 2.860$, $p = 0.063$, partial $\eta^2 = 0.067$) was found, with the Chinese L1-B participants exhibiting the biggest gain from the beginner to the intermediate group.

In other words, one significant finding is the underperformance of the participants in the Russian L1-A beginner group (i.e., Group 1) from that of their Chinese L1-A beginner counterparts in third person singular feminine, but of the two groups, the Russian participants alone (i.e., Group 3) exhibit a steady gain (see figure 4.3). A second finding indicates improvement of the Chinese L1-B participants (in particular from Group 1 to Group 2) in third person singular masculine. A third finding is convergence in the participants'

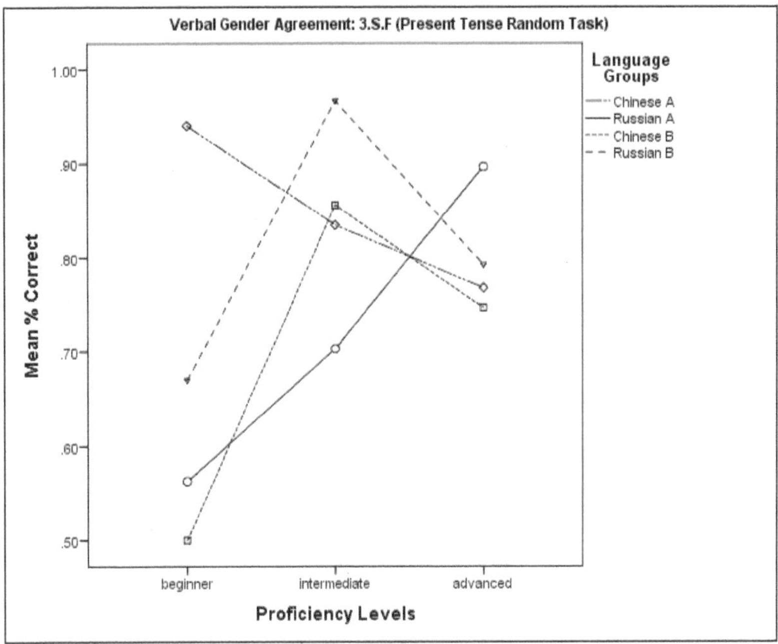

Figure 4.3 Boxplot of Mean % Correct for the Participants' Performance on Verbal Gender Agreement (3rd Person Singular Feminine in Present Tense Random Task) by Language Group and Proficiency Level

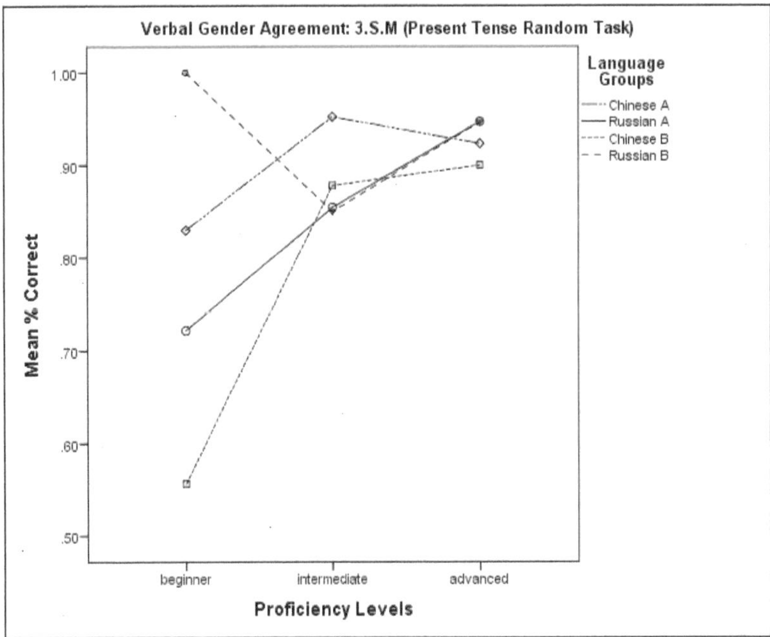

Figure 4.4 Boxplot of Mean % Correct for the Participants' Performance on Verbal Gender Agreement (3rd Person Singular Masculine in Present Tense Random Task) by Language Group and Proficiency Level

performance of third person singular feminine and masculine verbal agreement at the advance level (i.e., Group 3)—an observation that is true of all advanced groups on all forms of verbal agreement reported on above. This means that the main significant difference between the groups is at the beginner level, with the Chinese L1-A beginner participants starting off with an advantage over the beginner Russian L1-A group. In addition, subsequent Chinese L1-A Groups 2 and 3 (and unlike their performance on past and present tense tasks) seem to backslide in third person singular feminine, unlike the Russian L1-A participants.

4.4 Input Frequency

The above findings were obtained with the presentation of verbal gender agreement construction in the input of the participants as displayed in tables 1–4 in appendix B. In particular, the tables show how often and when verbal gender agreement patterns were presented in the textbooks of Group 1 of the Chinese L1-A, Chinese L1-B, Russian L1-A, and Russian L1-B participants. Although verbal gender agreement is a high-frequency structure, input information is provided only for Group 1 (corresponding to the first year of exposure) due to the variation in the introduction and presentation of the structure in Arabic first year curricula and due to introduction of Arabic letters and sounds. Recall, the target forms of verbal gender agreement are those involving third person singular masculine and third person singular feminine. Other agreement patterns are included in the tables to provide the bigger picture for the presentation of verbal gender agreement in the participants' formal instructional input.

With respect to the Chinese participants, tables 1a, 1b, 2a, and 2b (appendix B) display the distribution of their input of verbal gender agreement patterns in past and present tense. Tables 1a and 1b show that verbal gender agreement patterns in the instructional input of the Chinese L1-A participants were both informally present from early on since Lessons 3 and 4 (presented together with Arabic sounds and letters), were both formally introduced in Lesson 13, and were maintained thereafter consistently in the input throughout until Lesson 24. There were both focused and indirect focused attempts on the target forms and by far the Chinese L1-A received the most methodic and sustained input exposure of the overall verbal agreement patterns. Tables 2a and 2b (appendix B) show verbal gender agreement patterns in past and present tense were present sporadically (more so in the past tense) in the instructional input of the Chinese L1-B Group 1 in the two booklets teaching Arabic letters and sounds (left half of tables 2a and 2b, appendix B). The target forms (third person singular masculine and third person singular feminine) were later more consistently maintained (more so in the present tense) in the main textbook (right half of tables 2a and 2b, appendix B). In the latter, third person singular masculine in past and present tense was formally introduced in Lessons 7 and 5, respectively, and third person singular feminine was introduced later in Lesson 11 (right half of tables 2a and 2b, appendix B).

As for the Russian L1 participants, tables 3a and 3b (appendix B) show that verbal gender agreement patterns (including third person singular masculine and third person singular feminine) were present from early on in the instructional input of the Russian L1-A Group 1 somewhat consistently throughout, starting with Units 11–20/30 and Units 5 and 6 for past tense (left and right half of table 3a, respectively) and with Units 1–10 and Units 3–4 for present tense (left and right half of table 3b, respectively). It is not clear when the two forms were formally introduced, but it is likely that they had been introduced while teaching the Arabic letters and sounds informally (i.e., without use of specific texts for Arabic letters and sounds) or in the grammar reference book (Jushmanov 1999) in Lesson 3. Tables 4a and 4b show the distribution of third person singular masculine and third person singular feminine agreement in the instructional input of the Russian L1-B participants. Both forms (i.e., third person singular masculine and feminine) in the past tense were maintained somewhat consistently once formally introduced in Lesson 5 in the book, which focuses on Arabic phonology and orthography (left half of table 4a, appendix B). Later, in the main textbook, third person singular masculine (in the past tense) was present and maintained consistently from beginning to end, whereas third person singular feminine was present starting with Lessons 4 and 5 and was maintained throughout thereafter (right half of table 4a, appendix B). Table 4b shows that both forms (i.e., third person singular masculine and third person singular feminine) in the present tense were absent from the first book, which focuses on phonology and orthography (left half of table 4b, appendix B), but both forms were present in the subsequent/main textbook from early on and were maintained consistently, though more consistently so in the case of third person singular masculine (right half of table 4b, appendix B). In addition, unlike the instructional input of the Chinese participants, the instructional input of the Russian participants does not seem to contain direct and indirect focus on the two forms through, for example, conjugations charts and drills.

The foregoing description of input frequency of verbal gender agreement patterns in Group 1 of all the participants reflect some variations due to the need to introduce Arabic phonology and orthography. However, in subsequent input for subsequent years 2 and 3 (corresponding to Groups 2 and 3), the variation is likely minimized due to the high frequency of the structure itself. Three observations can be made here. First, the input frequency of the Chinese L1-A participants is a little less comparable to that of their Russian L1-A counterparts. The former maintains a slightly more intensive exposure of the target verbal forms as well as more sustained exposure of the overall verbal patterns throughout. Second, the input frequency of the Chinese L1-B participants is somewhat comparable to that of their Russian L1-B counterparts and less consistent than that of their Chinese L1-A and Russian L1-A counterparts. Recall that the former also happen to receive double the amount of exposure time than the latter (see table 2.1, chapter 2). Third, the instructional input of the Russian L1-A, Russian L1-B, and Chinese L1-B participants does not contain indirect focus on the two forms through conjugation charts and drills.

4.5 Summary

Based on the acquisition data for verbal gender agreement presented in this chapter, one general observation found is that all participants (across all L1 backgrounds) exhibit a tendency to converge together in their use of third person singular masculine as the default form for verbal gender agreement, especially in the past tense and present tense random tasks (for a similar observation, see Al-Hamad 2003). Another general observation is the convergence by all participants in their performance of third person singular feminine and masculine verbal agreement at the advanced level (i.e., Group 3). A third finding is that, in particular, the participants in the Chinese L1-A beginner group maintain a (statistically significant) advantage over their Russian L1-A counterparts in verbal masculine agreement in present tense and in verbal feminine agreement in the random present task. However, whereas the Russian L1-A participants at subsequent levels (Groups 2 and 3) achieved steady gains in their accuracy of rule application in verbal feminine agreement in random present tense, the Chinese L1-A Groups 2 and 3 showed a backsliding pattern (figure 4.3).

Notwithstanding the acquisition pattern of the verbal feminine agreement in the present tense random task by the Chinese L1-A versus Russian L1-A participants, no group difference was found between the groups in verbal gender agreement in past tense. Acquisition factor effects attributed to L1 transfer would predict an advantage by the Russian participants over their Chinese counterparts on their production of verbal agreement in the past tense. Recall, whereas Russian exhibits a gender feature in past tense (but does not in the present tense), Chinese does not exhibit a gender feature in any tense. However, the Russian L1 participants maintained no such advantage. The detected advantage found in the Chinese participants in the beginner group over their Russian counterparts (whether in verbal masculine agreement in the present tense or verbal feminine agreement in the random present tense) may likely be instead due to the nature or quality of the instructional input. However, more importantly, no significant difference in the performance of the Russian participants themselves on verbal gender agreement in the past was detected over that in the present tense. In fact, the Russian participants overall had higher accuracy ratios of verbal agreement in the present than in the past tense (see tables 4.1 and 4.2). The theoretical and practical implications of these observations and findings are further discussed in chapters 7 and 8.

Notes

1. However, Chinese does make a distinction between past versus present tense as examples (13)–(16) show.

2. In attributing parametric variation to strength of functional features, standard minimalist assumption is adopted here. On this account, due to rich verbal agreement features, both Arabic and Russian are analyzed with the functional feature strength set to [+strong] while functional feature strength in Chinese is set to [-strong].

3. Note, neither Chinese nor Russian allows postverbal subjects (i.e., VSO word order) unlike Arabic, as illustrated in (5)–(8) above.

4. The study elicited production data from forty Russian L1 and Chinese L1 learners (assigned to two intermediate and two advanced groups with ten participants in each group) during "guided conversations"/interviews for an average of ten minutes each. The interviews were about general topics to do with the participant's family, country, previous and current studies, plans for the future, and social life in their native country and in Saudi Arabia. The study investigated definiteness, gender, number, tense, and verbal agreement. However, the features (including verbal agreement) were analyzed as belonging to clusters rather than separately. Thus, verbal agreement was analyzed as either belonging to one of four categories (feminine verbs, masculine verbs, singular verbs, and plural verbs) or two categories (masculine and feminine verbs and singular and plural verbs) (Al-Hamad 2003, 90–92, 103–8). The features for person and dual were dropped from the investigation (Al-Hamad 2003, 75).

5. From the displayed data (Al-Hamad 2003, 91, table 4), it seems *both* the intermediate (32.16%) and advanced (56.64%) Chinese groups were slightly less successful in feminine verbal agreement than their Russian counterpart groups who

scored 45.2% and 70.97%, respectively. With respect to masculine verbal agreement, the Chinese intermediate (97.55%) and advanced (97.98%) groups seem to have performed similar to their Russian counterparts (97.27% and 98.62%, respectively) with high accuracy rates (Al-Hamad 2003, 91, table 4), indicating that the participants seem to rely on the masculine form as a default form in line with previous findings (e.g., Alhawary 2009a).

6. For more on null-subject use, see chapter 6.

7. Post hoc analyses using Tukey tests were not performed due to limited data, specifically in the Chinese L1-B Group 1 (see also table 4.1). However, it was possible to run Bonferroni post hoc analyses for fewer comparisons, mainly between and within groups rather than all possible comparisons. The following statement about the robustness of Bonferroni for fewer comparisons is noteworthy: "When testing a large number of pairs of means, Tukey's honestly significant difference test is more powerful than the Bonferroni test. For a small number of pairs, Bonferroni is more powerful" (IBM Knowledge Center 2017).

8. The low number of tokens, in particular by participants at the beginner level (i.e., Group 1), is in part due to inaccuracies in their production of the correct tense. For more on the use of tense (past versus present) by the participants, see chapter 5.

9. This had been anticipated in the pilot stage of the study as well as similar previous studies (e.g., Alhawary 2009a). Reverting to use of either of the nonintended tenses may happen despite the fact that special care was taken in explaining to participants each of the past and present narrative tasks. Therefore, the present tense random task was provided to control for the potential artifact of the instrumentation at least for the present tense and to allow for more confidence with the data and results.

10. This constant tendency to use the singular masculine as a default form indicates that actual acquisition tendencies may best be captured by focusing on the participant' rule application of singular feminine.

11. Post hoc analyses using Tukey tests were not performed due to limited data, specifically in the Chinese L1-B Group 1 (see also table 4.3). See also note 7 above.

Chapter 5

The Acquisition of Tense/Aspect

This chapter discusses the acquisition of tense/aspect based on the collected cross-sectional data from all of the Chinese L1 and Russian L1 groups.[1] As discussed in chapter 1, investigation of tense/aspect is focused on past/perfective and present/imperfective in the context of third person singular masculine and third person singular feminine use, as in (21)–(28) in chapter 1, restated below as (1)–(8).

(1) ʔakala ʔal-tˤālib-(u)
ate.3.s.m the-student.s.m-(Nom)
"The male student ate."

(2) ʔakala-t ʔal-tˤālib-a[t]-(u)
ate-3.s.f the-student-s.f-(Nom)
"The female student ate."

(3) ya-ʔkul-(u) ʔal-tˤālib-(u)
3.s.m-eat-(Indic) the-student.s.m-(Nom)
"The male student eats/is eating."

(4) ta-ʔkul-(u) ʔal-tˤālib-a[t]-(u)
3.s.f-eat-(Indic) the-student-s.f-(Nom)
"The female student eats/is eating."

(5) ʔal-tˤālib-(u) ʔakala
the-student.s.m-(Nom) ate.3.s.m
"The male student ate."

(6) ʔal-tˤālib-a[t]-(u) ʔakala-t
the-student-s.f-(Nom) ate-3.s.f
"The female student ate."

(7) ʔal-tˤālib-(u) ya-ʔkul-(u)
the-student.s.m-(Nom) 3.s.m-eat-(Indic)
"The male student eats/is eating."

(8) ʔal-tˤālib-a[t]-(u) ta-ʔkul-(u)
the-student-s.f-(Nom) 3.s.f-eat-(Indic)
"The female student eats/is eating."

As explained in chapter 1, investigation of the above target forms has been carried out irrespective of the participants' production of mood endings (on present tense forms of verbs). In other words, tense features are the focus alone and regardless as to whether or not the participants produced verbal mood endings appropriately, avoided producing them partially or wholly, or did not produce them at all. Furthermore, focus of the investigation is on the contexts of third person singular masculine and third person singular feminine regardless of the position of the subject (i.e., whether postverbally or preverbally), as in (1)–(4) versus (5)–(8), or if the subject is realized as null (for more on null subjects, see chapter 6).

5.1 Typological Pairings

Based on the participants' L1s, the investigation of Arabic tense features (past versus present tense) results in two similar typological pairings. In addition to exhibiting different verb forms for past versus present tense, Russian (like Arabic) exhibits a gender distinction between singular masculine and singular feminine verbal agreement in the past tense (but not person), as in (9) and (10), though it does not exhibit gender in non-past/present tense (but it exhibits person in addition to number), as in (11) and (12).

(9) studyent yel
student.s.m ate.s.m
"The (male) student ate."

(10) studyent-kə yel-a
student-s.f ate-s.f
"The (female) student ate."

(11) studyent yest
student.s.m eat.3.s
"The (male) student eats/is eating."

(12) studyent-kə yest
student-s.f eat.3.s
"The (female) student eats/is eating."

As for Chinese, although it does not exhibit a gender distinction (or any agreement features) between third person singular masculine and third person singular feminine in any tense, it distinguishes between past versus present tense, as illustrated in (13)–(16).

(13)	nan	xue sheng	chi	le
	male	study apprentice	eat	past
	"The male student ate."			
(14)	nu	xue sheng	chi	le
	female	study apprentice	eat	past
	"The female student ate."			
(15)	nan	xue sheng	(zai)	chi
	male	study apprentice	(is)	eat
	"The male student eats (is eating)."			
(16)	nu	xue sheng	(zai)	chi
	female	study apprentice	(is)	eat
	"The female student eats (is eating)."			

Sentences (13) and (14) show that Chinese essentially marks the distinction between past and present by means of the past tense marker *le* "past" placed after the verb (for past tense use) and uses the form of the verb as the default present tense. As discussed above, the past and present tense forms of the verb in Russian are not identical, and the verb in the past is additionally inflected for verbal gender agreement.[2] Accordingly, the yielded typological pairings are (a) and (b), exhibiting partial structural proximity due to lack of verbal agreement in Chinese.

(a) Russian participants who are speakers of a [+tense] and [+strong] L1, learning L2 Arabic [+tense] and [+strong], with previous knowledge of L2 English [+tense] and [-strong]

(b) Chinese participants who are speakers of a [+tense] and [-strong] L1, learning L2 Arabic [+tense] and [+ strong], with previous knowledge of L2 English [+tense] and [-strong][3]

5.2 Previous Findings

Data from previous studies that investigated the acquisition of tense by Arabic L2 learners who are speakers of English, Spanish, and Japanese as L1s resulted in the following findings:

- Arabic L2 learners across groups did not differ in their performance of past and present tense (on narrative tasks[4]), and they exhibited a greater degree of variability in their present tense use than in past tense (Alhawary 2007b, 141; 2009a, 106).

- Arabic L2 learners exhibited much less variability in their performance on a present tense random task than in the past tense, the Japanese L1 participants outperformed their English L1 counterparts and slightly so their Spanish counterparts, and the English L1 participants' performance improved significantly over time, but their Japanese and Spanish counterparts did not (Alhawary 2007b, 146–47; 2009a, 110–12).

Since no statistically significant effect was found in the performance of participants of all three L1 backgrounds (English, Spanish, and Japanese) on (past and present) narrative tasks and since the findings from the random present tense task revealed no particular trend, it has been suggested that such differences are "minimal" at best (Alhawary 2009a, 165).[5]

In addition, Al-Hamad (2003) reported findings on a cross-sectional study of intermediate and advanced groups of Chinese L1 and Russian L1 learners of Arabic as an L2. The study investigated the production of a set of morphosyntactic structures including tense (past and present).[6] The findings revealed that both the Russian and Chinese groups were "extremely successful" at acquiring both tenses. On past tense, the Russian intermediate and advanced groups scored 100% and 98.02%, and their Chinese counterparts scored 100% and 91.10%, respectively, and on present tense the Russian intermediate and advanced groups both scored 100%, and their Chinese counterparts scored 98.03% and 99.33%, respectively. According to predictions of L1 transfer effects, we would expect such a finding (i.e., the lack of any difference between the performance of the Russian L1 and Chinese participants) since both Russian and Chinese exhibit a feature that distinguishes between past and present tense.

The typological pairings of the present study—with participants who are Russian L1 and Chinese L1 speakers—are significant to further verify the conclusion reached above and whether such typological effects have a bearing (in this case, presence or absence of a feature in L1) on L2 grammatical development. Furthermore, the different groups and their exposure settings (i.e., with two sets of groups receiving double the amount of instruction than their two counterpart sets) is significant to examine the extent of such typological effects when particularly combined with input frequency.

5.3 Results

The four narrative tasks discussed in chapter 2 elicited descriptions of the activities of a female and a male character. Two of the narratives focused on past tense: one about a male character (i.e., where past tense verbs are inflected for third person singular masculine) and another about a female character (i.e., where past tense verbs are inflected for third person singular feminine). The two other narratives focused on the present tense: one about a male character (i.e., where present tense verbs are inflected for third person singular masculine) and another about a female character (i.e., where present tense verbs are inflected for third person singular feminine). Examples of correct past and present tense use (inflected for third person singular masculine and third person singular feminine) are illustrated in sentences (17)–(28) extracted from the respective participants' data samples.

(17)	IL:	wa	fi-s-sabt	ðahaba-t	ʔilā	bayt-i-hā
		and	in-the-Saturday	went-3.s.f	to	house-Gen-her
		"And on Saturday, she went to her house."				
		(Russian L1-A: Group 1)				
(18)	IL:	wa	hiya	laʕiba-t	fī tenis	
		and	she	played-3.s.f	in tennis	
	TL:	wa	(hiya)	laʕiba-t	ʔat-tenis	
		and	(she)	played-3.s.f	the-tennis	
		"And she played tennis."				
		(Russian L1-A: Group 2)				
(19)	IL:	wa	qabila-t	kaθīr	min	ʔal-nuqūd
		and	accepted-3.s.f	a lot	of	the-money
	TL:	wa	ʔaxaða-t	kaθīran	min	ʔan-nuqūd
		and	took-3.s.f	a lot	of	the-money
		"And she took a lot of money."				
		(Russian L1-A: Group 3)				
(20)	IL:	*wa	ðahaba	ʔilā	dīsko	
		and	went.3.s.m	to	disco	
	TL:	wa	ðahaba-t	ʔilā	ʔad-dīsko	
		and	went-3.s.f	to	the-disco	
		"And she went to the disco."				
		(Chinese L1-A: Group 1)				

(21) IL: wa hiya raqas^{ʕ}a-t maʕa ʔal-zuwwār
and she danced-3.s.f with the-visitors
TL: wa (hiya) raqas^{ʕ}a-t maʕa ʔaz-zuwwār
and (she) danced-3.s.f with the-visitors
"And she danced with the visitors."
(Chinese L1-A: Group 2)

(22) IL: wa θumma ʕāda-t ʔilā manzil-i-hā
and then returned-3.s.f to house-Gen-her
TL: wa/θumma ʕāda-t ʔilā manzil-i-hā
and/then returned-3.s.f to house-Gen-her
"And/then, she returned to her house."
(Chinese L1-A: Group 3)

(23) IL: šābb-un ya-kraʔ-u
youth.s.m-Nom 3.s.m-read-Indic
TL: ʔaš-šābb-u ya-qraʔ-u
the-youth.s.m 3.s.m-read-Indic
"The young man reads."
(Russian L1-B: Group 1)

(24) IL: ya-qūm-u min nawm
3.s.m-wake-Indic from sleep
TL: ya-qūm-u min ʔan-nawm
3.s.m-wake-Indic from the-sleep
"He wakes up from sleep."
(Russian L1-B: Group 2)

(25) IL: ya-tanāwal-u t^{ʕ}-t^{ʕ}aʕām
3.s.m-take-Indic the-food
"He eats food."
(Russian L1-B: Group 3)

(26) IL: ya-qlaʔ-u kitāb
3.s.m-read-Indic a book
TL: ya-qraʔ-u kitāb-an
3.s.m-read-Indic a book-Acc
"He reads a book."
(Chinese L1-B: Group 1)

(27) IL: ya-nām-u fi-l-bayt-i
3.s.m-sleep-Indic in-the-house-Gen
"He sleeps in the house."
(Chinese L1-B: Group 2)

(28)	IL:	*ta-ktub-u	r-risāla	ʔilā	ʔasˤdiqāʔ-i-hi
		3.s.f-write-Indic	the-letter	to	friends-Gen-his
	TL:	ya-ktub-u	risāla	ʔilā	ʔasˤdiqāʔ-i-hi
		3.s.m-write-Indic	a letter	to	friends-Gen-his
		"He writes a letter to his friends."			
		(Chinese L1-B: Group 3)			

Examples (17)–(22) illustrate the correct use of past tense and examples (23)–(28), the correct use of present tense. Examples (17)–(22) illustrate use of past tense (in the context of third person singular feminine), and examples (23)–(28) illustrate use of present tense (in the context of third person singular masculine). Some of the produced tokens may contain incorrect use of verbal agreement, as in examples (20) and (28), but these are considered correct instances of past and present tense use, respectively (for more on verbal agreement, see chapter 4).[7] The produced tokens contain verbs with explicit (pronominal and NP) subjects, as in (18), (21), and (23), and null subjects, as in (17), (19), (20), (22), and (24)–(28).[8]

Tokens of incorrect use of rule application of past and present tense occurred when the participants used the present tense form of the verb instead of the past tense form and vice versa, as illustrated in examples (29)–(39) extracted from the data samples.

(29)	IL:	*ya-shab-u [ya-ðhab-u]	ʔila	l-bank
		3.s.m-go-Inidc	to	the-bank
	TL:	ðahaba-t	ʔila	l-bank
		went-3.s.f	to	the-bank
		"She went to the bank."		
		(Russian L1-B: Group 1)		

(30)	IL:	*hiya	lā	ta-ʕmal-u	šayʔ-an
		she	no	3.s.f-work-Indic	a thing-Acc
	TL:	hiya	lam	ta-ʕmal/mā ʕamila-t	šayʔ-an
		she	no	3.s.f-work/not worked-3.s.f	a thing-Acc
		"She did not do anything."			
		(Russian L1-B: Group 3)			

(31)	IL:	*hiya	ta-zūr-u	sˤadīq-a
		she	3.s.f-visit-Indic	friend-s.f

	TL:	hiya	zāra-t	sˁadīq-a	
		she	visited-3.s.f	friend-s.f	
		"She visited a female friend."			
		(Chinese L1-B: Group 1)			
(32)	IL:	*wa	tu-māris	ʔar-riyādˁ-a	ʔaydˁan
		and	3.s.f-practice	the-sport-s.f	also
	TL:	wa	mārasa-t	ʔar-riyādˁ-a	ʔaydˁan
		and	practiced-3.s.f	the-sport-s.f	also
		"She practiced sport also."			
		(Chinese L1-B: Group 2)			
(33)	IL:	*ya-ðhab-u	ʔilā	ʔal-Hadīq-a	
		3.s.m-go-Indic	to	the-park-s.f	
	TL:	ðahaba-t	ʔilā	ʔal-Hadīq-a	
		went-3.s.f	to	the-park-s.f	
		"She went to the park."			
		(Chinese L1-B: Group 3)			
(34)	IL:	*wa	huwa	nām	
		and	he	slept.3.s.m	
	TL:	wa	(huwa)	ya-nām	
		and	(he)	3.s.m-sleep	
		"And he sleeps."			
		(Russian L1-A: Group 1)			
(35)	IL:	*katab-ti	fī	kitāb	
		wrote-2.s.f	in	a book	
	TL:	ya-ktub	fī	kitāb	
		3.s.m-write	in	a book	
		"He writes in a book."			
		(Russian L1-A: Group 2)			
(36)	IL:	*wa	laʕaba [laʕiba]	kura-t-a	l-qadam
		and	played.3.s.m	ball-s.f-Acc	the-foot
	TL:	wa	ya-lʕab	kura-t-a	l-qadam
		and	3.s.m-play	ball-s.f-Acc	the-foot
		"And he plays soccer."			
		(Russian L1-A: Group 3)			
(37)	IL:	*dārasa-t [darasa-t]	fī	Hudʒr-at-i	dars
		studied-3.s.f	in	room-s.f-Gen	lesson
	IL:	ya-drus	fī	Hudʒr-at-i	dars
		3.s.m-study	in	room-s.f-Gen	lesson
		"He studies in a classroom."			
		(Chinese L1-A: Group 1)			

(38)	IL:	*huw	mārasa	sˤarāt [sˤalāt]	maʕa	zumalāʔ-i-hi
		he	practiced.3.s.m	prayer	with	friends-Gen-his
	TL:	huw	yu-māris	ʔasˤ-sˤalāt/yu-sˤalli	maʕa	zumalāʔ-i-hi
		he	3.s.m-practice	prayer/prays	with	friends-Gen-his

"He prays with his colleagues."
(Chinese L1-A: Group 2)

(39)	IL:	*wa	ðahaba	ʔila	l-masdʒid	li-l-kiyām	bisˤalāt
		and	went.3.s.m	to	the-mosque	for doing	prayer
	TL:	wa	ya-ðhab	ʔila	l-masdʒid	li-sˤ-sˤalāt	
		and	3.s.m-go	to	the-mosque	for-the-prayer	

"And he goes to the mosque to pray."
(Chinese L1-A: Group 3)

Examples (29)–(33) illustrate incorrect use of past tense (in the context of third person singular feminine) where the participants instead used the present tense form of the verb. Examples (34)–(39) illustrate incorrect use of present tense (in the context of third person singular masculine) where the participants instead used the past tense form of the verb. Some of the produced tokens also contained incorrect verbal agreement, as in (29), (33), (35), and (37). However, the two types of incorrect use of rule application (i.e., of tense and verbal agreement) were coded separately (for more on verbal agreement, see chapter 4).

5.3.1 The Past Tense

A snapshot of the participants' production data of past tense inflected for third person singular feminine and third person singular masculine is provided in table 5.1 (see also figures 5.1 and 5.2 illustrating the production trends of all participants across all groups). Unlike verbal agreement, use of past tense does not indicate that the participants used third person masculine as the default form.

Full factorial two-way ANOVA tests of past tense—inflected for third person singular feminine—showed a main effect for L1 backgrounds ($F(3, 83) = 7.864$, $p < 0.001$, partial $\eta^2 = 0.221$), a main effect for proficiency ($F(2,83) = 5.528$, $p = 0.006$, partial $\eta^2 = 0.118$), and a main interaction effect between L1 backgrounds and proficiency ($F(6,83) = 4.188$, $p = 0.001$, partial $\eta^2 = 0.232$). Post hoc analyses using Tukey tests of all possible pairwise comparisons revealed that overall the Chinese L1-A, Russian L1-A, and Russian L1-B groups all differed significantly from the Chinese L1-B groups: $p = 0.015$, $p < 0.001$, and $p = 0.001$, respectively. The differences are mostly due to the (significant) underperformance of the Chinese L1-B beginner and intermediate groups in

Table 5.1 Production of past tense

L2 Arabic	*Past Tense (Feminine) Correct/Total*	*% Correct*	*Past Tense (Masculine) Correct/Total*	*% Correct*
Chinese L1-A				
Group1 (n = 10)	69/75	92	74/93	80
Group2 (n = 10)	87/115	76	105/152	69
Group3 (n = 10)	114/136	84	141/185	76
Chinese L1-B				
Group1 (n = 9)	6/14	43	9/16	56
Group2 (n = 10)	40/100	40	41/96	43
Group3 (n = 10)	95/99	96	101/117	86
Russian L1-A				
Group1 (n = 9)	81/82	99	77/79	97
Group2 (n = 9)	116/125	93	105/119	88
Group3 (n = 9)	97/98	99	106/114	93
Russian L1-B				
Group1 (n = 5)	11/15	73	13/15	87
Group2 (n = 6)	53/53	100	56/56	100
Group3 (n = 8)	81/82	99	101/104	97

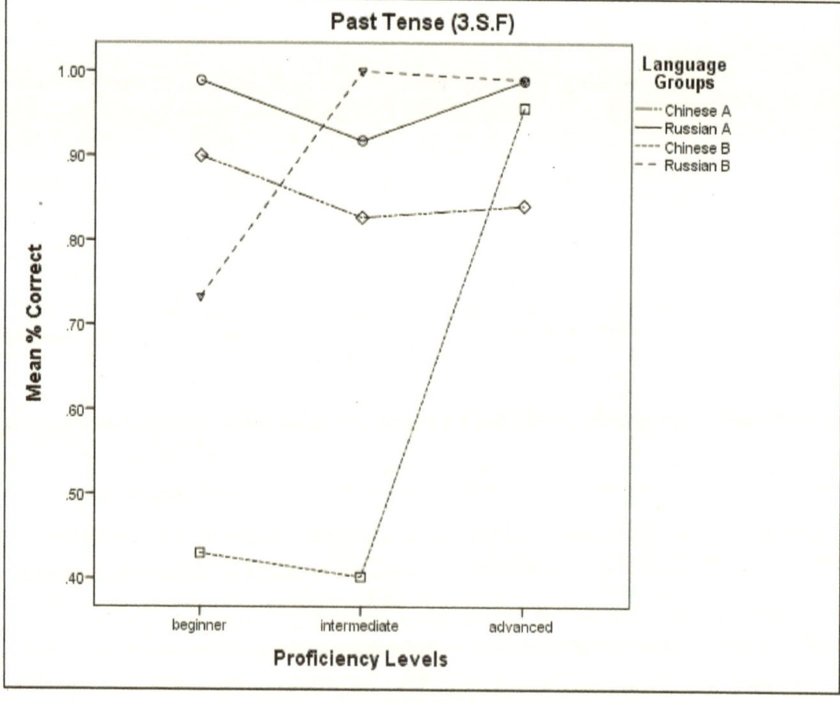

Figure 5.1 Interaction Plot of Mean % Correct for the Participants' Performance on Past Tense (inflected for 3.S.F) by Language Group and Proficiency Level

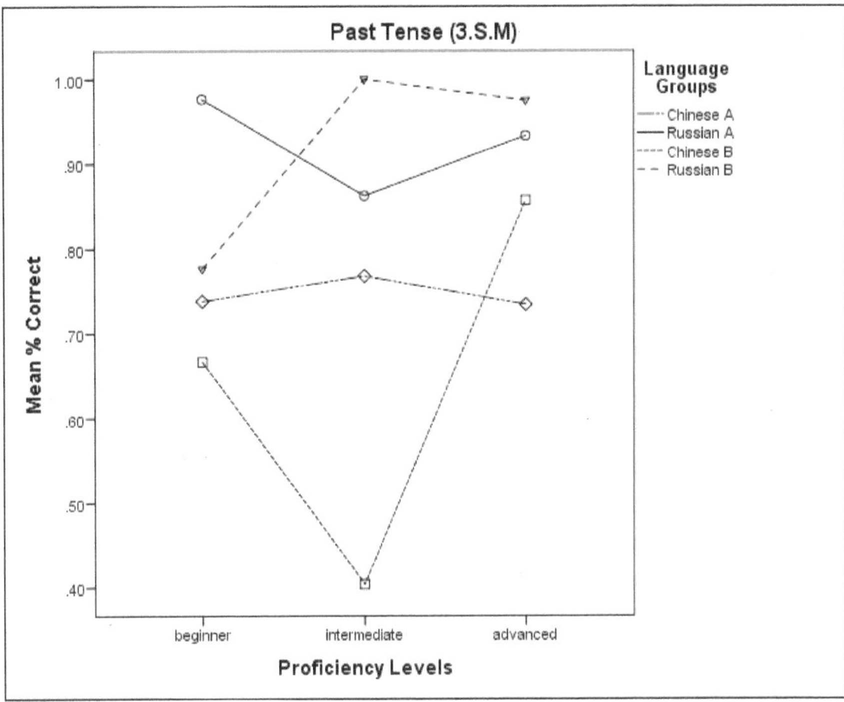

Figure 5.2 Interaction Plot of Mean % Correct for the Participants' Performance on Past Tense (inflected for 3.S.M) by Language Group and Proficiency Level

comparison with their other counterpart groups, with the advanced Chinese L1-B group catching up with their counterpart groups and differing significantly in particular from the intermediate Chinese L1-B group: $p < 0.001$ (see also figure 5.1).

Full factorial two-way ANOVA tests of past tense—inflected for third person singular masculine—revealed somewhat similar results to those of past tense use inflected for third person singular feminine. A main effect for L1 language backgrounds ($F(3,85) = 5.196$, $p = 0.002$, partial $\eta^2 = 0.155$) and a near main interaction effect between L1 backgrounds and proficiency ($F(6,85) = 2.093$, $p = 0.062$, partial $\eta^2 = 0.129$) were found. Post hoc analyses using Tukey tests revealed that overall the Russian L1-A groups differed significantly from the Chinese L1-B groups ($p = 0.001$) and nearly so from the Chinese L1-A groups ($p = 0.066$); so did the Russian L1-B groups from the Chinese L1-B groups ($p = 0.002$) and the Chinese L1-A groups ($p = 0.68$). The differences are mainly due to the (significant) underperformance of the Chinese L1-B intermediate group (i.e., Group 2) in comparison with their other counterpart groups, with the Chinese L1-B advanced group (i.e., Group 3) catching up with their counterpart groups and differing significantly from the Chinese L1-B intermediate group: $p = 0.014$ (see also figure 5.2).

In other words, the main (significant) findings that emerge about past tense is that the Chinese L1-B beginner and intermediate groups (i.e., Groups 1 and 2) underperformed their counterpart groups on past tense use inflected for third person singular feminine. Similarly, the Chinese L1-B intermediate group (i.e., Group 1) underperformed the other groups on past tense use inflected for third person singular masculine. In both cases, the Chinese L1-B groups improved significantly at the advanced level and caught up with the rest of their counterpart groups.

5.3.2 The Present Tense

Table 5.2 provides a snapshot of the participants' production data of present tense inflected for third person singular feminine and third person singular masculine (see also figures 5.3 and 5.4, illustrating the production trends of all participants across all groups). Unlike verbal agreement and like past tense use, use of present tense does not indicate the participants used third person masculine as the default form.

Full factorial two-way ANOVA tests of present tense—inflected for third person singular feminine—showed a main effect for L1 backgrounds ($F(3, 89) = 6.115$, $p = 0.001$, partial $\eta^2 = 0.171$) and a main interaction effect between L1 backgrounds and proficiency ($F(6,89) = 3.891$, $p = 0.002$, partial $\eta^2 = 0.208$). Post hoc analyses using Tukey tests of all possible pairwise comparisons revealed that overall the Chinese L1-A, Chinese L1-B, and Russian L1-A groups all differed significantly from the Russian L1-B groups: $p = 0.022$, $p < 0.001$, and $p = 0.011$, respectively. The differences are mainly due to the significant underperformance of the Russian L1-B intermediate and advanced groups as well as the near underperformance of the Russian L1-A beginner group (see also figure 5.3). In particular, and most importantly, the Chinese L1-B beginner group nearly differed from its Russian L1-A counterpart Group 1 ($p = 0.057$), the Chinese L1-B intermediate group significantly differed from its Russian L1-B counterpart Group 2 ($p = 0.002$), the Russian L1-A intermediate group significantly differed from its Russian L1-B counterpart Group 2 ($p = 0.032$), and the Russian L1-A advanced group significantly differed from its Russian L1-B counterpart Group 3 ($p = 0.016$).

Full factorial two-way ANOVA tests of present tense—inflected for third person singular masculine—revealed similar results to those of present tense use inflected for third person singular feminine. A main effect for L1 language backgrounds ($F(3,91) = 4.538$, $p = 0.005$, partial $\eta^2 = 0.130$), a main interaction

Table 5.2 Production of present tense

L2 Arabic	*Present Tense (Feminine) Correct/Total*	*% Correct*	*Present Tense (Masculine) Correct/Total*	*% Correct*
Chinese L1-A				
Group1 (n = 10)	24/56	43	18/52	35
Group2 (n = 10)	77/108	71	79/115	69
Group3 (n = 10)	77/133	58	92/135	68
Chinese L1-B				
Group1 (n = 9)	17/21	81	23/35	66
Group2 (n = 10)	87/88	99	102/104	98
Group3 (n = 10)	68/99	69	61/101	60
Russian L1-A				
Group1 (n = 9)	15/60	25	6/59	10
Group2 (n = 9)	75/88	85	69/87	79
Group3 (n = 9)	68/79	86	93/100	93
Russian L1-B				
Group1 (n = 5)	5/13	38	7/16	44
Group2 (n = 6)	10/42	24	16/43	37
Group3 (n = 8)	27/79	34	27/82	33

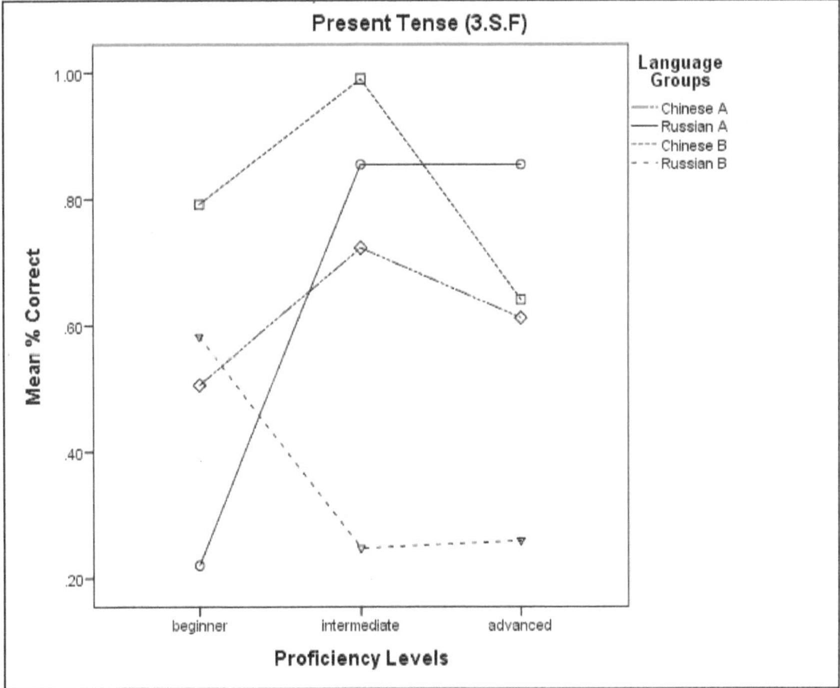

Figure 5.3 Interaction Plot of Mean % Correct for the Participants' Performance on Present Tense (inflected for 3.S.F) by Language Group and Proficiency Level

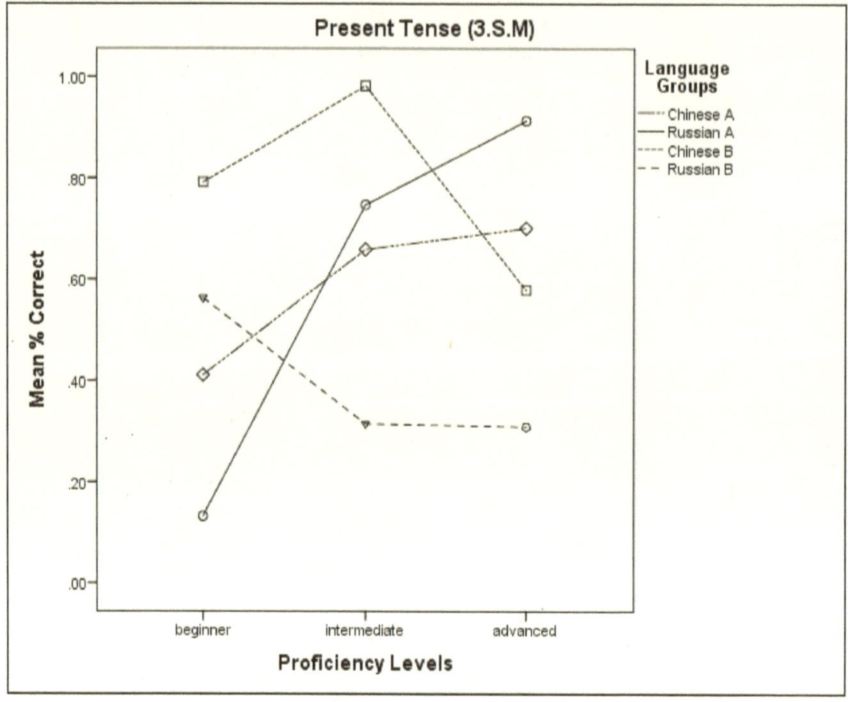

Figure 5.4 Interaction Plot of Mean % Correct for the Participants' Performance on Present Tense (inflected for 3.S.M) by Language Group and Proficiency Level

effect between L1 backgrounds and proficiency ($F(6,91) = 4.540$, $p < 0.001$, partial $\eta^2 = 0.230$), and a marginal effect for proficiency ($F(2,91) = 2.721$, $p = 0.071$, partial $\eta^2 = 0.056$) were found. Post hoc analyses using Tukey tests revealed that overall the Chinese L1-B groups as a whole differed significantly from the Russian L1-B groups ($p = 0.001$), with the former outperforming the latter. In addition, the Chinese L1-B beginner group differed from its Russian L1-A counterpart, Group 1 ($p = 0.009$); the Chinese L1-B intermediate group differed from both the Russian L1-B intermediate ($p = 0.016$) and advanced ($p = 0.005$) groups; and the Russian L1-A advanced group differed from its Russian L1-B counterpart Group 3 (p=0.024). The differences are mainly due to the significant underperformance of the Russian L1-B intermediate and advanced groups as well as the significant underperformance of the Russian L1-A beginner group (see also figure 5.4).

In other words, the main (significant) findings that emerge about present tense use (inflected for both third person singular masculine and feminine) is that the Russian L1-B intermediate and advanced groups (i.e., Groups 2 and 3) underperformed (in particular the Chinese L1-B intermediate group) and so did the Russian L1-A beginner group (in particular the Chinese L1-B beginner group). Although the performance of the Russian L1-B groups exhibited a decline beyond the beginner group, the Russian L1-A groups significantly improved in both present tense inflected for third person feminine ($p = 0.005$) and third person singular masculine ($p = 0.014$), starting from the intermediate level.

5.3.3 The Present Tense (Random Task)

Due to the nature of the narrative tasks where some participants may misunderstand the tasks and use the past tense in present tense narratives or the present tense in past tense narratives, participants' performance on a random present tense task was examined to provide additional evidence (see chapter 3).[9] Table 5.3 summarizes the performance of all participants of all L1 groups on the production of present tense use in the random task, inflected for third person singular masculine and feminine (see also figures 5.5 and 5.6). Like past and present tense, production of present tense in the random task does not indicate that the participants used third person masculine as the default form.

Table 5.3 Production of present tense random task

L2 Arabic	*Present Random (Feminine) Correct/Total*	*% Correct*	*Present Random (Masculine) Correct/Total*	*% Correct*
Chinese L1-A				
Group1 (n = 10)	22/23	96	40/42	95
Group2 (n = 10)	93/100	93	197/215	92
Group3 (n = 10)	186/198	94	218/251	87
Chinese L1-B				
Group1 (n = 9)	2/2	100	7/8	88
Group2 (n = 10)	68/68	100	117/119	98
Group3 (n = 10)	101/117	86	143/172	83
Russian L1-A				
Group1 (n = 9)	13/32	41	14/36	39
Group2 (n = 9)	86/93	92	126/135	93
Group3 (n = 9)	65/70	93	118/122	97
Russian L1-B				
Group1 (n = 5)	6/7	86	4/5	80
Group2 (n = 6)	14/22	64	18/32	56
Group3 (n = 8)	66/79	84	90/129	70

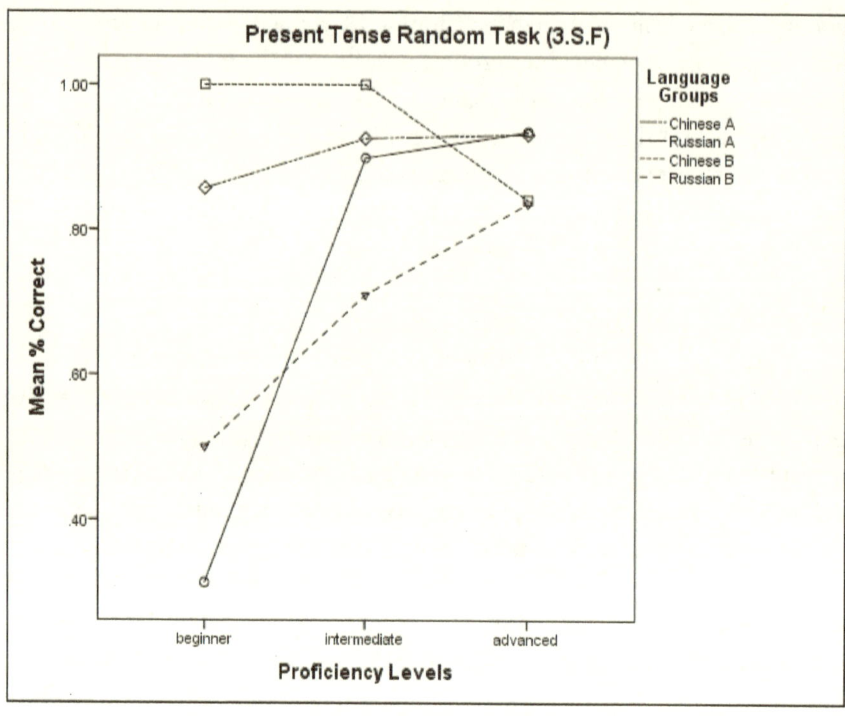

Figure 5.5 Interaction Plot of Mean % Correct for the Participants' Performance on Present Tense in Random Task (inflected for 3.S.F) by Language Group and Proficiency Level

Full factorial two-way ANOVA tests of present tense in the random task—inflected for third person singular feminine—revealed a main effect for L1 language backgrounds ($F(3,79) = 5.237$, $p = 0.002$, partial $\eta^2 = 0.166$), a main effect for proficiency ($F(2,79) = 4.454$, $p = 0.015$, partial $\eta^2 = 0.101$), and a main interaction effect between L1 backgrounds and proficiency ($F(6,79) = 3.601$, $p = 0.003$, partial $\eta^2 = 0.215$). Post hoc analyses using Tukey tests of all possible pairwise comparisons revealed that overall both the Chinese L1-A and Chinese L1-B groups as a whole differed significantly from the Russian L1-A groups ($p = 0.038$ and $p = 0.028$, respectively). The difference is mainly due to the underperformance of the Russian L1-A beginner group. The Chinese L1-A and Chinese L1-B beginner groups differed significantly from their Russian L1-A counterpart, Group 1: $p = 0.002$ and $p = 0.022$, respectively (see also figure 5.5). However, the Russian L1-A groups improve significantly over time, with the intermediate group differing significantly from the beginner group ($p < 0.001$), though the advanced group does not differ significantly from the intermediate one.

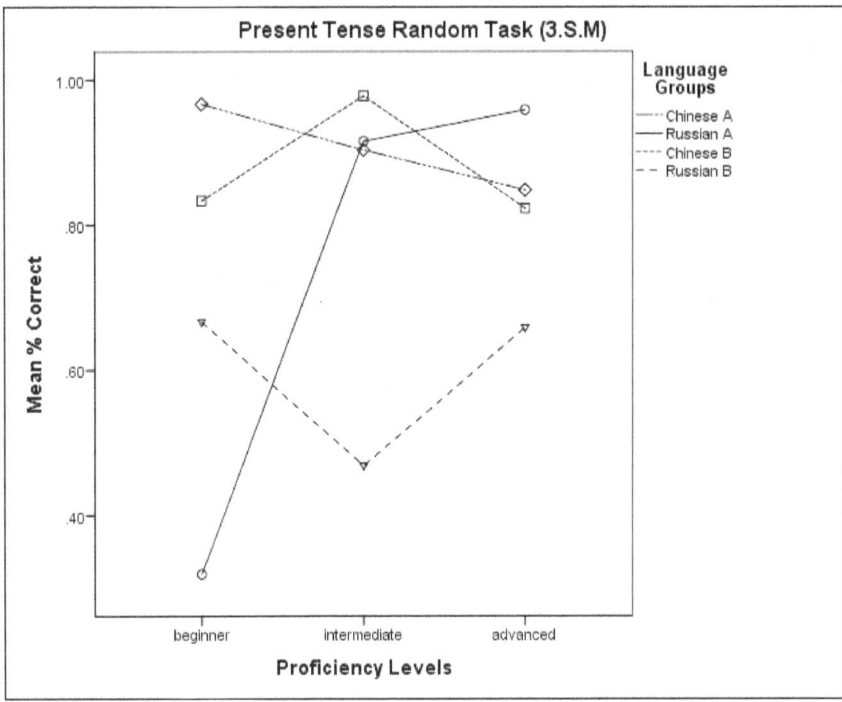

Figure 5.6 Interaction Plot of Mean % Correct for the Participants' Performance on Present Tense in Random Task (inflected for 3.S.M) by Language Group and Proficiency Level

Full factorial two-way ANOVA tests of present tense in the random task—inflected for third person singular masculine—revealed somewhat similar results to present tense use inflected with third person singular feminine, although here the difference between groups is due to the underperformance of the Russian L1-B intermediate group in addition to that of the Russian L1-A beginner group. The tests revealed a main effect for L1 language backgrounds ($F(3,84) = 7.778$, $p < 0.001$, partial $\eta^2 = 0.217$) and a main interaction effect between L1 backgrounds and proficiency ($F(6,84) = 6.849$, $p < 0.001$, partial $\eta^2 = 0.329$). Post hoc analyses using Tukey tests revealed that overall the Chinese L1-A groups differed significantly from their Russian L1-A ($p = 0.044$) and Russian L1-B ($p < 0.001$) counterparts, and the Chinese L1-B groups differed significantly from their Russian L1-B counterparts ($p < 0.001$). In particular, the Chinese L1-A beginner group differed significantly from the Russian L1-A beginner ($p < 0.001$) and the Russian L1-B intermediate ($p = 0.002$) groups, the Chinese L1-A intermediate group differed significantly from its Russian L1-B counterpart group ($p = 0.014$), the Chinese L1-B beginner group differed significantly from its Russian L1-A counterpart group ($p = 0.042$), the Chinese L1-B intermediate group differed significantly from its Russian L1-B counterpart group ($p = 0.002$), and the Russian L1-A intermediate group differed significantly from its Russian L1-B counterpart group ($p = 0.013$). Although the Russian L1-B groups seem to have improved over time (i.e., from the intermediate to the advanced level), the difference is not statistically significant. However, the improvement of the Russian groups (and catching up with the Chinese groups) is statistically significant; specifically, the Russian L1-A intermediate group differed significantly from the Russian L1-A beginner group: $p < 0.001$ (see figure 5.6).

In other words, the main (significant) findings that emerge about present tense use in the random task is that the Russian L1-A beginner group (i.e., Group 1) underperformed their Chinese L1-A and Chinese L1-B counterparts (with present tense inflected for both third person singular feminine and masculine). In addition, the Russian L1-B intermediate group (i.e., Group 2) underperformed their Chinese L1-A and Chinese L1-B as well as their Russian L1-A counterpart groups (with the present tense inflected for third person singular masculine). Although overall both Russian groups exhibited improvement along proficiency levels, only the Russian L1-A groups significantly improved in both present tense (in the random task) inflected for third person feminine and third person singular masculine starting from the intermediate level. Thus, the findings of the present tense random task seem to replicate somewhat the findings of the present tense narrative tasks reported on above.

5.4 Input Frequency

The above findings were obtained at least in part due to the participants' formal instructional input as displayed in tables 1–4 in appendix B. In particular, the tables show how often and when past and present tense (each inflected for third person singular masculine and feminine) were presented in the textbooks of Group 1 of the Chinese L1-A, Chinese L1-B, Russian L1-A, and Russian L1-B participants. Although past and present tense are high-frequency forms, input information is provided only for Group 1 (corresponding to the first year of exposure) due to the variation in the introduction and presentation of the two forms in Arabic first year curricula and due to the introduction of Arabic letters and sounds. Although focus of past and present tense investigation is in the context of third person singular masculine and third person singular feminine, other agreement patterns are included in the tables to provide the bigger picture for the presentation of past and present tense in the participants' formal instructional input.

Tables 1a and 1b (appendix B) show the presentation schedule of past and present tense, respectively, in the instructional input of the Chinese L1-A Group 1, the early presence of both tenses since Lessons 3 and 4 (presented together with Arabic sounds and letters), the formal introduction of both tenses at the same time in Lesson 13, and their consistent maintenance thereafter until Lesson 24. Participants in the Chinese L1-A groups do not seem to encounter difficulty acquiring past and present tense nor do they exhibit any asymmetry in the acquisition of both tenses, probably due to the introduction of both tenses at the same time and due to the nature and quality of the appropriate instructional input (including the direct and indirect focus on the two forms), although their performance seem to oscillate overall.

Tables 2a and 2b (appendix B) display past and present tense schedule in the instructional input of the Chinese L1-B Group 1 in the two booklets teaching Arabic letters and sounds (left half of tables 2a and 2b, appendix B) and the main textbook (right half of tables 2a and 2b, appendix B). Overall, past tense (table 2a, appendix B) is noticeably less consistently maintained than present tense (table 2b, appendix B), especially in the beginning six to seven lessons of the instructional materials. In addition, past tense inflected for third person singular feminine is noticeably less maintained than third person singular masculine throughout. Furthermore, present tense was introduced before past tense: in Lessons 5 and 7, respectively. This asymmetry in the instructional input of the two tenses seems to reflect the underperformance of the Chinese L1-B intermediate group (on past tense inflected for third singular masculine) as well as the beginner and intermediate groups (on past tense inflected for third person singular feminine).

Tables 3a and 3b (appendix B) show the scheduled presentation of past and present tense in the formal instructional input of the Russian L1-A Group 1. Both forms seem to be present somewhat consistently and comparably throughout, starting with Units 11–20/30 and Units 5 and 6 for past tense (left and right half of table 3a, respectively) and with Units 1–10 and Units 3 and 4 for present tense (left and right half of table 3b, respectively). It is not clear when both tenses were formally introduced, but it is likely that they were introduced while teaching the Arabic letters and sounds informally (i.e., without use of a specific text for Arabic letters and sounds) or in the grammar reference book (Jushmanov 1999) in Lesson 3, although the grammatical explanation is mostly relevant to past tense. The asymmetry in the performance of the Russian L1-A Group 1 (i.e., with their underperformance on present tense versus past tense) is not exactly clear, although the initial heavy emphasis on past tense forms in the grammatical explanation and the fact that past tense is slightly more consistently maintained in the instructional input may likely explain this trend.

Table 4a and 4b (appendix B) display past and present tense schedule in the instructional input of the Russian L1-B Group 1. Table 4a shows past tense was formally introduced in Lesson 5 in the book that focuses on Arabic phonology and orthography and was thereafter somewhat consistently maintained (left half of table 4a, appendix B). Later, in the main textbook, past tense inflected for third person singular masculine was present and maintained consistently from beginning to end, whereas past tense inflected for third person singular feminine was present starting with Lessons 4 and 5 and was maintained throughout thereafter (see right half of table 4a, appendix B). However, present tense is completely absent from the first book, which focuses on phonology and orthography (left half of table 4b, appendix B). It was later introduced in the main textbook from early on and was maintained thereafter, although more consistently so when inflected for third person singular masculine (right half of table 4b, appendix B). The underperformance of participants in the Russian L1-B Groups 2 and 3 on present tense as opposed to past tense is likely due to the deficiency of present tense in the input in comparison with the input of the past tense.

The foregoing description of input frequency of past and present tense in Group 1 of all the participants reflects some variations due in part to the need to introduce Arabic phonology and orthography. In subsequent input for subsequent years 2 and 3 (corresponding to Groups 2 and 3), the variation is likely minimized due to the high-frequency nature of the target (past and present) tense forms. However, what is crucial here is that the variations in the instructional input of the four different groups seem to reflect closely the participants' variable performance of past and present tense. Both past and present tense were introduced in the instructional input of the Chinese L1-A beginner participants at the same time and maintained consistently throughout; accordingly, the Chinese L1-A participants performed similarly in both. Past tense was introduced in the input of the Chinese L1-B beginner participants later than present tense (and the latter with slightly weaker frequency); accordingly, the Chinese L1-B participants performed better on present than past tense. Conversely, past tense was presented in the input of the Russian L1-B beginner participants before present tense (and the latter was totally absent from the entire first book); accordingly, the Russian L1-B participants performed better on past than on present tense. Finally, although past and present tense seem to have both been presented at the same time (but it could not be exactly determined when each was introduced), heavy emphasis on past tense forms in the grammatical explanation as well as more dense maintenance of past than present tense in the input may explain why the Russian L1-A participants performed better on past than present tense. A similar input exposure effect is found in Alhawary (2009a), where, for example, the English L1 beginner participants used past tense (91%) more accurately than present tense (67%) and present tense in the random task (57%), having been exposed to past tense much earlier than present tense based on Abboud and colleagues' (1983) textbook (Alhawary 2009a, 88, 107–11).

Thus, the preponderance of evidence here seems to indicate that the feature tense, given the present typological pairings, seems to be subject to input presentation bias depending on quality and timing of input presentation, where early exposure to a particular tense reflects accuracy in use of that tense. This explanation of input exposure effects is quite plausible, especially since the likelihood of (positive) L1 transfer effects is the same across all groups due to presence of the tense feature in both L1s: Chinese and Russian.

5.5 Summary

Based on the acquisition data for past and present tense presented in this chapter, a main observation is that, unlike their tendency with respect to nominal and verbal agreement, the participants did not exhibit a tendency to use third person singular masculine as the default form for either the past or the present tense. In addition, the following findings are revealed: (1) the Chinese L1-B beginner and intermediate groups underperformed their counterpart groups on past tense use (inflected for third person singular feminine), and the Chinese L1-B intermediate group underperformed their counterpart groups on past tense use (inflected for third person singular masculine), although Chinese L1-B participants improved significantly at the advanced level; (2) the Russian L1-B intermediate and advanced groups underperformed their Chinese L1-B intermediate counterparts on present tense, and the Russian L1-A beginner group underperformed its Chinese L1-B counterpart on present tense although the Russian L1-A groups significantly improved along proficiency; and (3) the Russian L1-B intermediate group underperformed its other counterparts, and the Russian L1-A beginner group underperformed its Chinese L1-A and Chinese L1-B counterparts on present tense use (in the random task), replicating somewhat the findings of the present tense narrative tasks. Thus, of all the groups, the Chinese L1-A groups seem to maintain their performance without showing any significant improvement or decline across groups. The crucial finding here, based on analysis of the formal instructional input of the participants, is that the variable performance or asymmetry in the performance of the participants is likely due to instructional input effects (i.e., quality and timing of the instructional input), since possible (positive) L1 transfer effects of tense are the same across all groups. Recall, both L1 Chinese and L1 Russian exhibit a tense feature (like Arabic and English). The theoretical and practical implications of past and present tense findings are further discussed in chapters 7 and 8.

Notes

1. As stated in chapter 1, the intention here is not to force a strict tense versus aspect analysis of the Arabic verb. Fassi Fehri argues that a proper characterization of Arabic is one that takes both into account with Arabic exhibiting "a dual tense-aspect" verbal inflectional system (1993, 146). For the purpose of the current study, reference is primarily made to tense, but this should not necessarily preclude an aspectual component or analysis.

2. Neither Chinese nor Russian allows postverbal subjects (i.e., SVO word order), unlike Arabic, as illustrated in (1)–(4), above.

3. In attributing parametric variation to strength of functional features, standard minimalist assumption is adopted here. On this account, due to rich verbal agreement features, both Arabic and Russian are analyzed with the functional feature strength set to [+strong] while functional feature strength in Chinese is set to [-strong].

4. These narrative tasks are similar to those discussed below in section 5.3 (see also section 2.5, chapter 2).

5. It has been claimed as a consequence that such findings are not in support of the Split-INFL hypothesis (see Alhawary 2009a, 165).

6. Al-Hamad (2003) also investigated definiteness, gender, number, and verbal agreement, in addition to tense. The study elicited production data from forty Russian L1 and Chinese L1 learners (assigned to two intermediate and two advanced groups with ten participants in each group) during "guided conversations"/interviews for an average of ten minutes each. The interviews were about general topics to do with the participant's family, country, previous and current studies, plans for the future, and social life in their native country and in Saudi Arabia (Al-Hamad 2003, 80 81).

7. Some of the produced tokens also contain phonological inaccuracies as indicated in the TL renditions.

8. For more on null-subject use, see chapter 6.

9. This had been anticipated in the pilot stage of the study as well as similar previous studies (e.g., Alhawary 2009a). Reverting to use of either of the non-intended tenses may happen despite the fact that special care was taken in explaining to participants each of the past and present narrative tasks. Therefore, the present tense random task was provided to control for the potential artifact of the instrumentation at least for the present tense and to allow for more confidence with the data and results.

Chapter 6

The Acquisition of Null Subjects

This chapter discusses the acquisition of null subjects based on cross-sectional data from all of the Chinese L1 and Russian L1 groups. The target structure of null subjects is of the main clause (i.e., non-embedded construction) type in both the past and present tense and inflected for third person singular masculine and third person singular feminine, as illustrated in sentences (29)–(32), discussed in chapter 1 and restated below as (1)–(4), where use of an overt/lexical pronominal or NP subject in matrix (or main) clause is optional.

(1) ʔakala
ate.3.s.m
"He ate."

(2) ʔakala-t
ate-3.s.f
"She ate."

(3) ya-ʔkul-(u)
3.s.m-eat-(Indic)
"He eats/is eating."

(4) ta-ʔkul-(u)
3.s.f-eat-(Indic)
"She eats/is eating."

As described in chapter 1, Arabic does not allow null-subject use in contexts such as embedded clauses following the complementizers *ʔinna* "that" and *ʔanna* "that" or any of their sisters *lākinna* "but," *kaʔanna* "it seems that/as though," *layta* "would that," and *laʕalla* "hope that," as in (5)–(7).

(5)	ʔa-ðˁunn-(u)	ʔanna-**hu**	ʔakala	
	1.s-think-(Indic)	that-**he**	ate.3.s.m	
	"I think that he ate."			
(6)	ʔana	ʤawʕān-(u)	lākinna-**hā**	ʔakala-t
	I	hungry-(Nom)	but-**she**	ate-3.s.f
	"I am hungry, but she ate."			

(7) ya-bdū kaʔanna-**hu** ya-ʔkul-(u)
3.s.m-seem as though-**he** 3.s.m-eat-(Indic)
"It/he seems as though he is eating."

Another context where use of pronominal subjects is obligatory includes constructions such as nominal sentences functioning as "adverbs of manner" or "circumstantial clauses" so long as the circumstantial clause is preceded by the conjunction particle *wa* "and" to trigger the requirement of a nominal rather than verbal circumstantial clause, as in (8).

(8) daxala wa **huwa** ya-ʜmil-(u) ʕulba
entered.3.s.m and he 3.s.m-carry-(Indic) a can
"He entered carrying a can."

A context that exhibits preference for use of pronominal subjects is when an NP subject is conjoined with a pronoun suffix of an immediately preceding verb, in which case a pronoun subject is preferably used to separate (or block the surface conjoining) between the verb and the lexical NP subject (if no other form is used to separate them), as in (9).[1]

(9) ʔarāda ʔan yu-sāfir-(a) **huwa** wa zawʤat-u-hu
Wanted.3.s.m to 3.s.m-travel-(Subjunc) he and wife-Nom-his
"He and his wife wanted to travel."

Additionally, pronominal subjects have a pragmatic function and are used when the subjects of two verbs are being contrasted or in focus whether they occur within SVO or VSO word order, as in (10) and (11), respectively.

(10) **huwa** ya-drus-(u) ʔal-handasa
he 3.s.m-study-(Indic) the-engineering
wa **hiya** ta-drus-u ʔal-tˤibb
and she 3.s.f-study-(Indic) the-medicine
"He studies engineering and she studies medicine."

(11) ʔin kun-ta **ʔan-ta** ʔal-qitˤtˤ-a fa-ʔayna ðahaba ʔal-laʜm
If were-2.s.m you-2.s.m the-cat-Acc so-where went.3.s.m the-meat
"If you yourself were the cat, where did the meat go?"

Although focus of the study does not include functional uses of pronominal subjects, the study nevertheless attempts to examine such uses in the instructional input to which the participants were exposed as well as production of prononminal subjects by the participants.

6.1 Typological Pairings

Based on the participants' L1s, the investigation of Arabic null subjects here results in two somewhat different typological pairings. On the one hand, there is a disagreement as to whether Russian is considered a null-subject language (e.g., Perlmutter and Moore 2002; Müller 2006, 2008) or that instances with contextually licensed subjectless positions in Russian are instead considered mere instances of ellipsis (e.g., Franks 1995; Avrutin and Rohrbacher 1997, as cited by Müller 2006). Based on the null-subject account, Perlmutter and Moore (2002) point out (following Franks 1995) that "pro-drop in Russian is subject to discourse conditions that make it much less common than pro-drop in Italian or Spanish" (Perlmutter and Moore 2002, 632). Müller adds that, in addition to null subjects use being "more restricted" than in other null-subject languages, "there is an asymmetry between 1./2. person vs. 3. person contexts, with the former ones permitting subject omission somewhat easier than the latter ones" (Müller 2008, 6). The analysis adopted here is that, following Franks (1995), Russian is a "mixed" null-subject language. Optional subject pronouns are illustrated in sentences (12)–(15), where the pronoun subjects can be dropped, for example, in answers to questions as to whether "he/she ate" and "he/she eats/is eating."[2]

(12) (on) yel
(he) ate.s.m
"He ate."

(13) (ona) yel-a
(she) ate-s.f
"She ate."

(14) (on) yest
(he) eat.3.s
"He eats/is eating."

(15) (ona) yest
(she) eat.3.s
"She eats/is eating."

In addition, Russian, like Arabic, exhibits gender and number (but not person) verbal agreement in past tense, as in (12) and (13), and exhibits person and number (but not gender) agreement in present tense, as in (14) and (15).

On the other hand, Chinese is more freely analyzed as a null-subject language, with the dropped subject in matrix clause being identified by a referent in the discourse. Thus, optional subject pronouns in sentences (17)–(20) can occur, for example, in answers to questions as to whether "he/she ate a meal" and "he/she eats or is eating a meal" (see also Huang 1989).

(17)	(ta)	chi	le	fan
	(he)	eat	past	meal
	"He ate a meal."			
(18)	(ta)	chi	le	fan
	(she)	eat	past	meal
	"She ate a meal."			
(19)	(ta)	chi	fan	
	(he)	eat	meal	
	"He eats a meal."			
(20)	(ta)	chi	fan	
	(she)	eat	meal	
	"She eats a meal."			
(21)	(ta)	zai	chi	fan
	(he)	is	eat	meal
	"He is eating a meal."			
(22)	(ta)	zai	chi	fan
	(she)	is	eat	meal
	"She is eating a meal."			

Sentences (17) and (18) express the Chinese past tense structures equivalent to those of Arabic in (1) and (2), and sentences (19)–(22) express the Chinese simple present and present progressive structures equivalent to those of Arabic in (3) and (4), above. In addition, as sentences (17)–(22) illustrate, Chinese (unlike Arabic) does not exhibit verbal agreement neither in the past nor present tense, though it exhibits a tense feature/distinction.

Accordingly, pairings (a) and (b) are yielded, where both Arabic and Chinese drop subject pronouns freely in matrix clauses whereas Russian exhibits mixed null-subject use.[3]

(a) Russian participants who are speakers of a [±null] and [+strong] L1, learning L2 Arabic [+null] and [+strong] L2, with previous knowledge of L2 English [-null] and [-strong]

(b) Chinese participants who are speakers of a [+null] and [-strong] L1, learning L2 Arabic [+null] and [+ strong], with previous knowledge of L2 English [-null] and [-strong][4]

6.2 Previous Findings

L2 studies on null subjects revealed that adult speakers of null- (such as Spanish) or non-null-subject languages (such as English and German) learning a null- or non-null-subject language seem to adjust to the L2 system, and in all such language pairings L2 learners produce subjectless clauses from their early stages of L2 acquisition. Studies also showed that speakers of non-null-subject languages learning a non-null-subject language reject more subjectless sentences than speakers of null-subject languages learning a non-null-subject language (see Alhawary 2007a for a detailed review).

As for Arabic studies on null subjects, data from previous studies, which investigated the acquisition of null subjects use by Arabic L2 learners who are speakers of English [-null], Spanish [+null], and Japanese [+null] as L1s, yielded the following findings:

- Arabic L2 learners who are English L1, Japanese L1, and Spanish L1 speakers seem to adjust to the Arabic L2 system and drop lexical subjects (in narrative tasks[5]) from early on (Alhawary 2007a; 2009a, 120–21).
- Arabic L2 learners who are Spanish L1 speakers (especially the beginner group) drop significantly fewer lexical subjects than their English L1 and Japanese L1 counterparts (Alhawary 2007a; 2009a, 120–22).
- A contingent relationship was found between the production of subjectless sentences and verbal agreement, explaining the unexpected finding in the Spanish L1 participants. It was found that in addition to producing far fewer sentences with null subjects (than their English L1 and Japanese L1 counterparts), the Spanish L1 (beginner) participants produced far lower ratios of verbal agreement but with more exposure to Arabic L2 input over time; the Spanish participants (the intermediate and advanced group) exhibited an increase in both null-subject production and correct verbal agreement accuracy (Alhawary 2007a; 2009a, 112–24).[6]
- The Arabic L1 control group dropped by far more lexical subjects than any of the three English L1, Japanese L1, and Spanish L1 groups (Alhawary 2007a; 2009a, 120–22).

The novel typological pairings of the present study—with participants who are Russian L1 and Chinese L1 speakers learning Arabic as an L2—are crucial to further verify the findings of previous studies as well as, in particular, null subjects use by L1 speakers of a mixed null-subject language (such as Russian) that exhibits null subjects partially or less freely in main clause than Chinese and Arabic.

6.3 Results

6.3.1 Null-Subject Production

The focus of null-subject production is on third person singular masculine and feminine as null or lexical subjects. Analysis of the participants' null-subject use is based on their spontaneous performance on four narrative tasks: two in the present tense and two in the past tense (for a detailed description, see chapter 2, section 2.5). Since each of the four narrative tasks is on a specific character (male or female), one would expect each of the six native (control) speakers to produce between 0–4 contexts with overt lexical subjects (NPs or pronouns), with one token for each task to introduce the first event. In Arabic, once the first event in each narrative is bound by an explicit pronominal or NP subject (or a known referent in the discourse), producing a lexical subject for each subsequent event of a narrative becomes redundant.[7] The control participants produced tokens within the predicted range. All of the six native Arabic speakers produced eleven overt subjects (four pronouns and seven NPs), and all except one occurred as a description of the first event of a narrative. Apart from one token, all contexts occurred with the overt subjects in a preverbal position. Only one control participant produced 100% null-subject contexts.

In addition, the control group occasionally produced (obligatory) overt pronominal subjects in embedded clauses with verbs such as *yabdū* "it seems," *kaʔanna* "looks like," and *yumkin* "it is possible" and following the complementizer *ʔanna*, as illustrated in (23) and (24).

(23)	ya-bdū	ʔanna-**hā**	ta-sˤʜū	bākira
	3.s.m-seem	that-she	3.s.f-wake up	early
	"It seems that she wakes up early."			
(24)	kaʔanna-**hu**	kāna	ya-ʔkul-u	kaθīran
	looks.like-he	was.3.s.m	3.s.m-eat-Indic	a lot
	"It looks like he was eating a lot."			

The control participants produced a total of twenty-four such tokens in the narratives. As for the four groups of participants (Chinese L1-A, Chinese L1-B, Russian L1-A, and Russian L1-B), they produced a small number of such tokens: a total of forty-eight tokens of obligatory overt pronominal subjects mainly in embedded clauses as displayed in table 6.1. Sentences (25)–(35) are representative examples extracted from the data.

(25) IL: lākinna-**hu** ðahaba ʔilā ʔal-shopping
but-he went.3.s.m to the-shopping
"... but he went shopping."
(Chinese L1-A: Group 1)

(26) IL: liʔanna-**hu** ya-ʜibb kura-t-a l-qadam
because-he 3.s.m-like ball-s.f-Acc the-foot
"... because he likes soccer."
(Chinese L1-A: Group 2)

(27) IL: ʔa-ðˤunn ʔinna-**hā** tˤālib-a tˤayyib-a
1.s-think that-she student-s.f kindhearted-s.f
TL: ʔa-ðˤunn ʔanna-**hā** tˤālib-a tˤayyib-a
1.s-think that-she student-s.f kindhearted-s.f
"... and I think she is a kindhearted student."
(Chinese L1-A: Group 2)

(28) IL: ʔa-ðˤunn ʔinna-**hā** šābb-at-un ʔūrūppiyy-a
1.s.-think that-she young-s.f-Nom European-s.f
TL: ʔa-ðˤunn ʔanna-**hā** šābb-at-un ʔūrūppiyy-a
1.s.-think that-she young-s.f-Nom European-s.f
IL: liʔanna-**hā** ta-drus fi-l-ʤāmiʕa
because-she 3.s.f-study in-the-university
"I think she is a young European woman because she studies in college."
(Chinese L1-A: Group 2)

(29) IL: ya-bdū ʔanna-**hā** ðahaba-t ʔilā mustašfā
3.s.m-seem that-she went-3.s.f to hospital
"It seems that she went to hospital."
(Chinese L1-A: Group 3)

(30) IL: wa baʕda ðālik fa-ya-ʕūd-u ʔilā bayt-i-hi
and after that so-3.s.m-return-Indic to house-Gen-his
wa ʔinna-**hu** ya-šʕur-u bi-l-ʤūʕ
and indeed-he 3.s.m-feel-Indic with-the-hunger

"And after that, he returns home and indeed he feels hungry."
(Chinese L1-A: Group 3)

(31)		li?anna-**hu**	?arāda	baʕdˤ-a	nuqūd [?an-nuqūd]
		because-he	wanted.3.s.m	some-Acc	money

"… because he wanted some money."
(Chinese L1-B: Group 2)

(32)	IL:	wa	mumkin	huwa	muslim
		and	maybe	he is	Muslim
		li?anna-**hu**	ya-ðhab	l-l-māsdʒid [?ila-l-masdʒid]	
		because	3.s.m-go	to-the-mosque	

"And maybe he is Muslim because he goes to mosque."
(Russian L1-A: Group 3)

(33)	IL:	wa	hiya	saʕīd-at-un		
		and	she	happy-s.f-Nom		
		li?anna-**hā**	ta-fʕal-u		mā	tu-rīd-u
		because-she	3.s.f-do-Iindic		what	3.s.f-want-Indic

"And she is happy because she does what she wants."
(Russian L1-B: Group 3)

(34)	IL:	*wa	ya-bdū	?anna-**hā**	nāma	dʒayyid-an
		and	3.s.m-seem	that-she	slept.3.s.m	well-Acc
	TL:	wa	ya-bdū	?anna-**hā**	nāma-t	dʒayyid-an
		and	3.s.m-seem	that-she	slept-3.s.f	well-Acc

"And it seems that she slept well."
(Chinese L1-A: Group 3)

(35)	IL:	*li?anna	ʕarafa-t	?anna	hunāka	Hayāt	saʕīda
		because	knew-3.s.f	that	there	life	happy
	TL:	li?anna-**hā**	ʕarafa-t	?anna	hunāka	Hayāt	saʕīda
		because-she	knew-3.s.f	that	there	life	happy

"… because she knew there was a happy life."
(Russian L1-A: Group 2)

In all of the obligatory overt pronoun contexts in clauses (listed in table 6.1), the participants produced the required overt pronouns as illustrated in (25)–(35), except for three tokens (two by a Russian L1-A Group 2 participant and one by a Chinese L1-A Group 3 participant), as in (35). Of all the contexts (i.e., out of the total forty-eight tokens), only two contexts were produced with incorrect verbal agreement—by the Chinese L1-A Group 3, as in (34). A few tokens were produced with the wrong complementizer, as in (27)–(28).

Table 6.1 Production of non-null-subject contexts

Participants	*Total Correct Overt Subjects*	*Total Incorrect Overt Subjects*
Arabic L1		
Controls (n = 6)	24	0
Chinese L1-A		
Group1 (n = 10)	1	0
Group2 (n = 10)	4	0
Group3 (n = 10)	20	3
Chinese L1-B		
Group2 (n = 10)	1	0
Group3 (n = 10)	4	0
Russian L1-A		
Group2 (n = 9)	7	2
Group3 (n = 9)	5	0
Russian L1-B		
Group3 (n = 8)	1	0

The quantity of obligatory overt subject contexts reflects the amount of input exposure to the target language that each of the four groups of participants received, with the Chinese L1-A participants having produced the highest number (a total of twenty-eight tokens), followed by the Russian L1-A groups who produced a total of fourteen tokens, who in turn are followed by the Chinese L1-B groups who produced a total of five tokens, then the Russian L1-B groups who produced one token. Obligatory overt subject contexts (mainly in embedded clauses[8]) were coded differently from the null-subject contexts discussed below. In addition, to avoid skewing the null-subject data, contexts with newly introduced referents are excluded from null-subject contexts since they constitute obligatory overt subject contexts. Such contexts were occasionally produced when some participants introduced events/verbs related to a referent other than the two characters in the narratives such as *zārahu ʔabūhu* "His father visited him" or *sˤadīqatuhā kānat marīdˤa* "Her friend was sick."

The four groups mainly produced main clauses with overt (lexical NPs and pronouns) and null subjects. Sentences (36)–(47) are representative examples of overt subject use of third person singular masculine and third person singular feminine in both past and present tense.

(36) IL:	radʒul	ðahaba	fī	ʔalāskā
	man	went.3.s.m	in	Alaska

TL: ʔar-radʒul ðahaba ʔilā ʔalāskā
the-man went.3.s.m to Alaska
"the man went to Alaska."
(Russian L1-A: Group 1)

(37) IL: šābb-u-n kitba fī daftar
young man-Nom-Indef wrote.3.s.m in note-book
TL: ʔaš-šābb-u kataba fī daftar
the-young man-Nom wrote.3.s.m in note-book
"The young man wrote on a notebook."
(Russian L1-B: Group 1)

(38) IL: ʔal-walad-u ya-stayqiðˤ-u fi sˤ-sˤabāʜ
the-boy-Nom 3.s.m-wake-Indic in the-morning
"The boy wakes up in the morning."
(Chinese L1-B: Group 2)

(39) IL: marʔ-a ta-ðhab ʔilā ʔal-mirʔān
person-s.f 3.s.f-go to the-mirʔān
TL: ʔal-marʔ-a ta-ðhab ʔilā ʔal-matˤʕam
the-person-s.f 3.s.f-go to the-restaurant
"The woman goes to the restaurant."
(Chinese L1-B: Group 2)

(40) IL: hāzihi l-marʔ-at-u zahaba-t ʔilā ʔal-zū
this.s.f the-person-s.f-Nom went-3.s.f to the-zoo
TL: hāðihi l-marʔ-at-u ðahaba-t ʔilā
this.s.f the-person-s.f-Nom went-3.s.f to
ʜadīqat-i l-ʜayawān
park-Gen the-animal
"This woman went to the zoo."
(Russian L1-B: Group 3)

(41) IL: zāra-t hāðihi ʔal-ʔimraʔ-a marīdˤ-a-n
visited-3.s.f this.s.f the-person-s.f sick person-Acc-Indef
fī l-mustašfā
in the-hospital
TL: zāra-t hāðihi ʔal-marʔ-a…
visited-3.s.f this.s.f the-person-s.f
"This woman visited a sick person in the hospital."
(Chinese L1-A: Group 3)

(42) IL: hiya ta-ʔkul-u ʔal-qahw-at-a
she 3.s.f-eat-Indic the-coffee-s.f-Acc

	TL:	hiya	ta-šrab-u	ʔal-qahw-at-a		
		she	3.s.f-drink-Indic	the-coffee-s.f-Acc		
		"She drinks coffee."				
		(Chinese L1-A: Group 1)				
(43)	IL:	wa	huwa	nām		
		and	he	slept.3.s.m		
	TL:	wa	huwa	ya-nām		
		and	he	3.s.m-sleep		
		"And he sleeps."				
		(Russian L1-A: Group 1)				
(44)	IL:	wa	hiya	ðahaba-t	ʔilā	xāliʤ [ʔal-xāriʤ]
		and	she	went-3.s.f	to	outside
		"And she went abroad."				
		(Chinese L1-B: Group 2)				
(45)	IL:	wa	hiya	raqasˤa-t	maʕa	z-zuwwār
		and	she	danced-3.s.f	with	the-visitors
		"And she danced with the visitors."				
		(Chinese L1-A: Group 2)				
(46)	IL:	wa	huwa	ya-drus-u	fī	l-madrasa
		and	he	3.s.m-study-Indic	in	the-school
		"And he studies at school."				
		(Russian L1-A: Group 3)				
(47)	IL:	hiya	tu-māris-u	riyādˤa-t ʔal-tennis		
		she	3.s.f-pratices	sport-s.f the-tennis		
		"She plays tennis."				
		(Russian L1-B: Group 3)				

Overt subjects occurred in both preverbal, as in (36)–(40) and (42)–(47), and postverbal positions, as in (41), although they occurred much more in the former than the latter. Overall, the participants produced more overt pronominal subjects than NP subjects (see table 6.2).[9]

As for null-subject contexts, sentences (48)–(53) are representative examples of null subject use of third person singular masculine and third person singular feminine and in both past and present tense.

(48)	IL:	wa	fī	l-sabt	ðahaba-t	ʔilā	bayt-i-hā
		and	in	the-Saturday	went-3.s.f	to	house-Gen-her
		"And on Saturday, she went to her house."					
		(Russian L1-A: Group 1)					

(49)	IL:	kataba	wādʒib-i-hi	fī	masāʔ
		wrote.3.s.m	homework-Gen-his	in	evening
	TL:	kataba	wādʒib-a-hu	fī	ʔal-masāʔ
		wrote.3.s.m	homework-Acc-his	in	the-evening

“He wrote his homework in the evening.”
(Chinese L1-A: Group 1)

(50)	IL:	ya-nām-u	fi	l-bayti
		3.s.m-sleep-Indic	in	the-house

“He sleeps at home.”
(Chinese L1-B: Group 2)

(51)	IL:	ya-ðhab-u	ʔila	l-madrasa
		3.s.m-go-Indic	to	the-school

“He goes to school.”
(Russian L1-B: Group 2)

(52)	IL:	laʕiba-t	kur-at-a	t-tennis
		played-3.s.f	ball-s.f-Acc	the-tennis

“She played tennis.”
(Chinese L1-A: Group 3)

(53)	IL:	fī	yawm	ʔas-sabt	ʕāda	ʔila	bayt-i-hi
		in	day	the-Saturday	returned.3.s.m	to	house-Gen-his

“On Saturday, he returned to his house.”
(Chinese L1-B: Group 3)

Table 6.2 displays the distribution of the production data (of all participants) in null and overt contexts, including those of the control group (see also figure 6.1). The data show that the Chinese L1 participants combined produced far more subjectless clauses than their Russian L1 counterparts. The Chinese L1-A groups produced almost twice the number of subjectless clauses than their Russian L1-A groups (1,027 versus 691, respectively); so did the Chinese L1-B than their Russian L1-B counterparts (549 versus 380, respectively). Although the Chinese L1-B participants were noticeably conservative in dropping subjects at the intermediate level (i.e., Group 2), they almost caught up with their Chinese L1-A counterpart at the advanced stage (i.e., Group 3) with both dropping subjects at high rates (93% and 84%, respectively). The Russian L1 participants exhibited a different trend. At the beginner level (i.e., Group 1), they emerged dropping subjects at relatively high rates (79% and 75%), but they ended (at the advanced level in Group 3) being more conservative and converged on dropping subjects at 53%.

Table 6.2 Distribution of null-subject contexts in the participants' IL systems

Participants	*Null/Total Subjects*	*%*	*Overt NP/ Pronominal Subjects*
Arabic L1			
Controls (n = 6)	264/275	96	7/4
Chinese L1-A			
Group1 (n = 10)	178/262	68	1/83
Group2 (n = 10)	356/468	76	28/84
Group3 (n = 10)	493/529	93	19/17
Chinese L1-B			
Group1 (n = 9)	56/86	65	1/29
Group2 (n = 10)	150/381	39	30/201
Group3 (n = 10)	343/408	84	24/41
Russian L1-A			
Group1 (n = 9)	217/275	79	3/55
Group2 (n = 9)	271/389	70	5/113
Group3 (n = 9)	203/381	53	2/176
Russian L1-B			
Group1 (n = 5)	44/59	75	5/10
Group2 (n = 6)	156/191	82	8/27
Group3 (n = 8)	180/337	53	72/85

Table 6.2 also lists the number of contexts where overt subjects are used. The data reveal that contexts with pronominal subjects represented the largest number of contexts with overt subjects; contexts with NP subjects were far fewer. The data also show that the control group by far outperformed all three L1 groups, dropping subjects in 264 out of 275 contexts (i.e., producing overt NP or pronominal subjects in 11 contexts only).

Full factorial two-way ANOVA tests revealed a near effect for L1 backgrounds ($F(4, 96) = 2.328$, $p = 0.062$, partial $\eta^2 = 0.088$) and a main interaction effect between L1 backgrounds and proficiency ($F(6, 96) = 4.830$, $p < 0.001$, partial $\eta^2 = 0.232$). Post hoc analyses using Tukey tests of all possible pairwise comparisons revealed that, overall, the control group differed marginally from the Russian L1-A groups ($p = 0.099$) and nearly from the Chinese L1-B groups ($p = 0.057$). The Chinese L1-A Group 3 differed nearly significantly from the Russian L1-A Group 3 ($p = 0.069$) and marginally so from the Russian L1-B Group 3 ($p = 0.095$). In addition, the Chinese L1-B Group 3 differed significantly from its Group 2 counterpart ($p = 0.010$), and while the Chinese L1-A Group 3 differed significantly from the Chinese L1-B Group 2 ($p = 0.001$), it did not differ from the Chinese L1-B Group 3.

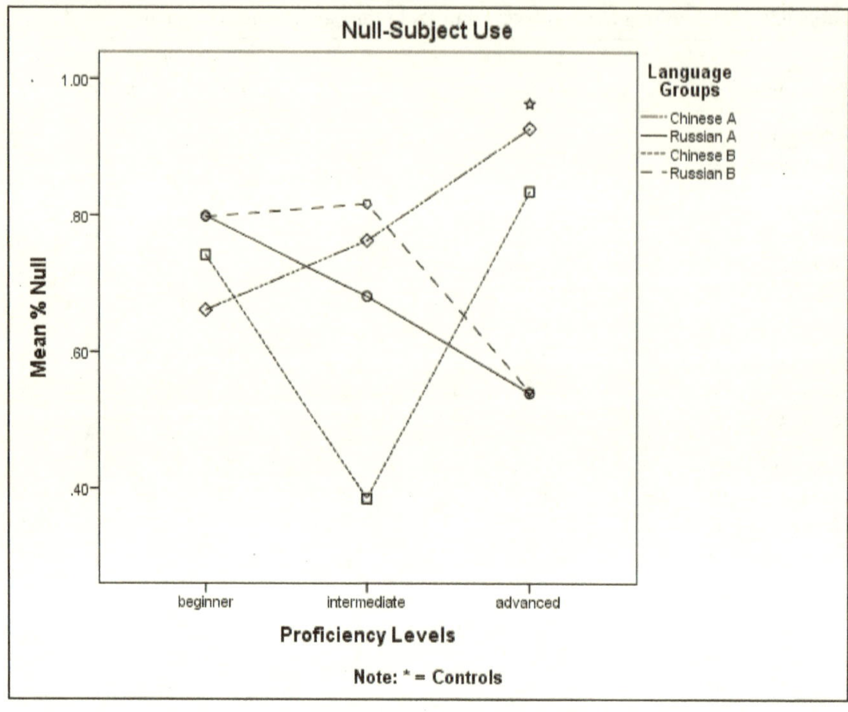

Figure 6.1 Interaction Plot of Mean % for the Participants' Performance on Null-Subject Use by Language Group and Proficiency Level

In other words, the Chinese L1 participants (in particular the Chinese L1-A groups) dropped noticeably more than their Russian L1-A and Russian L1-B counterparts, and although the performance of the Chinese L1-A participants (in particular Group 3) differed from that of the Russian L1-A and Russian L1-B Group 3 participants, their performance did not differ significantly from that of their Chinese L1-B Group 3 counterparts. Additionally, as can be seen from figure 6.1, whereas the advanced (Group 3) participants in the Chinese L1 groups seem to converge in dropping more subjects, the advanced participants (Group 3) in the Russian L1 groups seem to converge in the opposite direction of dropping far fewer subjects.

6.3.2 Null Subjects and Verbal Agreement Production

To explore use of null subjects by the four groups of participants further, the data were analyzed for verbal agreement. Sentences (54)–(63), which are extracted from the data, illustrate inaccurate rule applications of verbal agreement in null and overt subjects contexts.

(54)	IL:	*ʔal-bint	ðahaba	fī	Las Vegas
		the-girl	went.3.s.m	in	Las Vegas
	TL:	ʔal-bint	ðahaba-t	ʔilā	Las Vegas
		the-girl	went-3.s.f	to	Las Vegas
		"The girl went to Las Vegas."			
		(Russian L1-A: Group 1)			
(55)	IL:	*ʔaš-šābb	ta-stayqið-u		
		the-young man	3.s.f-wake-Indic		
	TL:	ʔaš-šābb	ya-stayqiðˤ-u		
		the-young man	3.s.m-wake-Indic		
		"The young man wakes up."			
		(Chinese L1-B: Group 2)			
(56)	IL:	*hāzihi	l-fatā-t	ʔakala	
		this.s.f	the-young-s.f	ate.3.s.m	
	TL:	hāðihi	l-fatā-t	ʔakala-t	
		this.s.f	the-young-s.f	ate-3.s.f	
		"This girl ate."			
		(Russian L1-B: Group 2)			
(57)	IL:	*ya-ʕūd-u	hāðihi	l-marʔ-a	
		3.s.m-return-Indic	this.s.f	the-person-s.f	
	TL:	ta-ʕūd-u	hāðihi	l-marʔ-a	
		3.s.f-return-Indic	this.s.f	the-person-s.f	
		"This woman returns."			
		(Chinese L1-A: Group 2)			
(58)	IL:	*wa	huwa	ʤāʔa-t	
		and	he	came-3.s.f	
	TL:	wa	huwa	ʤāʔa	
		and	he	came.3.s.m	
		"And he came."			
		(Chinese L1-A: Group 1)			
(59)	IL:	*wa	hiya	yu-ʜibb	ʔusrat-i-hā
		and	she	3.s.m-like	family-Gen-her
	TL:	wa	hiya	tu-ʜibb	ʔusrat-a-hā
		and	she	3.s.f-like	family-Acc-her
		"And she likes her family."			
		(Chinese L1-A: Group 2)			
(60)	IL:	*ðahaba	hiya	ʔilā	Las Vegas
		went.3.s.m	she	to	Las Vegas

	TL:	ðahaba-t	(hiya)	ʔilā	Las Vegas
		went-3.s.f	(she)	to	Las Vegas
		"She went to Las Vegas."			
		(Russian L1-A: Group 3)			
(61)	IL:	*ta-šrab-u	huwa	ʔaš-šāy	
		3.s.f-drink-Indic	he	the-tea	
	TL:	ya-šrab-u	(huwa)	ʔaš-šāy	
		3.s.m-drink-Indic	(he)	the-tea	
		"He drinks tea."			
		(Russian L1-A: Group 2)			
(62)	IL:	*wa	ʕāda	ʔilā	bayt-i-hā
		and	returned.3.s.m	to	house-Gen-her
	TL:	wa	ʕāda-t	ʔilā	bayt-i-hā
		and	returned-3.s.f	to	house-Gen-her
		"And she returned to her house."			
		(Chinese L1-B: Group 3)			
(63)	IL:	*ta-ktub	waʤabāt-u-hu		
		3.s.f-write	assignments-Nom-his		
	TL:	ya-ktub	wāʤibāt-i-hi		
		3.s.m-write	assignments-Acc-his		
		"He writes his homework assignments."			
		(Chinese L1-B: Group 3)			

Sentences (54)–(57) exhibit incorrect verbal agreement with overt NP subjects, sentences (58)–(61) display incorrect verbal agreement with overt pronoun subjects, and sentences (62) and (63) show incorrect verbal agreement with null subjects. The extracted sentences (in past and present tense) also illustrate use of preverbal subjects, as in (54)–(56), (58), and (59), as well as postverbal subjects, as in (57), (60) and (61).

Table 6.3 displays the distribution of correct rule application of verbal agreement in null and overt subject contexts (see also figure 6.2). The snapshot of the data (in table 6.3) shows the beginner Russian L1-A and Russian L1-B groups emerging with the lowest accuracy rates in their performance of rule application of verbal agreement in null-subject contexts (at 58% and 45%, respectively) and the beginner Chinese L1-A and Chinese L1-B groups exhibiting relatively higher rates (at 68% and 82%, respectively). However, the accuracy rates of verbal agreement in null (and overt) subject contexts show improvement along proficiency by all groups, especially by the Russian L1-A

Table 6.3 Distribution of verbal agreement in the participants' IL systems

Participants	*Correct Agreement Null Subjects: Correct/Total*	%	*Correct Agreement Overt Subjects: Correct/Total*	%
(Arabic L1)				
Controls (n = 6)	264/264	100	11/11	100
Chinese L1-A				
Group1 (n = 10)	121/178	68	61/84	73
Group2 (n = 10)	323/356	91	98/112	88
Group3 (n = 10)	447/493	91	33/36	92
Chinese L1-B				
Group1 (n = 9)	46/56	82	19/30	63
Group2 (n = 10)	133/150	89	217/231	94
Group3 (n = 10)	303/343	88	57/65	88
Russian L1-A				
Group1 (n = 10)	125/217	58	46/58	79
Group2 (n = 10)	244/271	90	98/118	83
Group3 (n = 9)	197/203	97	159/178	89
Russian L1-B				
Group1 (n = 5)	20/44	45	11/15	73
Group2 (n = 6)	123/156	79	30/35	86
Group3 (n = 8)	160/180	89	140/157	89

(at 58%, 90%, and 97%) and Russian L1-B (at 45%, 79%, and 89%) groups, who showed steady improvement across all three levels.

Full factorial two-way ANOVA tests of verbal agreement in null-subject contexts revealed a main effect for L1 backgrounds ($F(4, 94) = 3.930$, $p = 0.005$, partial $\eta^2 = 0.143$), a main effect for proficiency ($F(2, 94) = 28.397$, $p < 0.001$, partial $\eta^2 = 0.377$), and a main interaction effect between L1 backgrounds and proficiency ($F(6, 94) = 2.294$, $p = 0.041$, partial $\eta^2 = 0.128$). Post hoc analyses using Tukey tests revealed that Group 1 of both of the Chinese L1-A and Chinese L1-B participants differed significantly from the Russian L1-B Group 1 ($p = 0.019$ and $p = 0.008$, respectively), and the control group differed significantly from the Russian L1-A ($p = 0.001$) and Russian L1-B ($p < 0.001$) Group 1 and marginally so from the Chinese L1-A Group 1 ($p = 0.082$).[10]

In other words, and in light of the null-subject data (see table 6.2 and figure 6.1), the higher verbal agreement accuracy rates along proficiency development did not translate into higher rates of subject dropping in the case of the Russian L1-A and Russian L1-B participants (particularly Group 3). However,

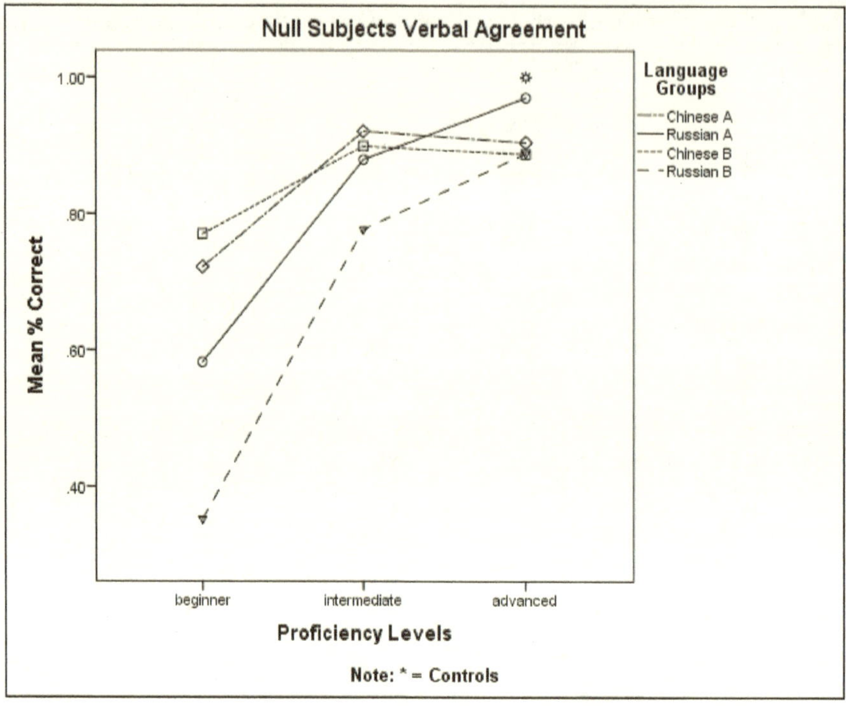

Figure 6.2 Interaction Plot of Mean % Correct for the Participants' Performance on Null-Subject Verbal Agreement by Language Group and Proficiency Level

higher accuracy rates along proficiency development did result in higher rates of subjectless sentences in the case of the Chinese L1 groups.

Finally, null-subject data were analyzed for verbal agreement in the past tense versus verbal agreement in the present tense (see table 6.4). The analysis revealed similar findings to those of verbal agreement in null-subject contexts in general; i.e., with the beginner Russian L1-A and Russian L1-B participants (Group 1) exhibiting lower accuracy rates than their Chinese L1-A and Chinese L1-B counterparts in past tense at 58% and 48% versus 64% and 92%, respectively (see also figure 6.3). The beginner (i.e., Group 1) Russian L1-A and Russian L1-B participants also exhibited lower accuracy rates than their Chinese L1-A and Russian L1-B counterpart groups in present tense at 55% and 41% versus 82% and 79%, respectively.

Full factorial two-way ANOVA tests of past tense verbal agreement in null-subject contexts revealed a main effect for L1 backgrounds ($F(4, 84) = 3.658$, $p = 0.009$, partial $\eta^2 = 0.148$), a main effect for proficiency ($F(2, 84) = 17.828$,

Table 6.4 Distribution of past and present verbal agreement in the participants' IL systems

Participants	*Correct Agreement Null Subjects: Past/Total*	*%*	*Correct Agreement Null Subjects: Present/Total*	*%*
(Arabic L1)				
Controls (n = 6)	137/137	100	127/127	100
Chinese L1-A				
Group1 (n = 10)	89/139	64	32/39	82
Group2 (n = 10)	166/185	90	157/171	92
Group3 (n = 10)	263/291	90	184/202	91
Chinese L1-B				
Group1 (n = 9)	12/13	92	34/43	79
Group2 (n = 10)	43/51	84	90/99	91
Group3 (n = 10)	187/211	89	116/132	88
Russian L1-A				
Group1 (n = 10)	113/195	58	12/22	55
Group2 (n = 10)	145/162	90	99/109	91
Group3 (n = 9)	110/113	97	87/90	97
Russian L1-B				
Group1 (n = 5)	13/27	48	7/17	41
Group2 (n = 6)	106/139	76	17/17	100
Group3 (n = 8)	141/159	89	19/21	90

$p < 0.001$, partial $\eta^2 = 0.298$), and a main interaction effect between L1 backgrounds and proficiency ($F(6, 84) = 2.389$, $p = 0.035$, partial $\eta^2 = 0.146$). Post hoc analyses using Tukey tests revealed the control group differed significantly from Group 1 of both the Russian L1-A ($p = 0.005$) and the Russian L1-B ($p < 0.001$) as well as the Chinese L1-A Group 1 ($p = 0.037$) participants. Full factorial two-way ANOVA tests of present tense verbal agreement in null-subject contexts revealed a main effect for proficiency ($F(2, 82) = 11.621$, $p < 0.001$, partial $\eta^2 = 0.221$). Post hoc analyses using Tukey tests showed the control group differed nearly significantly from the Russian L1-A Group 1 ($p = 0.055$) and significantly from the Russian L1-B Group 1 ($p = 0.011$).

Thus, as in the general verbal agreement data, null subjects in past and present tense data reveal the opposite trends for the Chinese L1 and Russian L1 groups. Although the beginner Russian L1 participants emerged with noticeably lower accuracy agreement rates than their Chinese L1 counterparts (tables 6.3 and 6.4), both dropped subjects at relatively high rates with no

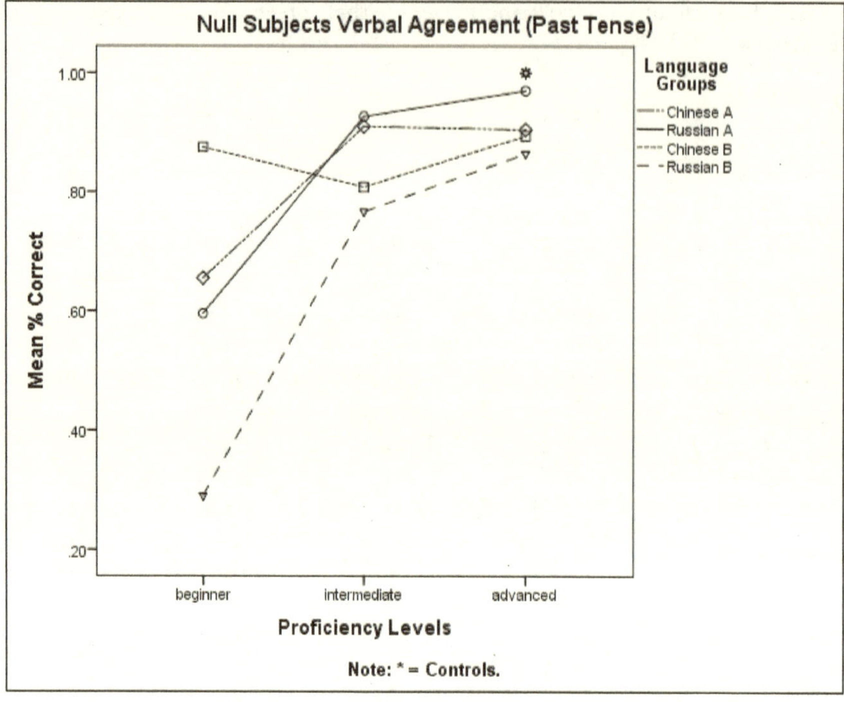

Figure 6.3 Interaction Plot of Mean % Correct for the Participants' Performance on Null-Subject Verbal Agreement in Past Tense by Language Group and Proficiency Level

significant difference (table 6.2). However, as past and present verbal accuracy rates improved significantly at later stages (especially at the advanced level corresponding to Group 3), such accuracy rates resulted, for the advanced Russian L1 participants, in dropping significantly fewer subjects, whereas higher accuracy rates in past and present verbal agreement, for the Chinese L1 advanced groups (Group 1), resulted in significantly more dropped subjects.

6.4 Input Frequency

The above null-subject findings were yielded despite the participants' exposure to the formal instructional input shown in tables 6.5–6.8. The tables display how often and when explicit pronoun subjects were used: (1) in optional contexts, where a pronoun is not required, and (2) in contrastive contexts, where use of an explicit pronoun serves a functional use indicating that the particular subject (pronoun) is in focus versus another. The latter is exemplified in sentences (10) and (11) above. Although focus is on pronoun subjects

Table 6.5 Frequency of pronominal subjects use in the textbook of the Chinese L1-A Group 1

Unit[a]	*Optional*		*Contrastive*	
13	**3.s.m (1)**[b]			
16	**3.s.m (2)**	**3.s.f (1)**	**3.s.m (1)**	
22				**3.s.f (1)**
23	**3.s.m (1)**			

[a] The textbook used is *al-Jadīd fī al-Lugha al-ʿArabiyya*, vol. 1 (Guo and Zhou 2002).
[b] Number in parentheses ( ) = total contexts.

Table 6.6 Frequency of pronominal subjects use in the textbook of the Chinese L1-B Group 1

Unit[a]	*Optional*		*Contrastive*	*Unit*[b]	*Optional*		*Contrastive*	
1–40	1.s (1)[c]			1				
1				2				
2	1.s (3)	1.p (3)		3				
3				4	**3.s.m (1)**			
4				5				
5				6				
6				7	**3.s.m (1)**	**3.s.f (1)**		
7				8	**3.s.m (1)**	**3.s.f (1)**		2.s.m (2)
					1.s (4)			
8				9		**3.s.f (1)**		
9				10	**3.s.m (1)**			
10				11				
11				12			**3.s.m (2)**	**3.s.f (2)**
								2.s.m (1)
12				13	**3.s.m (1)**	**3.s.f (1)**		
13				14	**3.s.m (4)**	**3.s.f (1)**		

[a] The textbook used for the left half of the table is *Kitāb al-Qirāʾa* & *Mudhakkira ʾIḍāfiyya li-l-Mustawā al-ʾAwwal* (Saudi Teaching Delegates, n.d.).
[b] The textbook used for the right half of the table is *al-ʿArbiyya bayna Yadayk*, vol. 1 (Al-Fawzān et al. 2003).
[c] Number in parentheses ( ) = total contexts.

of third person singular masculine and third person singular feminine, other pronouns (such as second person singular masculine and feminine, first person singular and plural, and third person masculine dual and plural) occurred

Table 6.7 Frequency of pronominal subjects use in the textbook of the Russian L1-A Group 1

Unit/ Lesson[a]	*Optional*		*Contrastive*		*Unit/ Lesson*[b]	*Optional*		*Contrastive*
1–10	1.s (2)[c]	1.p (3)		1.p (1)	1–2			
11–20	1.s (4)	3.p.m (1)	2.s.m (1)	1.s (1)	3–4			
21–30	1.s (2)	**3.s.f (1)**	2.s.f (1) 2.s.m (2)	**3.s.f (1)** 1.s (3)	5–6			
31–40	1.s (2)			1.s (3)	**7–8**		1.p (1)	
41–50	1.s (4)	**3.s.f (1)**			9–10			
51–60	1.s (1)	2.s.m (2)			11–12			
61–70	1.s (2)				13–14			
71–80	1.s (2)	2.s.m (1)			15–16			
81–90	1.s (1)				**17–18**		1.p (1)	
91–110	1.s (5)		2.s.m (1)	1.s (1) **3.s.m (1)**	19–20			
101–10	1.s (2) **3.s.f (1)**	**3.s.m (1)** 3.p.m (1)	2.s.m (1)	1.s (1)	21–22			
111–20	1.s (2)	2.s.f (1) **3.s.m (1)**		1.s (1)	**23–24**			2.s.m (1)
121–30	1.s (2) **3.s.f (2)**	1.p (4) **3.s.m (1)**			25–**26**	**3.s.m (1)**	**3.s.f (1)**	
131–40	1.s (3)	**3.s.f (2)** 1.p (1)			27–28			
141–50			2.s.m (1)	1.s (2)	29–**30**	**3.s.m (1)**	1.p (1)	

[a] The textbook used for the left half of the table is *Povsednevnyarabskijjazyk* (Franka 2007).
[b] The textbook used for the right half of the table is *Literaturnyarabskyjazyk* (Khanna 2006).
[c] Number in parentheses ( ) = total contexts.

in the textbooks of Group 1 of the Chinese L1-A, Chinese L1-B, Russian L1-A, and Russian L1-B participants. The rest of the instructional input contains explicit NP subjects and null subjects, with null subjects being the prevalent feature (see also appendix B for all verb contexts).[11] Presence of such pronouns is significant to indicate the extent to which the participants were encouraged to drop or not drop subjects.

Accordingly, tables 6.5 and 6.8 show that the Chinese L1-A and Russian L1-B Group 1 had the fewest instances of explicit pronoun use in their instructional input, a total of seven tokens in each. If pronouns other than those for third person singular masculine and feminine are excluded, the Russian L1-B participants would end up with even fewer tokens (a total of three). Table 6.6 shows that the participants in the Chinese L1-B Group 1 had more exposure

Table 6.8 Frequency of pronominal subjects use in in the textbook of the Russian L1-B Group 1

Unit/ Lesson[a]	*Optional*		*Contrastive*		*Unit/ Lesson*[b]	*Optional*		*Contrastive*	
1					1	**3.s.m (1)**[c]	**3.s.f (1)**		
2					2			2.s.m (1)	
3					3		3.d (1)		1.p (1)
4					4		**3.s.f (1)**		
					12				1.s (1)

[a] The textbook for the left half of table is *Vvodno Foneticheskii Koors Arabskovo Yezika* (Semyonova and Lukyanova 2004).
[b] The textbook for the right half of table is *Oochebna-Metodicheskoye Possobiye Po Arabskomu Yaziku* (Semyonova and Lukyanova 2005).
[c] Number in parentheses ( ) = total contexts.

to explicit pronoun use: a total of thirty-two tokens of all types of pronouns and eighteen tokens of third person singular feminine and third person singular masculine pronouns. By far, the participants in the Russian L1-A Group 1 (table 6.7) seem to have exposure to the largest number of tokens of explicit pronoun use: a total of eighty-seven tokens of all types of pronouns and fifteen tokens of third person singular feminine and third person singular masculine pronouns.

Given the small number of tokens of explicit pronouns, it would not be unexpected to find the Chinese L1-A and, to a lesser extent, the Chinese L1-B participants (in Group 1) encouraged to drop subjects from early on at higher rates than random hits (68% and 65%, respectively) and end up dropping subjects at even higher rates later at the advanced stage (93% and 84%, respectively), although the intermediate Chinese L1-B participants were, for some reason, noticeably conservative in dropping subjects (at 39%). However, input alone cannot explain the data of the Russian L1-A and Russian L1-B participants. Although the Russian L1-A participants had a significant number of redundant explicit pronouns (in comparison with their Chinese L1 counterparts) in their instructional input, they started dropping subjects at an even higher rate (79%) at the beginner stage than their Chinese L1 counterparts and continued the trend in the intermediate stage (70%), but they ended up dropping far fewer subjects, at 53%. Similarly, although the input of the Russian L1-B participants may explain the high rates at which they dropped subjects at the beginner and intermediate stages (75% and 82%, respectively), it is unclear, based on input exposure alone, how their null-subject use declined noticeably at the advanced stage, dropping subjects at 53% much like their Russian L1-A counterparts.

The foregoing description of input frequency of explicit pronominal subjects use in optional and contrastive contexts does not account alone for the patterns of null-subject use exhibited by the four groups of participants. Although input may explain null-subject use by the Chinese L1 participants, input alone cannot explain the patterns of null-subject use by the Russian L1 participants. It is likely that the resulting null-subject use patterns by the participants are due to L1 transfer effects. As discussed above (section 6.1), unlike Arabic and Chinese, Russian drops subjects less freely due to noted restrictions in null-subject use (hence, it was analyzed as a mixed null-subject language).

6.5 Summary

The data revealed that the Chinese L1 and Russian L1 participants dropped subjects at somewhat high rates (i.e., higher than mere random hits) at the beginner and intermediate stages of their Arabic L2 acquisition (except for the participants in the Chinese L1-B Group 2). However, although the Chinese L1-A and Chinese L1-B in Group 3 ended up dropping more subjects at the advanced level (in comparison with those in Group 1), their Russian L1-A and Russian L1-B counterparts showed the opposite trend. Instead of approximating more toward the performance of the control group by dropping more subjects, the performance of the Russian L1-A and Russian L1-B participants backslid at the advanced level, and both ended up converging at 53% of dropping subjects from their initial rates of 79% and 75%, respectively.

Similarly, when the null-subject patterns exhibited by the participants were analyzed with respect to verbal agreement production (including the distinction between past and present verbal agreement), two different patterns of findings emerged. Higher verbal accuracy rates along proficiency development yielded higher rates of null-subject production for the Chinese L1 participants. However, this was not the case with the Russian L1 participants. Higher verbal accuracy rates along proficiency development did not result in higher rates of null-subject production by the Russian L1 participants. The former finding is congruent with previous findings based on English L1, Spanish L1, and Japanese L1 learners of Arabic, where a close correlation was found between the production of null subjects and verbal agreement development (Alhawary 2007a, 2009a). The latter finding, where there is no correlation between production of null subjects and verbal agreement, seems to indicate this is due to the role of L1 transfer (due to typological or structural dissimilarities), especially given the nature of input exposure and frequency of null subjects therein, which cannot explain the detected null-subject use patterns. Recall, whereas in general Arabic and Chinese drop null subjects freely as null-subject languages, Russian drops subjects more conservatively, since it is a mixed null-subject language. The theoretical implications of such typological and L1 transfer effects are addressed in chapter 7.

Notes

1. However, it is to be noted here that such a preference rule is usually not taught in Arabic as a foreign/second language. Instead, either such a rule is not observed altogether (i.e., treating the construction as a purely null-subject construction) or the construction is reintroduced with a preposition, circumventing the need for invoking a pronoun preference use, as in (i).

(i) ʔarāda ʔan yu-sāfir-(a) **maʕa** zawdʒat-i-hi
wanted.3.s.m to 3.s.m-travel-(Subjunc) with wife-Gen-his
"He wanted to travel with his wife."

2. A specific example with a full context where the referent/subject can be identified in the discourse and the pronoun subject can consequently be dropped is illustrated in (ii) (cited from Tsedryk 2013, 2).

(ii) Q: Gde Lena$_i$?
where Lena.Nom
"Where is Lena?"
A: ____$_i$ u sebya v komnate. ____$_i$ delaet uroki.
(she) at herself in room (she) do.3.s home-work.Acc
"(She is) in her room. (She) is doing her homework."

3. However, unlike Arabic, both Chinese and Russian allow null subjects in embedded clauses, particularly when the embedded null subject is bounded by the subject in the matrix clause as in (iii) (cited from Huang 1989, 193) and (iv) (cited from Tsedryk 2013, 2).

(iii) Zhangsan$_i$ shuo [_$_i$ hen xihuan Lisi].
Zhangsan said very like Lisi
"Zhangsan said that he liked Lisi."
(iv) Lena$_i$ skazal-a čto ____$_i$ delaet uroki.
Lena.Nom said-s.f. that do.3.s homework.Acc
"Lena said that she is doing her homework."

Sentences (iii) and (iv) contrast with sentences (5)–(7) in Arabic, above, where a lexical subject/pronoun is obligatorily used in the embedded clause following complementizers such as *ʔinna* "that" and its sisters. However, as noted above, the focus here is mainly on null-subject use in matrix clause.

4. In attributing parametric variation to strength of functional features, standard minimalist assumption is adopted here. On this account, due to rich verbal agreement features, both Arabic and Russian are analyzed with the functional

feature strength set to [+strong], while functional feature strength in Chinese is set to [-strong]. More recent reformulations of null subjects such as radical pro-drop (à la Neeleman and Szendrői 2005) are not adopted here since such a proposal would lump together languages such as Arabic [+null], Spanish [+null], and English [-null] as nonradical pro-drop languages as opposed to Chinese [+null] and Japanese [+null] as radical pro-drop languages (for a similar criticism, see Lardiere 2009a; cf. Liceras 2009).

5. These narrative tasks are similar to those discussed below in section 6.3 (see also section 2.5, chapter 2).

6. The qualitative difference in the formal input of all three groups of participants (English L1, Japanese L1, and Spanish L1) was suggested as a possible explanation for the low accuracy rates of verbal agreement in the production of the Spanish L1 participants. Although the instructional materials of all three groups of participants focus on form from early on, only those belonging to the English L1 and Japanese L1 participants recycle verbal agreement rigorously throughout, whereas those used by the Spanish L1 participants hardly do so (Alhawary 2009a, 166).

7. Due to shared knowledge between the interviewee and interviewer as the instruction about performing the task is introduced, even producing an overt subject (a pronoun or NP) with the first event may not be necessary. Hence, not all the control participants produced an overt subject at the beginning of each of the four tasks.

8. Of the forty-eight tokens of obligatory overt pronominal contexts, all but two occurred in embedded clauses. The two remaining tokens occurred in main clauses following the complementizer *ʔinna* "that," which can precede a main clause to mean "verily" or "indeed," as in (30).

9. The participants produced a small number of contexts with overt (NP and pronominal) subjects where they contrasted between the male and female character at the end of a narrative. These contexts, where a pronoun is expected to be used, were not coded in order to avoid skewing the data of null subjects. Recall, in order to help elicit spontaneous production data, the participants were asked to describe the vacations of the two characters and to decide whether they make a compatible couple based on what they did during their vacations (chapter 2, section 2.5).

10. As for verbal agreement in overt subject contexts, full factorial two-way ANOVA tests revealed only a main effect for proficiency ($F(2, 86) = 3.519$, $p = 0.034$, partial $\eta^2 = 0.076$). Post hoc analyses using Tukey tests revealed that the control group differed significantly from the Chinese L1-A Group 1 ($p = 0.029$).

11. In addition, a few tokens of adverbial of manner clauses of the nominal sentence type, where an explicit pronoun subject is obligatory, as in sentence (8) above, were found in the textbooks of the Chinese L1-A and Russian L1-A Group 1 participants.

Chapter 7

Theoretical Implications

This chapter discusses the acquisition findings of the morphosyntactic target structures reported in the foregoing chapters (3–6) in view of ongoing debates, models, and hypotheses posited in the second language acquisition literature as they relate to language transfer and other contributing factors, such as input frequency, proficiency, typological and structural proximity, and universal grammar access/transfer effects. The chapter discusses specific ways that the findings contribute to our understanding of these aspects and the resulting crosslinguistic evidence of these and other related issues, such as usage-based learning and speech processing prerequisites.

7.1 Preliminaries

The central focus of this chapter is language transfer. However, in addition to the role of language transfer, a number of factors are generally agreed to play a role in second language acquisition (SLA). One such factor is input frequency. The frequency of occurrence of forms in L2 input is generally found to be a significant acquisition factor in that the more frequent the form, the more likely for it to be transferred and acquired in L2 (e.g., Hatch 1974; Larsen-Freeman 1976; Lightbown 1980; and other studies cited by Larsen-Freeman and Long 1991, 132–34).[1] Recent frequency research has also shown that high-frequency structures and high token/type frequency (such as certain verbs and their subcategorization frames) can facilitate the acquisition of L2 structures (e.g., Mellow 2006; Schwartz and Causarano 2007; Rhode 2009; Thomas 2010; Valian and Coulson 1988; Ellis 2002; Goldberg, Casenhiser, and Sethuraman 2004; Ellis and Ferreira Junior 2009; McDonough and Kim 2009; Agren and Van de Weijer 2013). Similarly, research on input frequency and morphological and lexical processing has shown that frequent morphological and lexical patterns can be acquired and predicted to be acquired sooner than others (e.g., Bybee and Newman 2006; Portin, Lehtonen, and Laine 2007; Carlson 2009).[2] Recall, the target morphosyntactic structures here—which include nominal and verbal gender agreement, past and present tense, and null subjects—are among the most high-frequency structures in Arabic. Sentences in Arabic are either nominal or verbal, and each necessarily involves gender agreement. Both sentence types may also contain demonstrative pronouns and noun phrases (NP) of the type consisting of a head noun followed by an attributive adjective. In addition, all verbal sentences (i.e., all sentences that start with a verb where the referent subject is already known from the discourse) involve null-subject use. Accordingly, in attempting to account for the present acquisition findings, frequency effects are taken into account here, at least as far as the target forms are high-frequency forms in Arabic. Furthermore, to ascertain that the target forms are high-frequency structures and, indeed, available in the formal input to which the participants were exposed, the learning schedules of the target forms are examined and analyzed in the participants' first-year instructional materials. First year instructional input, in particular, exhibits variation, since each language curriculum may approach the teaching and introduction of Arabic phonology and orthography differently.

A second factor that has a role in L2 acquisition in relation to L1 transfer is the L2 learner's proficiency level.[3] It is generally observed that L1 transfer (particularly negative transfer of morphosyntactic features) is noticeably exhibited in lower proficiency levels (e.g., Odlin 1989; Poulisse and Bongaerts 1994; Fuller 1999). It has also been observed that more exposure to L2 and higher proficiency in L2 can result in more L2 transfer in L3 acquisition (e.g., Stedje 1977; Williams and Hammarberg 1998; Hammarberg 2001; Ringbom 2001). However, whether or not increased proficiency leads to a decrease in L1 transfer, studies produced mixed evidence (see studies cited in Jarvis 2000, 247). Recently, a few studies seem to indicate that increased proficiency in the L2 can override L1 transfer effects (e.g., Hopp 2010; Ionin and Montrul 2010). Recall, the present data was collected from twelve groups of participants at three proficiency levels, half of whom received twice the amount of input exposure than the other half. Thus, the data examined here allows for both factors to be taken into account: proficiency as well as input exposure effects. Accordingly, the present study attempts to account for L1 transfer at various levels of L2 development (first year through third year) and the extent to which (negative) transfer effects can or cannot be overridden by extra exposure to L2 input at the three different proficiency levels.

A third factor that has a bearing on L2 acquisition, especially in connection with L1 and L2 transfer, is related to typological and structural proximity.

Typologically similar or dissimilar languages are found to exhibit crosslinguistic effects (positive/facilitative and negative/non-facilitative) in L2 (e.g., Weinreich 1953; Anderson 1983; Gass 1983; Odlin 1989; Jarvis and Odlin 2000; Selinker and Lakshmanan 1993; Kellerman 1995; Cadierno 2008; Römer, Ellis, and O'Donnell 2014) and L3 acquisition (e.g., Flynn, Foley, and Vinnitskaya 2004; Berkes and Flynn 2012; Bardel and Falk 2007, 2012; Falk and Bardel 2011; Rothman 2010, 2011, 2013, 2015; Rothman and Cabrelli Amaro 2010; Rothman, Bañón, and Alonso 2015). Recall, the L1s of the participants of the present study belong to geographically and culturally distant languages (Chinese and Russian) from Arabic and are either additionally similar or dissimilar to Arabic with respect to the target structures, resulting in five typological language pairings in 1(a)–(d), and accordingly the data of the present study allows for accounting for such understudied language pairings.

1(a) Nominal gender agreement:
L1 Chinese as a language distant (from Arabic) geographically, culturally, and linguistically *versus* L1 Russian as a language close structurally but distant geographically and culturally

1(b) Verbal gender agreement:
L1 Chinese as a language distant (from Arabic) geographically, culturally, and structurally *versus* L1 Russian as a language close structurally (especially in past tense) but distant geographically and culturally

1(c) Tense/aspect:
L1 Chinese as a language close (to Arabic) structurally but distant geographically and culturally *similar* to L1 Russian as a language that is close (to Arabic) structurally but distant geographically and culturally (since both exhibit a distinction between past and present tense)

1(d) Null subjects:
L1 Chinese as a language close (to Arabic) structurally but distant geographically and culturally versus Russian as a language that is not quite similar structurally (i.e., as a mixed null-subject language, dropping subjects less freely) and distant geographically and culturally

The Arabic L2 language pairings displayed in 1(a)–(d), together with the input exposure and proficiency factors taken into account, are significant for examining most recent accounts related to L1 and L2 transfer, usage-based learning, and speech processing prerequisite constraints.

7.2 L1 Transfer and Usage-Based Learning and Typological Effects

While no direct claims are made here about L1 speaker knowledge and acquisition of the target forms from usage-based perspectives (in absence of relevant research on Arabic L1 acquisition), the data of the present study have implications for usage-based accounts with respect to the yielded L1 transfer findings. Usage-based accounts, among others, are based on the assumptions that language processing is sensitive to input frequency in that language users register occurrence of forms in processing, that users have devoted considerable resources to the computation and expectation of their L1 features resulting in language-specific tuned expectations and selective attention, and that learned attentional biases from L1 accordingly influence ultimate attainment of L2 (Römer, Ellis, and O'Donnell 2014, 953).[4] Since the equivalent target structures in the participants' L1s (i.e., nominal and verbal constructions with or without the gender feature, tense, and null or non-null subjects) are high-frequency structures, they are likely well entrenched in the minds of Chinese and Russian speakers according to what is exhibited and processed in their L1s. Hence, we would expect asymmetrical acquisition patterns in their Arabic L2 IL systems reflecting the typological differences (and how entrenched processing routines in conceptual systems) exhibited between their L1s and Arabic as their L2. The data of the present study seems to provide strong evidence for usage-based typological effects underlying attentional or processing bias from L1, although falling a little short from accounting for the full range of the data.

With respect to nominal gender agreement, the findings seem to provide evidence that the processing of nominal constructions in absence of the gender agreement feature is expectedly, according to usage-based accounts, more entrenched in the Chinese participants than the Russian counterparts, where only the L1 of the former does not exhibit the gender feature (see section 3.3.1). The findings show that the performance of the beginner Russian L1-A and Chinese L1-A participants (Group 1) differed significantly from that of their Russian L1-B and Chinese L1-B counterparts (the former received double the amount of input than the latter) but that, more importantly, the intermediate and advanced Russian L1-A participants (Groups 2–3) maintained an advantage (though not statistically significant) over their Chinese L1-A counterparts in both feminine and masculine agreement; so did the Russian L1-B participants in Groups 1–3 over their Chinese L1-B counterparts in Groups 1–3 as well as the Chinese L1-A counterparts in Group 3 in feminine agreement (tables 3.1–3.3, section 3.3.1: chapter 3; for a similar finding, based on a study on L1 Russian and L1 Chinese learners of Arabic, see Al-Hamad 2003).

Moreover, where both Russian and Chinese do not exhibit demonstrative gender agreement (unlike Arabic), there was no statistical differences between and within groups in the performance of all groups. Previous studies on English L1, French L1, and Japanese L1 speakers learning Arabic as an L2 produced the same findings where both English L1 and Japanese L1 underperformed their French counterparts on nominal gender agreement constructions (both noun–adjective and demonstrative agreement) since the latter exhibits gender agreement in both types of nominal constructions and the former do not (see Alhawary 2009a, 2009b).[5]

Similarly, assuming that Russian and Chinese are typologically different, where Russian is a mixed null-subject language and drops subjects less freely than Chinese (as a null-subject language), the participants' developmental data of null subjects over time does seem to overall reflect an attentional or processing bias from their L1s. Whereas the advanced participants in the Chinese L1 groups seem to converge in dropping more subjects, the advanced participants in the Russian L1 groups seem to converge in the opposite direction of dropping far fewer subjects.

As for the tense data, these too seem to predictively offer evidence in support of usage-based/typological effects and attentional bias from L1. Recall that both Russian and Chinese exhibit a tense distinction, like Arabic. The data mainly showed that whereas the Chinese L1-B (Groups 1 and 2) underperformed their counterparts groups on past tense, the Russian L1-A (Group 1) and Russian L1-B (Groups 2 and 3) underperformed their counterpart groups on present tense.[6] Previous Arabic L2 studies, with English, Spanish, and Japanese as L1s, produced a similar finding. The participants of these studies similarly, expectedly, did not differ in their performance of past and present tense since all three L1s exhibit a distinction between past and present tense (Alhawary 2009a).

However, counter evidence for usage-based/typological effects and attentional bias from L1 seems to be yielded from the verbal gender agreement data. The data revealed a (statistically significant) advantage in particular of the Chinese L1-A beginner group over its Russian L1-A counterpart in verbal masculine agreement in the present tense and verbal feminine agreement in the present random tense task. L1 transfer effects in this case would instead predict an advantage by the Russian participants over their Chinese counterparts on their production of verbal agreement in the past tense. Recall that only Russian exhibits verbal gender agreement in the past tense, yet no evidence suggests learned attentional or processing bias from their L1 in their L2 acquisition of Arabic, so—at least according to usage-based accounts—they should have maintained an advantage in the processing of verbal gender agreement in the past tense over their Chinese counterparts. At the very least, we would expect the performance of the Russian L1-A and Russian L1-B groups on verbal gender agreement in the past to be significantly different (i.e., better) than that in the present tense (due to structural proximity between Russian verbal agreement in the past tense and Arabic verbal agreement). In fact, contrary to this prediction, the Russian participants overall had higher accuracy ratios of verbal agreement in the present than in the past tense (see tables 4.1 and 4.2). Previous L2 Arabic studies on verbal gender agreement, with English, French, and Japanese as L1s, showed that all groups achieved high levels of accuracy on verbal gender agreement, that the French maintained an advantage (though not statistically significant) over their English and Japanese counterparts, and that the Japanese participants maintained an advantage (though not statistically significant) over their English counterparts. Since none of the three L1s exhibits a distinction in verbal gender agreement between third person singular masculine and third person singular feminine, the findings were claimed not to necessarily provide evidence for or against L1 transfer (see Alhawary 2009a, 2009b; cf. Al-Hamad 2003, who reports Russian L1 intermediate learners being more successful in acquiring Arabic verbal gender agreement than their Chinese L1 counterparts, but verbal agreement data in the past and present tense were not reported separately).

The above explanation, relevant to usage-based accounts, can also be traced to a similar trend of explaining crosslinguistic effects based on Selinker's notion of "latent psychological structures" (cited in Odlin 2014, 35) and the assumption that the "psycholinguistic foundations of IL are embedded in cognitive systems." Accordingly, examining candidate domains that motivate L2 learners to look for similarities and to cope with dissimilarities between the forms in their L1 system and those in the L2 become crucial to understanding L1 transfer and other phenomena. Among such likely candidates are meaning based or conceptual domains such as those related to "the communicative value of semantics and pragmatics of the structures" (Odlin 2014, 35).[7] From this perspective, following Odlin (and Ferguson and Barlow 1988; Corbett 1999), since gender agreement can be considered to serve "important communicative goals" of establishing discourse coherence (i.e., by allowing the speaker and listener to keep track of referents in a discourse), the typological traits of the use of gender agreement categories allow for drawing generalizations about L2 "learner motivations to use their native language when they seek to construct coherent discourse representations" (Odlin 2014, 36–37). Accordingly, the data of the current study indicates that the production of Arabic nominal constructions exhibiting gender agreement resulted in positive transfer for the Russian L1 participants but negative transfer for Chinese L1 participants.

The same generalization can be drawn from the null-subject data. Since pronoun use, like gender agreement use, serves to establish discourse coherence, the typological traits of the use of null- or non-null-subject patterns allow us to detect learners' motivations to use null- or non-null-subject patterns in their L1s when they seek to construct coherent discourse representations involving the constructions. Accordingly, the data of null subjects indicates that the production of Arabic null subjects resulted in positive transfer for the Chinese L1 participants (whose L1 exhibits null-subject use) but somewhat negative or conservative transfer for Russian L1 participants.

Similarly, by implication, the above generalizations can be extended to present and past tense use. Since both Russian and Chinese exhibit a tense distinction like Arabic, expectedly, no distinction in the performance between the two sets of participants was yielded and instead positive transfer resulted for several groups across and between the Russian and Chinese groups likely subject to input presentation timing.

However, contrary to the expected generalization of the typological traits of the use of verbal gender agreement, and on a par with nominal gender agreement, one would expect the production data of the Russian verbal gender agreement in the past tense to result in positive transfer for the Russian L1 speakers. Recall, among the L1s of the participants, only Russian exhibits a gender distinction in the past tense. The lack of any typological effects with respect to verbal agreement remains unclear under crosslinguistic typological effects and usage-based accounts—unless, as suggested by Odlin (2014), the lack of positive transfer here is due to presence of language-specific constraints and variations in processing routines: "the psycholinguistic literature on native speaker performance also gives reasons to believe that processing routines are to some extent language-specific, and the routines may vary even between highly similar languages" (Odlin 2014, 37).

Kellerman's (1977, 1978, 1979, 1983) notion of psychotypology may be relevant to why speakers of a language—such as Russian, which exhibits verbal gender agreement in the past tense but which is geographically and culturally far removed from Arabic—could not capitalize on the structural similarity with their L1. The notion hypothesizes that learners' perception of language distance plays a role in L1 transfer in triggering or constraining language transfer without necessarily corresponding to the actual distance between languages (see also Ringbom 2001). Although no data has been collected about the participants' perception of the typological distance between their L1s and Arabic, it is likely that they did not perceive a structural closeness, due perhaps to the geographic distance. However, this would not explain the advantage maintained by the Russian participants over their Chinese counterparts with respect to nominal gender agreement or the advantage maintained by the Chinese participants in dropping far more subjects than their Russian counterparts. Therefore, a less ad hoc explanation is needed to explain the full range of the findings from a usage-based and crosslinguistic (psycho)typological effect accounts.

7.3 L1 Transfer and Universal Grammar Access Accounts

In terms of parametric and feature L2 acquisition accounts within principles and parameters (of the generative framework), a number of hypotheses have been proposed in the literature that are relevant to the present data. Such hypotheses are claimed to account for ultimate attainment in L2 acquisition as well as variability in the use of inflections either due to L1 transfer effects (i.e., whether or not feature values associated with functional categories are transferable from L1) or being superficially missing in L2 surface forms but entail a learning task of disentangling the form–function relationship in L2 depending on the extent that such a relationship is configured similarly or differently from that in L1.[8] At least four proposals representing the main current approaches on universal grammar (UG) access and L1 transfer have been advanced: the representational deficit / interpretability hypothesis, the organic grammar hypothesis, the full transfer / full access model, and the feature reassembly hypothesis. In this section a brief description of each of the four hypotheses is offered, followed by a discussion of the specific predictions that each makes and whether such predictions are borne out by the present data.

The representational deficit / interpretability hypothesis (e.g., Hawkins 2005, 2009; Hawkins and Hattori 2006; Hawkins et al. 2008; Tsimpli 2003; Tsimpli and Dimitrakopoulou 2007; Tsimpli and Mastropavlou 2008; Franceschina 2005), which is a reformulation of the failed functional features hypothesis (Hawkins and Chan 1997; Hawkins 1998, 2001), posits that uninterpretable ϕ-features (such as agreement features of person, number, and gender) are subject to maturational constraints (i.e., critical period effects) and, therefore, if such features are not instantiated (in L1) prior to the critical period, they become no longer accessible later (i.e., they become unavailable in the UG inventory for L2 acquisition). Such features are part of the feature-checking mechanism and structural derivation in the minimalist framework and are deleted when checked against relevant features (e.g., Chomsky 1995, 1998, 1999, 2001a; see also Carstens 2000; White et al. 2004). In other words, L2 morphological development related to uninterpretable features is constrained by what is available in L1 and, therefore, may be permanently impaired depending on the nature of the L1 system. By contrast, interpretable ϕ-features required for semantic interpretation (i.e., those encoding specific lexical items such as gender feature/assignment on nouns) are acquirable in L2 even if such features are not available in L1 (cf. Carroll 1989).[9] In other words, the hypothesis claims that the presence or absence of (uninterpretable) features in L1 makes a difference in L2 acquisition and accounts for the variability or optionality in the use of inflectional features throughout the stages of L2 development due to partial unavailability of UG.[10] Accordingly, the hypothesis makes three predictions: (1) an asymmetry would result in the acquisition of nominal gender agreement by L1 speakers of languages (such as Russian) that exhibit the nominal gender agreement feature versus those whose L1s (such as Chinese) that do not; (2) uninterpretable features (i.e., agreement features such as *u*Gender), if not instantiated in L1, are not acquirable whereas interpretable features (such as gender assignment on nouns) are acquirable regardless of whether such features are available in L1; and (3) the learning mechanism of agreement features by L2 learners whose L1 does not exhibit nominal gender agreement (such as the uninterpretable gender ϕ-features) is permanently impaired in L2.

The organic grammar hypothesis (Vainikka and Young-Scholten 2006, 2007, 2009), formerly known as "minimal trees" (proposed by the same authors: Vainikka and Young-Scholten 1994, 1996, 1998), makes three related claims: (1) initial variability in the use of inflection is due to lack of transfer of functional categories in L1, (2) only lexical categories are transferred from L1 to L2 initial state, and (3) L2 minimal trees become target-like based on evidence from L2 input. In the event uninterpretable features become inaccessible in L2 (à la the representational deficit hypothesis), the full house principle (Vainikka and Young-Scholten 1994) will help fill an empty functional category in L2 (Vainikka and Young-Scholten 2009).[11]

The full transfer / full access model, which has not undergone any recent reformulations, adopts a strong L1 transfer and UG access approach (Schwartz and Sprouse 1994, 1996; Schwartz 1998; see also Epstein, Flynn, and Martohardjono 1996).[12] It posits that the entirety of L1 grammar, including lexical categories, functional categories, and feature values associated with functional categories (excluding the phonetic matrices of lexical/morphological items), is available to L2 learners from the early stages of L2 acquisition; restructuring (or approximation of the L2 system) takes place upon exposure to input of the target language, and that obscurity in input leads to fossilization.

The feature reassembly hypothesis is a reformulation of an earlier hypothesis known as the missing surface inflection hypothesis.[13] It attempts at refining the full transfer / full access model (Schwartz and Sprouse 1994, 1996; Schwartz 1998). Departing from a parametric feature-setting approach, feature reassembly hypothesis "adopts a comparative linguistic feature-based approach in which ultimate attainment of nativelike L2 morphosyntactic knowledge depends on the extent to which learners are able to reconfigure the feature values in functional categories and lexical items, and the conditions under which these are realized, from those of the [L1] to the L2 in cases where these differ" (Hwang and Lardiere 2013, 58; see also Lardiere 2008, 2009b). The main assumption of the hypothesis is based on the notion of L2 learners' task being involved in "reassembling" or "reconfiguring" the features in conformity with those of L2 since L2 learners are assumed to initially transfer from their L1 (à la the full transfer / full access model) knowledge of functional categories and how morpholexical items are assembled.[14] In addition, "eventual native-like attainment is at least possible for some learners" regardless of the presence or absence of features in L1 (Hwang and Lardiere 2013, 75).

The data reported on here suggest that none of the current L2 proposals discussed above can fully account for the data, although the full transfer / full access model may provide the closest explanation. Thus, according to one prediction of the representational deficit / interpretability hypothesis, we would expect an asymmetry in the acquisition of nominal (noun–adjective) gender agreement by the Russian L1 speakers versus the Chinese L1 speakers. The former have instantiated the (uninterpretable) feature gender agreement in their L1 (and therefore the feature remains accessible for L2 acquisition) whereas the latter do not (due to the feature's disappearance from the UG inventory). This seems to be borne out by the data since the Chinese L1 speakers seem to encounter more difficulty learning nominal gender agreement than their Russian counterparts (see chapter 3). This finding is particularly strong since the Chinese L1-A groups received about double the amount of input as that of the Chinese L1-B groups (so did the Russian L1-A than the Russian L1-B groups); yet both Chinese groups seem to find nominal gender agreement more difficult than their Russian counterparts. Recall, both the Russian L1-A and Russian L1-B groups maintained an advantage over their Chinese

L1 participants.[15] This finding is consistent with that reported in Al-Hamad's (2003) study, which revealed the Russian L1 participants were more accurate in their suppliance of gender markings on nouns and adjectives than their Chinese L1 counterparts. This finding is further corroborated by previous findings from Arabic L2 studies where French L2 learners (whose L1 exhibits the nominal gender agreement feature) outperformed their English L1 and Japanese L1 counterparts (whose L1s do not exhibit the nominal gender agreement feature) in almost all groups (Alhawary 2009a, 2009b).

According to a second prediction of the representational deficit / interpretability hypothesis, uninterpretable features (i.e., agreement features), if not instantiated in L1, are not acquirable whereas interpretable features (such as gender assignment on nouns) are acquirable regardless of whether or not such features are available in L1. We find some evidence for this prediction through participants' limited novel use of gender assignment (i.e., their use of interpretable ϕ-features), where they produced only a small number of tokens with feminine nouns as masculine nouns and masculine nouns as feminine nouns (see chapter 3, section 3.3.1.2; see also section 3.3.2.2, where three Russian L1-A beginner participants produced a good number of feminine nouns as masculine nouns with a masculine demonstrative). This finding suggests that, apart from a few individual cases, all participants (the Russian L1 as well as the Chinese L1 participants) seem to have acquired the proper gender assignment on nouns from early on and regardless of L1 (see also Sabourin, Stowe, and de Haan 2006; cf. White et al. 2004). This is also in line with previous data from Arabic L2 learners with other L1s, including English, French, and Japanese (Alhawary 2009a, 2009b). By the same token, the finding that the Russian participants, in particular the Russian L1-A groups, had far more such tokens than their Chinese L1-A counterparts may also indicate that the Russian participants' learning of nominal gender agreement (i.e., their use of uninterpretable ϕ-features) is more robust than their Chinese counterparts, and they seem to be more aware of the gender agreement feature due to the feature being present and instantiated in their L1 (see chapter 3, sections 3.3.1.2 and 3.3.2.2).

Finally, as far as the representational deficit / interpretability hypothesis is concerned, according to a third prediction of the hypothesis, the learning mechanism of agreement features by L2 learners whose L1 does not exhibit nominal gender agreement (i.e., in this case use of uninterpretable gender ϕ-features) is predicted to be permanently impaired or unacquirable in L2. In order for this prediction to be confirmed, the performance of the participants would have to exhibit variability or optionality in gender agreement across all Chinese participants and none would achieve a performance level similar to that of native speakers. Upon looking at the performance of individual participants, the findings reveal that there is nothing to suggest that impairment is permanent in this case since some Chinese L1 participants within all groups (except for the Chinese L1-B Group 1) exhibited high accuracy performance on nominal gender agreement, especially singular feminine, with four scoring within 80% range and one in the 90% range in the Chinese L1-A Group 1, five within 80% range and one in the 90% range in the Chinese L-A Group 2, four within 80% range and one in the 90% range in the Chinese L1-A Group 3, two within 80% range and one in the 90% range in the Chinese L1-B Group 2, and one within 80% range and three in the 90% range in the Chinese L1-B Group 3. More importantly, two participants in the Chinese L1-A Group 1 even performed at ceiling level (100% correct rule application) in both singular feminine and singular masculine (versus one participant in the Russian L1-A Group 2), as shown in figure 7.1. This is in line with previous findings where at least one English L1 participant performed at ceiling level (100% correct) in singular feminine (noun–adjective) agreement and verbal agreement contexts (Alhawary 2009a, 159–60). This finding suggests acquirability and even full attainment of uninterpretable features in L2, in particular the [*u*Gender] feature, may be possible regardless of the status of L1 and impairment may not be permanent (see also Gess and Herschensohn 2001; Bruhn de Garavito and White 2002; White et al. 2004), contrary to the representational deficit / interpretability hypothesis (e.g., Hawkins 2005, 2009; Hawkins and Hattori 2006; Hawkins et al. 2008; Tsimpli 2003; Tsimpli and Dimitrakopoulou 2007; Tsimpli and Mastropavlou 2008; Franceschina 2005; for claims related to non-attainability of L2 nativelike proficiency due to critical period effects, see, for example, Hyltenstam and Abrahamsson 2003 and Abrahamsson and Hyltenstam 2008).[16]

According to a main prediction of the organic grammar hypothesis, we would expect low performance and variability in the use of, for example, verbal gender agreement and tense at early stages of development (due to lack of transfer of functional categories in L1). The strongest evidence against the prediction of the organic grammar hypothesis comes from the high performance of the beginner groups on past tense (especially by the Chinese L1-A Group 1, the Russian L1-A Group 1, and the Russian L1-B Group 1) as well as present tense random task (especially by the Chinese L1-A Group 1, the Chinese L1-B Group 1, and the Russian L1-B Group 1) (see tables 5.1 and 5.3, chapter 5). This is also supported by previous data (both longitudinal and cross-sectional)

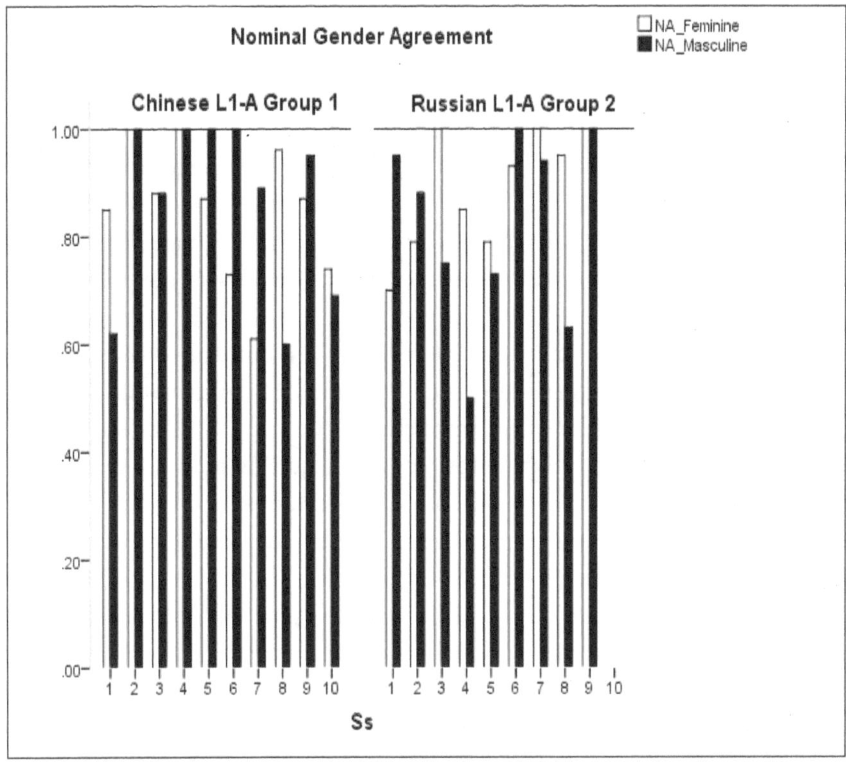

Figure 7.1 Bar Chart of % Correct Performance on Nominal Gender Agreement (Feminine and Masculine) by individual participants of the Chinese L1-A Group 1 and Russian L1-A Group 2

where English L1, Spanish L1, and Japanese L1 participants achieved high accuracy rates in their use of verbal agreement (Alhawary 2009a, 2009b) and tense (Alhawary 2009a). In addition, the organic grammar hypothesis does not predict the asymmetry in the acquisition of nominal (noun–adjective) gender agreement by the Chinese L1 and Russian L1 participants, as mentioned above.

As for the feature reassembly hypothesis, it predicts that acquiring uninterpretable features not present in L1 is possible (Hwang and Lardiere 2013). However, in the event that morphosyntactic features (such as those of verbal and nominal gender agreement in Arabic) involve a challenging learning task of reassembling such features in L2, then we would expect low performance on such forms at early stages of L2 development (see Hwang and Lardiere 2013, 58). In other words, the degree of complexity that such reassembling or reconfiguring process entails would necessarily reflect the amount of learning difficulty encountered by the L2 learners. With respect to the acquisition of

Arabic nominal gender agreement in feature reassembly hypothesis's terms, the L2 learner will have to learn to associate gender marking with the appropriate morpholexical items, which means the initial establishment of a feature-checking relation between the interpretable feature of gender (on nouns) and the assignment of an uninterpretable [*u*Gender] feature of the feminine -*a* marker (on adjectives). The data of the present study partly confirms the prediction of the feature reassembly hypothesis in that eventual native-like attainment is possible, at least for some learners regardless of the presence or absence of the feature in L1. Since at least two of the Chinese L1 participants were able to perform at ceiling (100% correctly) on both singular masculine and feminine agreement, as illustrated in figure 7.1, there is nothing to suggest that there is a permanent impairment in UG access (to the feature gender agreement from the UG inventory) or that acquiring new uninterpretable features is not possible in adult SLA, as discussed above. However, the feature reassembly hypothesis fails to predict the acquisition asymmetry of nominal gender agreement by the Chinese L1 versus the Russian L1 participants (for a similar finding, see also Al-Hamad 2003). The learning task (of reassembling) the feature gender in Arabic seems to be more challenging for the former than the latter, although it is hardly complex, neither in and of itself nor in relation to Chinese L1 or Russian L1.

The second part of the (nonconfirmed) prediction of the feature reassembly hypothesis does not mean that Arabic does not exhibit features that entail a complex feature reassembly task, as indeed there are some such features.[17] The findings presented in support of the hypothesis are arguably convincing, where the learning of the Korean plural feature (by English L1 speakers) does seem to exhibit a complex feature reassembly task as reflected by the conditions governing its use as illustrated in (2) (cited from Hwang and Lardiere 2013, 64).

(2) [n] = noun (feature associated with nP)
[group] = plural
[individuation] = classifier (two relevant subtypes:)
    [+human]
    [−human]
[q] = quantity (two subtypes:)
    [q-rel] = "relative" = nonnumerical quantifier (e.g., *many, some*)
    [q-abs] = "absolute" = numerical quantifier (e.g., *three*)
[specific] = "i.know"

However, unlike the plural feature in Korean, the learning (of reassembly) task is hardly complex when it comes to Arabic nominal gender agreement (between the head noun and an attributive adjective within Arabic NPs) and instead nominal gender agreement is to a large extent regular and exhibits phonological regularity (with the exception of a small subset of crypto-feminine nouns not included in the target forms). As explained in chapter 3, in the vast majority of cases, nominal agreement for singular feminine is achieved by attaching the suffix {*-a*} in word final (salient) position on both nouns and adjectives, resulting in a rhyming effect that can serve as a phonological clue to the Arabic L2 learner. For singular masculine, gender agreement is realized as zero {*-0*}, the stem being the default masculine form (see also section 1.1, chapter 1). Accordingly, gender (singular feminine and singular masculine) agreement in Arabic is transparent and quite unlike that in Spanish, for example, which has been cited as potentially problematic for adult L2 learners (e.g., Bruhn de Garavito and White 2002; White et al. 2004; Franceschina 2005).[18] Yet the present data reveal an asymmetry in the acquisition of Arabic nominal gender agreement by Chinese L1 and Russian L1 speakers, with the former finding the form more challenging than the latter and the latter showing an advantage over the former with their higher accuracy rates, especially in the intermediate and advanced groups (for a similar finding based on Russian L1 and Chinese L1 learners of Arabic, see also Al-Hamad 2003). The only distinction between the two is that whereas the nominal gender agreement feature is present in the L1 of the Russian participants, it is absent in the L1 of the Chinese participants (for similar findings based on data from English L1, Japanese L1, and French L1 learners of Arabic, see Alhawary 2009a; see also Sabourin et al. 2006, for compatible findings on Dutch L2 grammatical gender).

Thus, whereas the findings are partially in support of the feature reassembly hypothesis for revealing that even native-like performance is possible at least for some learners, the hypothesis fails to account for the asymmetry in the acquisition patterns of nominal gender agreement. By focusing on the complexity of features and the conditions for their realization, the feature reassembly hypothesis attempted to advance a comparative feature-based approach to "further refine the construct of L1 influence" and explain a possible source that may account for obscurity in the input à la full transfer / full access model, which may result in possible fossilization or learning problems (Hwang and Lardiere 2013, 81). However, in the case of the transparent input related to Arabic nominal gender agreement (singular feminine and singular masculine), it would be unwarranted to assume complexity of feature realization (which does not exist in this case) to result in added learning burden or difficulty. It seems rather that absence of a feature in L1 in and of itself plays a role in adult L2 acquisition. As mentioned above, certain other features do entail a complex learning task, but relying on the notion of task complexity involved in figuring out the (re)configuration of features in L2 as a factor alone does not provide a satisfactory explanation of the data of nominal gender agreement reported on here.

Of all four proposals, the full transfer / full access model seems to provide the closest adequate explanation, especially if an additional refinement is added: that the presence or absence of a feature in L1 plays a role in L2 acquisition. Accordingly, the main prediction of the hypothesis that full UG access is possible through L1 seems to be confirmed by the data. If lexical categories, functional categories, and possibly abstract features associated with functional categories (not the surface, phonetic matrices of lexical/morphological items) are available for transfer from the early stages of L2 acquisition in the sense that the L2 learner knows to check for certain features if present in their L1, then we would predict an asymmetry in the performance of L2 learners whose L1 exhibits such features versus those whose L1 does not (see also Lardiere 1998, 2000; Alhawary 2009a, 154). Accordingly, whereas the Russian L1 speakers are more likely to check (for feature checking) for the nominal gender feature present in their L1 when they produce Arabic NPs, the Chinese L1 speakers are less likely to do so and would find such a feature more problematic to acquire since the gender feature is absent in their L1. This is borne out by the data. Recall, the performance of the beginner Russian L1-A and Chinese L1-A participants (Group 1) differed significantly from that of their Russian L1-B and Chinese L1-B counterparts (the former received double the amount of input than the latter), but, more importantly, the intermediate and advanced Russian L1-A participants (Groups 2 and 3) maintained an advantage (though not statistically significant) over their Chinese L1-A counterparts in both feminine and masculine agreement; so did the Russian L1-B participants in Groups 1–3 over their Chinese L1-B counterparts in Groups 1–3 as well as the Chinese L1-A counterparts in Group 3 in feminine agreement (see tables 3.1–3.3, section 3.3.1, chapter 3; see also Al-Hamad 2003; for similar findings based on data from English L1, Japanese L1, and French L1 learners of Arabic, see Alhawary 2009a). Thus, the nominal gender (noun–adjective) findings here point to two conclusions. First, the maintained advantage exhibited by the Russian participants over their Chinese counterparts point to the robust role of L1 transfer, which seems to extend to even the advanced/third-year level of Arabic (intensive and nonintensive) instruction. Second, the role of L1 transfer can be overridden or minimized by increased input exposure or proficiency, where due to the (double) extra input exposure, the beginner Chinese L1-A participants (Group 1) were able to minimize the impact resulting from absence of the nominal (noun–adjective) gender feature versus the Chinese L1-B participants who could not (for a similar conclusion about the extent of the role of L1 transfer, see Hopp 2010; Ionin and Montrul 2010).[19]

Similarly, on the above L1 transfer account, since gender is absent in nominal demonstrative agreement in both Russian and Chinese, we would expect no significant difference between the performance of the Russian L1 and Chinese L1 participants. This prediction, too, is borne out by the data. There were no between and within group differences in the performance of participants on demonstrative gender agreement (see chapter 3, section 3.3.2 and tables 3.10 and 3.12, in particular).[20] This finding is corroborated by previous studies based on data from English L1, Japanese L1, and French L1 learners of Arabic, where French L1 participants, whose L1 alone exhibits gender demonstrative agreement, outperformed their English L1 and Japanese L1 counterparts on demonstrative singular feminine agreement (Alhawary 2009a, 2009b). Accordingly, it is reasonable to assume that presence or absence of a feature in L1 plays a role in L2 acquisition even when no obvious complexity of feature realization (entailing a challenging learning task to figure out the (re)assembly or (re)configuration of features in L2) is observed.

However, with respect to verbal gender agreement, the prediction of the full transfer / full access model falls short of accounting for the full range of the data. Recall only Russian has verbal gender agreement albeit in the past tense. Accordingly, if the newly introduced prediction of the full transfer / full access model were to be maintained here too (i.e., presence or absence of a feature in L1 makes a difference), we would expect an asymmetry in the performance of Russian L1 and Chinese L1 participants, with the former performing better than the latter, at least with respect to verbal gender agreement in the past tense. However, this prediction is not supported by the data. The findings revealed no group difference in the performance of the Russian L1 and Chinese L1 participants on past tense verbal gender agreement (see chapter 4, section 4.3.1 and table 4.1). Previous studies that included L1 English, L1 French, and L1 Japanese learners of Arabic did not reveal significant L1 group differences with respect to verbal agreement, understandably since none of the L1s of the participants exhibits singular masculine and feminine agreement (Alhawary

2009a, 157; 2009b; cf. Al-Hamad 2003, who reported Russian L1 intermediate learners being more successful in acquiring Arabic verbal gender agreement than their Chinese L1 counterparts though verbal agreement data in the past and present tense were not reported separately). However, a slight advantage (though not statistically significant) was reported for the performance of the French L1 participants over their English and Japanese counterparts and another for the performance of the English L1 participants over their Japanese counterparts. Although the three L1s do not exhibit verbal gender agreement, the three differ in that only Japanese exhibits zero verbal agreement morphology, both English and French do have verbal agreement features, with English having a more impoverished paradigm than French (Alhawary 2009a, 157). Hence, this may explain, from the perspective of the full transfer / full access model, the slight advantage of the French L1 participants (over the English and Japanese counterparts) and that of the English L1 participants (over their Japanese counterparts) due perhaps to the contributing (positive transfer) effect of the presence of the verbal agreement feature paradigm in the participants' L1.

With respect to the present data and the qualitative difference in the verbal agreement paradigms of Russian (exhibiting a rich verbal agreement paradigm, including a singular gender agreement feature in the past tense) and Chinese (exhibiting zero verbal agreement morphology), the full transfer / full access model does not seem to account for the lack of asymmetry in the performance of the participants on verbal gender agreement on par with that of nominal gender agreement within a purely feature-based approach. However, if we consider the nature of the target verbal agreement form as a contributing factor to the finding, a likely explanation may be advanced. Since tense is conflated with verbal morphological agreement features (where, for example, the prefix for agreement is also traditionally analyzed as a present tense marker and its absence corresponds to the past tense), Arabic L2 learners (of L1s that do not exhibit verbal gender agreement including Chinese) are somehow able to learn verbal gender agreement while being aided by positive L1 transfer of tense, since both L1s of the participants exhibit the feature tense.[21]

Thus, of all current formal/generative UG and L1 transfer models, the full transfer / full access model seems to provide the closest adequate explanation with the additional stipulation that presence or absence of a feature in L1 plays a role in further predicting L1 transfer effects. However, the nature of the target form as an additional contributing acquisition factor, must also be taken into account. Otherwise, the process of L1 transfer may appear to be randomly selective.

7.4 Null Subjects: More on L1 Transfer

Investigating the acquisition of null subjects has occupied center stage in SLA for over three decades although interest in pursuing further research seems to have somewhat waned in recent years. At least, four main questions have preoccupied second language researchers: setting the null-subject parameter, the association between the development of verbal inflection and null subjects, access to UG, and L1 transfer. Study results are summarized as follows (for a detailed review, see Carroll 2001; Sauter 2002; Alhawary 2007a, 2009a):

- There is no agreement whether the L2 learner can reset the parameter in L2; studies produced mixed evidence on resetting the null-subject parameter, especially with respect to the clustering effect, where the setting of the value of one parameter should trigger the resetting of other parameters belonging to the same cluster.
- Studies generally reveal that adult speakers of null-subject and non-null-subject languages learning a null-subject language produce subjectless clauses from early on. Conversely, speakers of null-subject and non-null-subject languages learning a non-null-subject language do supply overt subjects from early on.
- Studies provide mixed evidence for the association between development of verbal inflection and null subjects.
- Evidence in support of L1 transfer comprise three strands of findings: (1) speakers of null-subject languages learning null-subject languages produce null-subject clauses and seem to adjust to the L2 system from early on; (2) speakers of null-subject languages learning non-null-subject languages (for example, English and German) seem to adjust to the system of L2 from early on although they still produce some subjectless clauses; and (3) speakers of non-null-subject languages learning non-null-subject languages noticeably reject more subjectless clauses than speakers of null-subject languages learning non-null-subject languages.

It is worth mentioning here that the vast majority of such studies have been conducted on three languages as L2s: English [-null], German [-null], and

Spanish [+ null], many of which relied on grammaticality judgment tasks in assessing participants' use of null subjects.[22]

With respect to Arabic SLA studies, findings from previous studies on adult speakers of English [-null], Japanese [+null], and Spanish [+null] provide evidence for UG access, L1 transfer, and the association between the development of verbal inflection and null subjects (see Alhawary 2007a, 2009a).[23] The production data reported on in chapter 6 (similar to those employed in previous Arabic L2 studies) contribute further to general SLA as well as Arabic L2 findings, especially with respect to both the association between verbal agreement and null-subject use and L1 transfer. Moreover, the data here are collected from two novel typological constellations: L1 Chinese and L1 Russian speakers learning Arabic as an L2, resulting in the pairings (3) and (4).

(3) Russian participants who are speakers of a [±null] and [+strong] L1, learning L2 Arabic [+ null] and [+ strong], with previous knowledge of L2 English [-null] and [-strong]

(4) Chinese participants who are speakers of a [+null] and [-strong] L1, learning L2 Arabic [+null] and [+ strong], with previous knowledge of L2 English [-null] and [-strong][24]

Although Chinese is a [+null] language, as discussed in chapter 6, Russian is a mixed null-subject language [±-null], suggesting that null subject in Russian is not as freely used as in Chinese and Arabic.

Accordingly, if L1 transfer effects were to be detected in the present data, we would expect: (1) above chance performance levels on dropping null subjects by the Chinese and Russian participants (especially by the former) in their early and/or subsequent stages of Arabic L2 acquisition and (2) an asymmetry in the use of null subjects by both groups, where we would expect the Russian L1 participants to exhibit a conservative use in null subjects and the Chinese L1 participants to use null subjects more freely. In fact, the two predictions are borne out by the data. That the participants of both L1 language backgrounds dropped a significant number of subjects is evident in all groups of beginners at the rate of 68% by the Chinese L1-A Group 1, 65% by the Chinese L1-B Group 1, 79% by the Russian L1-A Group 1, and 75% by the Russian L1-B Group 1 (see table 6.2, chapter 6).

With respect to the second prediction of an asymmetrical pattern in null-subject use by both groups of participants, this is manifested by means of two observations. First, despite performance above chance by all participants in the beginner groups (see table 6.2, chapter 6) and despite improvement in performance on verbal agreement in subsequent stages (Groups 2 and 3) by all participants (see table 6.3, chapter 6), the Chinese L1 participants eventually converged on progressively dropping more subjects (in particular, the advanced Chinese L1-A and Chinese L1-B Group 3 dropped subjects 93% and 84% of the time, respectively), and the Russian L1 participants converged progressively on dropping fewer subjects to a low random chance level, with both the advanced Russian L1-A and Russian L1-B Group 3 dropping subjects only 53% of the time (see table 6.2, chapter 6; see also figure 6.1, chapter 6). Second, consider the number of individual cases of participants who dropped subjects in comparison with those of the native controls. Based on the range where the native controls dropped subjects 92–100% of the time, we find far more individual participants in the Chinese groups along the three proficiency levels to have performed within the native speakers' range than in the Russian groups—as many as fourteen in the Chinese L1-A groups and ten in the Chinese L1-B groups versus four in the Russian L1-A groups and five in the Russian L1-B groups (see figure 7.2).

Thus, as the case with acquisition of nominal gender agreement, the data of the null subjects provide strong evidence for the role of L1 transfer—a positive/

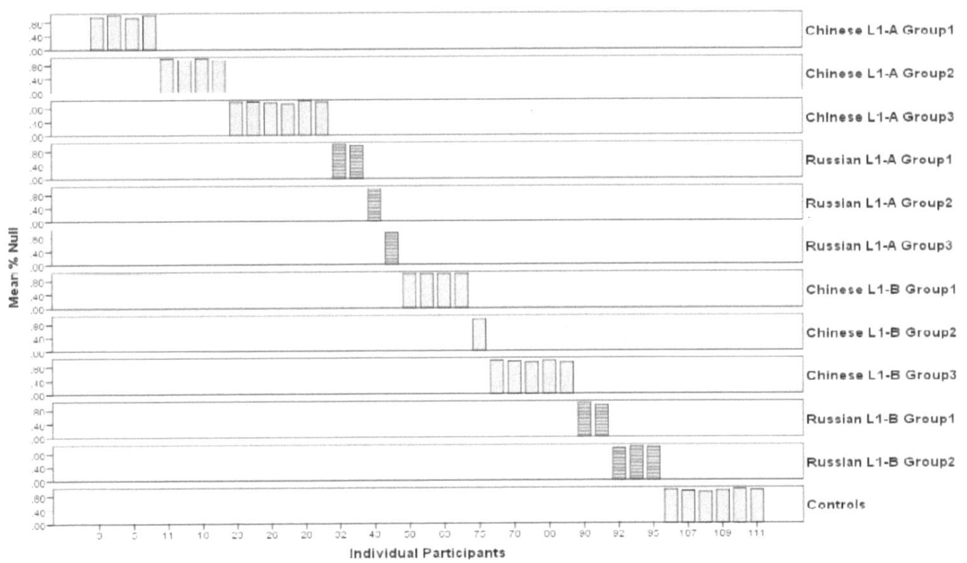

Figure 7.2 Bar Chart of Individual Participants Who Dropped Subjects within Range of the Native Controls

facilitative role for Chinese and a negative/non-facilitative role for Russian. The findings are particularly strong since this finding was obtained irrespective of the amount of input exposure, where the Russian L1-A groups received about double the amount of input as that of the Russian L1-B groups (so did the Chinese L1-A than the Chinese L1-B groups); yet both groups converged on dropping conservatively far fewer subjects (than the Chinese L1-A and Chinese L1-B groups) toward the advanced proficiency level, reflecting the degree of freedom with which subjects are dropped in Chinese versus Russian. Future research should include participants at higher advanced or near-native levels in order to examine the near-native status of the null-subject parameter in Arabic L2 participants in similar language pairings (e.g., à la Sorace 2003). Null-subject use is especially intriguing to examine since it involves optional use of the target form itself.

7.5 L2 or L1 Transfer?

In the event the L2 learner had exposure to more than one L2 linguistic system, it may be proposed that the L1 may not be the only source of transfer and that other L2 systems may also transfer. This is a relatively new area in SLA, which is also referred to as "L3 transfer." At least three main morphosyntactic L3 transfer proposals with specific claims have so far been advanced and have received significant attention in the past decade: the cumulative enhancement model (e.g., Flynn et al. 2004; Berkes and Flynn 2012), the L2 status factor (e.g., Williams and Hammarberg 1998; Bardel and Falk 2007, 2012; Falk and Bardel 2011), and the typological primacy model (e.g., Rothman 2010, 2011, 2013, 2015; Rothman and Cabrelli Amaro 2010; Rothman et al. 2015). According to the cumulative enhancement model (CEM), the learner's L1 does not play a privileged role in L3 acquisition, learning is a cumulative process and consequently both L1 and any previously learned L2s (regardless of order of acquisition of the L2s) can be possible sources for transfer, and such a process is selective whereby it may either play an exclusively facilitative role or remain neutral (i.e., allowing only positive transfer to the exclusion of negative transfer). The L2 status factor model (L2SFM) similarly posits that the L1 does not play a privileged role in L3 acquisition, but it is further claimed that the L2 supersedes the L1 as the source of transfer (both negative/non-facilitative and positive/facilitative), irrespective of whether or not transfer from L1 would lead to target-like L3 production. This strong role for L2 transfer is claimed to be due to a higher degree of sociolinguistic and neurocognitive similarities between L2 and L3 (being distinct from L1), such as learning setting, age of onset, learning outcome, awareness of language learning, use of learning strategies, and the nature of L2 (metalinguistic) knowledge being declarative rather than procedural and memory storage of such knowledge system. As for the typological primacy model (TPM), it adopts similar claims to those of the CEM (i.e., in allowing both L1 and L2 transfer to occur) but diverges from it in

1. Allowing negative/non-facilitative transfer to take place (in addition to positive/facilitative transfer);
2. Stipulating transfer (positive or negative) as being conditioned by typological/structural similarity between the languages at play, based on linguistic cues in the input and assessed from early on by the internal linguistic parser (a.k.a., the Language Acquisition Device/LAD);
3. Making no predictions where "the structurally similar language is not predicted to be assessed by the internal parser as the typologically similar language at a holistic level" despite presence of structural similarity; in this case, transfer is claimed to "not obtain" (Rothman 2015, 186);
4. Assuming that the internal parser is guided by a set of implicationally hierarchical linguistic cues (Lexical > Phonological > Morphological > Syntactic) to determine the previous L1 or L2 system which is closest holistically (or most typologically/structurally similar) to that of the L3; and
5. Claiming that transfer (from L1 or L2) is full rather than partial and occurs at the initial stage, similarly to the full transfer / full access model (e.g., Schwartz and Sprouse 1996; see section 7.3, above).

Such stipulations are claimed based on "general cognitive economy and cognitive processing factors" attributed to the bilingual mind (Rothman 2015, 184).

As mentioned in chapter 2 (section 2.3), to control for L1 and L2 transfer effects, language background data were collected from participants through a short survey and a follow-up interview (see also appendix A). According to the language backgrounds of the study participants, and in addition to self-reported knowledge of English as an L2 ranging from "fair" to "good" in all but one participants (who reported "weak" knowledge in the Russian L1-A Group 1), a number of participants reported knowledge of other L2s (see table 2.3, chapter 2). With respect to the Chinese L1 participants, one Chinese L1-A participant (Group 2) reported L2 knowledge of Japanese; and three Chinese L1-B (Groups 2 and 3) participants reported knowledge of one additional L2

(German, Spanish, or Polish), three reported knowledge of Japanese L2, and one reported knowledge of Korean. As for the Russian L1 participants, twelve Russian L1-A participants reported L2 knowledge of additional languages: three in Group 1 (one reported knowledge of French, one of Hindi, and one of both French and Spanish), five in Group 2 (one of French, one of Spanish, two of German, and one of both French and German), and four in Group 3 (one of French, one of Spanish, one of German, and one of both French and German). Five of the Russian L1-B participants reported L2 knowledge of French L2: two in Group 1 and three in Group 3.

As discussed in chapter 2 (section 2.3), the English L2 knowledge of the Chinese and Russian participants was an L2, and other languages were L3s similar to Arabic since they ranked their knowledge of L2 English consistently higher than other L2s (except for three participants who ranked their knowledge of English as an L2 similar to other L2s: one in the Russian L1-A Group 3 with L2 Spanish and L2 English being at the same level and one in each of the Russian L1-B Group 1 and Group 3 with L2 French and L2 English being at the same level) and Arabic.

To test whether there was any L2 transfer effects and whether the data can be accounted for by any of the L2 transfer models, performance of individual participants was examined, including performance of those who had other previous L2 knowledge besides English in comparison with those who had not. The results, together with implications for L2 transfer models in L3 acquisition, are provided in the four subsections immediately below. In general, with respect to L2 transfer from English, the findings seem to rather point to a strong L1 transfer role (whether positive/facilitative or negative/non-facilitative). For example, contrary to the CEM and the L2SFM, whereas Chinese L1 seems to play a negative role in nominal (noun–adjective) gender agreement, Russian L1 seems to play a positive role, and in both cases L1 transfer seems to be superseding L2 transfer and the role of English L2. In addition, the role of typological proximity seems to be more evident in L1 transfer than L2 transfer from English. Thus, typological proximity seems to be operative in (positive) L1 transfer from Russian in nominal (noun–adjective) gender agreement, an observation that is congruent with the predictions of the TPM. However, contrary to the TPM, L1 transfer from L1 Chinese in nominal gender agreement and null-subject use (negative and positive transfer, respectively) seems to be operative on a structural/linguistic proximity level rather than on a typologically "holistic" level, as discussed below.

7.5.1 L2 or L1 Transfer: Nominal (Noun-Adjective) Gender Agreement

With respect to nominal (noun–adjective) gender agreement, all participants with knowledge in other L2s performed within range of those who had knowledge of only English as an L2, except for two participants, both of whom scored noticeably below range of other participants within their own respective groups, as shown in table 7.1. Since German (in the case of the Chinese L2-B participant) and both Spanish and French (in the case of the Russian L1-A participant) exhibit nominal gender agreement similar to that in Arabic, no L2 (positive/facilitative) transfer effect of the three L2s can be detected here, contrary to the CEM, which would predict only positive transfer from an L2 to occur.

As for English L2 transfer effects, and based on the performance of the two participants (in table 7.1) alone, the prediction of a negative transfer effect from English L2 (since English does not exhibit nominal gender agreement) would be consistent with the L2SFM. However, based on the performance of all the participants, specifically the Chinese L1 versus the Russian L1 groups (see table 3.1, chapter 3), for whom English was a strong (and earlier) L2, the L2SFM cannot account for the difference in the acquisition pattern and the advantage of the Russian participants over their Chinese counterparts—due to L1 transfer, as argued in the above sections. According to the L2SFM, due to their similar exposure to English as an L2, the Chinese L1 and Russian L1 participants should demonstrate the same level of difficulty and should perform similarly on Arabic nominal (noun-adjective) gender agreement, since English does not exhibit such feature agreement. However, recall that, whereas Chinese does not exhibit nominal (noun–adjective) gender agreement, Russian does.

Table 7.1 Participants who scored out of range on nominal gender agreement (NGA)

	L2	*L2*	*L2*	*NGA Correct/ Total*	*%*
Chinese L1-B Mandarin					
Group2 (n=1)	English = G	German = F	—	1/11	9
Russian L1-A					
Group1 (n=1)	English = N	French = F	Spanish = F	1/21	5

Self-rated L2 Proficiency: N = Near-native; G = Good; F = Fair.

As for TPM's predictions, the data seem to provide mixed evidence. On one hand, TPM's predictions seem to be confirmed with (positive/facilitative) L1 transfer occurring from Russian, since Russian is more typologically similar to Arabic (than English) on a holistic level (considering their rich morphological systems[25]). On the other hand, TPM predictions are disconfirmed if Chinese is the source of negative (L1) transfer, since Chinese and Arabic are dissimilar typologically (and structurally). Similarly, the findings would still be problematic for TPM's predictions if the source of negative transfer in the Chinese participants were attributed to English L2, since the TPM does not make predictions on a structural proximity level, not to mention this would render the positive L1 transfer effects in the Russian participants unaccounted for (for additional counter evidence to the TPM where, for example, L1 transfer seems to obtain from the typologically most distant language, based on structural than typological proximity, see Jin 2009; Hermas 2014; see also Westergaard et al. 2017, who accordingly advanced the linguistic proximity model, and Slabakova 2017, who proposed the scalpel model).

7.5.2 L2 or L1 Transfer: Verbal Gender Agreement

When examining the individual performance of the participants on verbal gender (feminine) agreement, there was no clear pattern across the three narrative tasks of verbal agreement (i.e., in the past tense, present tense, and random present tense) except for one participant (in the Russian L1-A Group 3) who scored noticeably lower (across all three narrative tasks) than other participants within the same group. The participant self-reported L2 knowledge of Spanish (and English). The few remaining cases were of participants with other L2 knowledge (besides English L2) where the participants either scored slightly (by around 10% accuracy) lower or higher than other participants with

Table 7.2 Participants who scored out of range on verbal gender agreement (VGA)

	L2	*L2*	*VGA*	*Correct/Total*	*%*
Chinese L1-B Mandarin					
Group3 (n = 2)	English = N	Korean = F	Present	5/6	83 L
	English = G	Polish = F	Random	4/9	44 L
Russian L1-B					
Group3 (n = 2)	English = G	French = G	Past	9/9	100 H
	English = F	French = F	Past	11/11	100 H

N = Near-native; G = Good; F = Fair; L = lower than other participants within the same group; H = higher than other participants with the same group.

only L2 English knowledge (in the same group), as shown in table 7.2. The former are two Chinese L1-B participants who reported L2 knowledge of Korean and Polish (in addition to English), and the latter are two Russian L1-B participants who reported knowledge of L2 French (in addition to English).

Accordingly, no significant or clear L2 transfer effects can be detected here. In particular, although the slight underperformance of the two Chinese L1-B participants may be attributed to negative L2 transfer from Korean and Polish (for not exhibiting verbal gender agreement in the present tense[26]) à la the L2SFM, the outperformance of the two Russian L1-B participants cannot be attributed to positive L2 transfer from French (or English). In addition, negative transfer effects from Chinese cannot be ruled out in the case of the two Chinese L1-B participants; nor can positive transfer effects be ruled out from Russian in the two Russian L1-B participants since Russian exhibits verbal gender agreement in the past tense (table 7.2). Thus, overall, the above cases are too few and contradictory to allow any noticeable L2 transfer effects on the participants' performance of verbal gender agreement and, therefore, the data cannot be explained by L2 transfer models such as the L2SFM.

7.5.3 L2 or L1 Transfer: Tense/Aspect

Not unlike verbal gender agreement, the data of tense/aspect reveals no clear pattern across the three narrative tasks: past tense, present tense, and random present tense. Recall also that the data overall revealed no significant group differences (see chapter 5). The performance of individual participants that differed from other participants within their respective groups reveals a small number of cases in the production of tense (inflected for third person singular feminine), as displayed in table 7.3. As table 7.3 shows, these individual cases are scattered among the groups and seem to be random, with some cases having higher accuracy percentages and others lower than those of other participants within their respective groups, and some differing only by a small margin of 10%. Since all the languages involved in the pairings (including both L1s and all L2s) exhibit at least a distinction between past and present tense, no particular L2 effect can be detected for any of the participants' L2s, except that of English L2 (which is shared by all the participants), their L1s, or some other factors.

7.5.4 L2 or L1 Transfer: Null Subjects

The analysis of the participants' individual production of null subjects also revealed no transfer effect of L2s other than English (see table 7.4). The

Table 7.3 Participants who scored out of range on tense/aspect

	L2	*L2*	*Tense*	*Correct/Total*	*%*
Chinese L1-B Mandarin					
Group3 (n = 2)	English = G	Polish = F	Present	0/8	0 L
	English = N	Korean = F	Present	3/6	50 L*
Russian L1-A					
Group1 (n = 1)	English = N	French = F	Present	4/7	57 H*
Group3 (n = 1)	English = G	Spanish = G	Present	1/8	13 L
			Random	4/8	50 L
Russian L1-B					
Group1 (n = 1)	English = G	French = F	Past	1/5	20 L
Group3 (n = 1)	English = F	French = F	Present	6/7	86 H

N = Near-native; G = Good; F=Fair; L = lower than other participants within the same group; H = higher than other participants within the same group; *= slightly (higher or lower) by 10% (in)accuracy rate.

individual cases form slight outliers and point to contradictory predictions of L2 effects. This is true of all participants in the Russian L1-A and Russian L1-B groups displayed in table 7.4. Despite the fact that all of the L2s of the Russian L1-A participant in Group 2 (i.e., English, German, and French) are all non-null-subject languages, the participant had the highest percentage of dropped subjects, contrary, for example, to the negative transfer prediction of the L2SFM. The performance of the other Russian L1-A participant in Group 3 is also not exactly consistent with the L2SFM of transfer, which would have to allow mostly for negative (rather than positive) transfer to occur, since two of the participant's stronger L2s (English and French) are non-null-subject

Table 7.4 Participants who scored out of range on null subjects

	L2	*L2*	*L2*	*Null/Total*	*%*
Russian L1-A					
Group2 (n = 1)	English = N	German = G	French = F	25/26	96 H*
Group3 (n = 1)	English = N	French = G	Spanish = F	33/35	94 H
Russian L1-B					
Group3 (n = 2)	English = G	French = G	—	32/36	88 H*
	English = F	French = F	—	8/42	19 L*

N = Near-native; G = Good; F = Fair; L = lower than other participants within the same group; H = higher than other participants within the same group; *= slightly (higher or lower) within 10% (in)accuracy rate.

languages while the third weaker one (Spanish) is. Similarly, the performance of the two Russian L1-B participants provides contradictory evidence to L2 transfer effects. Although both of the participants' L2s (English and French) are non-null-subject languages, their productions formed slight outliers to their group in two opposite directions, and neither the L2SFM nor the CEM can account for both at the same time.

As for English L2 transfer effects alone, given that all the participants share English as an L2 (see table 6.2, figure 6.1, chapter 6), the L2SFM cannot account for the difference in the production pattern and the conservative dropping of subjects by the Russian L1 participants versus that of their Chinese L1 counterparts, who dropped subjects more freely—due most likely to L1 transfer effects, as argued in the above sections. According to the L2SFM, we would expect only negative (L2) transfer to occur since English is the L2 of all the participants and since English does not allow null subjects. Similarly, the TPM does not make the right prediction about transfer effects and the production data of both the Chinese L1 and Russian L1 participants. Recall, the TPM predicts that (L1) transfer would obtain in Russian participants since Russian seems to be typologically more similar to Arabic "at a holistic level" (at least morphologically), while it does not in Chinese participants since Chinese is not typologically more similar to Arabic (than English) "at a holistic level," although they share a structural similarity (of null subjects). However, while the former exhibited negative transfer, the latter exhibited positive transfer. Thus, in addition to disconfirming strong L2 transfer effects and rather confirming a strong role for L1 transfer, the data indicate that none of three L2 transfer models accounts for the data adequately.

To conclude this section, upon further analysis of the individual performance of participants in all groups, no evidence of L2 transfer effects (including of English L2 and other languages) could be detected, especially with respect to the participants' production of nominal (noun–adjective) gender agreement and null subjects. As for participants' production of verbal gender agreement and tense/aspect, individual performance of participants with different L2s did not reveal any clear patterns. These cases were contradictory and too few to reveal any significant effect for L2 transfer, and despite the fact that L2 transfer effects may be possible, L1 transfer effects from L1 Chinese and L1 Russian could not be ruled out. In sum, the findings, at least those related to nominal (noun–adjective) gender agreement and null subjects, leave little doubt that the role of L1 transfer is far more robust than admitted by any of the three L2 transfer models and provide concomitantly some counterevidence to their claimed predictions.

7.6 L1 Transfer and Speech Processing Prerequisites

Finally, processability theory is a well-known L2 grammatical development model based on a cognitive processing approach (Pienemann 1998, 2005; Pienemann and Håkansson 1999; Pienemann and Keßler 2011; Keßler 2008; Baten et al. 2015). Processability theory (PT) stipulates that speech production is by nature constrained since working memory is a "limited capacity" processor of information. Therefore, additional "memory buffers" are posited in which "processing procedures" deposit grammatical information for temporary storage (Pienemann1998, 60). The processing procedures, following Levelt (1989) and Kempen and Hoenkamp (1987), are further claimed to operate hierarchically in an implicational set sequence. From an L2 perspective, these procedures are considered to be language-specific. Accordingly, the L2 learner would have to create language-specific prerequisites necessary for L2 grammatical development. In L2 grammar terms, the L2 learner cannot initially process L2 grammatical structures since the learner cannot yet code conceptual information into L2 syntactic structures for two reasons. First, the lexicon is not fully annotated. Second, even if the lexical annotation were transferred into L2, the syntactic procedures "have not specialized to hold the specific L2 syntactic information" in the proposed memory buffers (Pienemann 1998, 76). The extent of this specialization is claimed to be the principle or "core" mechanism of L2 processability (Pienemann and Håkansson 1999, 384).

Accordingly, three morpheme types are identified to be held in temporary memory buffers: lexical morphemes, phrasal (i.e., "phrasal" as in phrase structure à la lexical functional grammar, or LFG) morphemes, and interphrasal morphemes.[27] The three types of morphemes are assumed to be processable by the L2 learner along five distinct stages in an implicational order, as follows (Pienemann 1998, 83–85):

Stage 1	Absence of any language-specific procedures where words are entered into the lexicon and conceptual structures are simply mapped into individual words and fixed phrases
Stage 2	Development of "category procedures" where grammatical categories (that is, S, V, N, etc.) are assigned and "lexical morphemes" (for example, the {-ed} tense marker in English)

are produced; these morphemes can be activated and realized in the same location once grammatical categories are assigned

Stage 3 Development of "phrasal procedures" where development from word level to phrase level becomes possible and "phrasal morphemes" are produced (that is, lexical morphemes, such as tense, number, gender, and case markers when unified between a head of a phrase and its modifier/s)

Stage 4 Development of "S-procedures" where "Inter-phrasal morphemes," involving exchange of information across phrases, are developed (for example, subject–verb agreement features); here, functional destinations are determined and sentences assembled

Stage 5 Development of "S-procedures" where subordinate/embedded clauses are developed.

Table 7.5 illustrates the hierarchical stages of speech processing procedures (also known as "speech processing prerequisites"), where the implicational nature of the hierarchy "derives from the assumption that the processing resources developed at one stage are necessary prerequisites for the following stage" (Pienemann 1998, 87).

Based on PT's notion of hierarchical stages of processing procedures, two other relevant learnability/teachability claims follow, as shown in (6) and (7).

6. Stages cannot be skipped [even] through formal instruction.
7. Instruction will be beneficial if it focuses on structures from the next stage (Pienemann 1998, 250).[28]

The first claim, stated in (6), makes a strong prediction that "stages cannot be skipped [even] through formal instruction" since skipping a stage is

Table 7.5 PT hierarchy of implicational sequence of speech processing procedures

	Developmental Stages				
Procedures	*T1*	*T2*	*T3*	*T4*	*T5*
S-procedure	-	-	-	-	+
S-procedures/interphrasal procedures	-	-	-	+	+
Phrasal procedures	-	-	+	+	+
Category procedures	-	+	+	+	+
Word or lemma access	+	+	+	+	+

"T" = time/stage, "+" = emergence, "-" = non-emergence.

hypothesized to cause the hierarchy to be "cut off in the learner grammar at the point of the missing processing procedure and that the rest of the hierarchy will be replaced by a direct mapping of conceptual structures onto surface form" (Pienemann and Håkansson 1999, 391; also Pienemann 1998, 250). The second claim, stated in (7), makes a weak prediction that instruction is beneficial if it focuses on structures from the next stage. Pienemann (1998) qualifies the second claim as "optimistic" since "there is no reason to assume that learners will acquire a structure just because they can process it; [a] functional need would have to be present for the structure to emerge" (1998, 250).[29]

Although the current study was not initially intended to test the prediction that PT makes (in particular with respect to the claim that stages cannot be skipped), the data of nominal gender agreement (between the attributive adjective and the head noun within the Arabic NP) and verbal gender agreement (i.e., between the subject and the verb in past and present tense) are relevant for testing such a prediction. According to PT, since nominal gender agreement involves agreement between the attributive adjective and head noun within the noun phrase, the structure is hypothesized to be processable (or to emerge) at stage 3, whereas verbal gender agreement (involving agreement between the noun phrase and the verb phrase) is hypothesized as a stage 4 structure (see also table 7.6 listing the two agreement forms accordingly). To illustrate the points of comparison between the two structures and the types of agreement procedures involved, figure 7.3 offers an example of a simplified constituent structure (c-structure) of the two forms à la LFG (as a notational framework adopted by PT), where grammatical information of singular feminine agreement is shared between the attributive adjective *ʔal-ʤadīd-**a*** "the new female" and the head noun *ʔal-tˤālib-**a*** "the female student" (requiring phrasal procedures acquirable at stage 3) and between the noun phrase *ʔal-tˤālib-**a** ʔal-ʤadīd-**a*** "the new female student" and the verb ***ta**-ʔkul* "she eats/is eating" (requiring interphrasal procedures acquirable at stage 4).

The most relevant part of the data of nominal and verbal gender agreement are those produced by the beginner and intermediate groups since the claims made by PT ultimately rest on the notion of "emergence" of the ability to process

Table 7.6 Two target structures

Processing Prerequisites	*Arabic L2 Structures*	*Stage*
Interphrasal procedures	Verbal gender agreement (S-V)	4
Phrasal procedures	Nominal gender agreement (N-A)	3

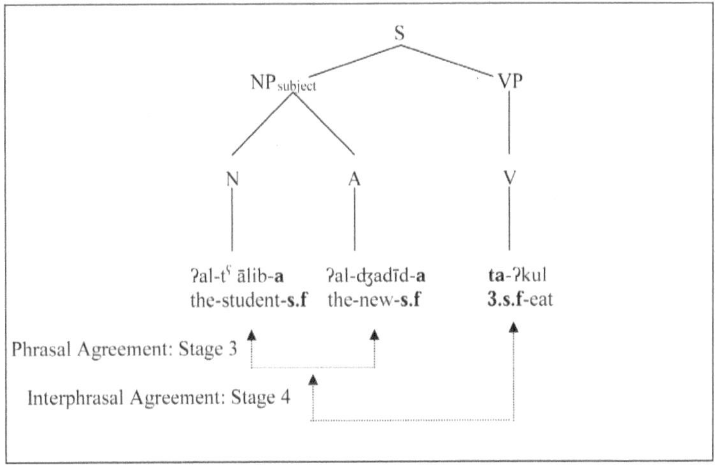

Figure 7.3 Simplified C-Structure of "The new (female) student eats/is eating." Illustrating Phrasal and Interphrasal Agreement

a form.[30] According to PT prediction of a processability hierarchy, we would expect all participants to process nominal (noun–adjective) gender agreement (a stage 3 structure) before verbal gender agreement (a stage 4 structure). In turn, we would expect all participants to encounter less difficulty processing nominal gender agreement than verbal gender agreement. Based on the performance of the beginner Chinese L1 as well as the beginner and intermediate Russian L1 participants on nominal gender agreement versus verbal agreement in the past tense, the data seem to be in support of the prediction made by PT, where these participants had higher percentages of accuracy on nominal than verbal agreement in the past tense, in particular singular feminine and third person singular feminine, respectively (see chapter 3, section 3.3.1 and table 3.1; chapter 4, section 4.3.1 and table 4.1). However, when considering the performance of the beginner and intermediate Chinese L1-B and Russian L1-B groups on verbal gender agreement (third person singular feminine) in the present tense, the data are contrary to PT's prediction where these participants exhibited the opposite pattern; i.e., they had noticeably lower accuracy percentages on nominal gender (singular feminine) agreement (see chapter 3, section 3.3.1 and table 3.1) than they did on verbal gender (third person singular feminine) agreement in the present tense (see chapter 4, section 4.3.2 and table 4.2). The same is true with respect to the distinction between nominal gender agreement versus verbal gender agreement in the present tense random task by the (same) beginner and intermediate Chinses L1-B and Russian L1-B groups (see chapter 4, section 4.3.3 and table 4.3). Additionally, the Chinese L1-A beginner group scored a little higher (91% accurate) on verbal gender (third person singular feminine) agreement in the random present tense task than they did (85% accurate) on nominal gender (singular feminine) agreement (see chapter 4, section 4.3.3 and table 4.3; chapter 3: section 3.3.1 and table 3.1). According to PT predictions, we should expect nominal gender agreement (a stage 3 structure) to be processable with more ease or more accurately than verbal gender agreement (a stage 4 structure), not conversely. Thus, based on the participants' performance on nominal gender agreement versus verbal gender agreement, the findings here seem to provide mixed evidence at best with respect to PT's claim about the presence of a processability hierarchy in L2 grammatical development. Furthermore, that the participants seem to process verbal agreement in the present tense more accurately than verbal agreement in the past tense (based on accuracy percentages) indicates that there may be other acquisition factors involved such as perceptual salience, where the agreement prefix (in the present tense) may have been more salient for those participants than the agreement suffix in the past tense.[31]

In addition, the asymmetry in the acquisition of nominal (noun–adjective) gender agreement by the Chinese L1 versus the Russian L1 participants, discussed in the previous sections, cannot be accounted for by PT. Recall, the Russian L1 participants seem to maintain an advantage over their Chinese L1 counterparts (see chapter 3, section 3.3.1 and table 3.1). PT claims related to the presence of a speech processing hierarchy in L2 acquisition cannot fully account for the present data or the similar data and findings reported in Al-Hamad (2003). Instead, the data can be better explained by an L1 transfer model, such as the full transfer / full access model, allowing for a role for the presence or absence of a feature in L1. Accordingly, the performance advantage maintained by the Russian L1 participants over their Chinese L1 counterparts is likely due to the presence of the nominal gender feature in their L1 and its transfer during their learning of Arabic (which also exhibits the same feature) as an L2.

Although the data here (in particular those of the verbal gender agreement) are somewhat limited, other (stronger) findings of previous studies that were intended to test the PT predictions directly (based on both longitudinal and cross-sectional data and use of two different acquisition and emergence criteria) corroborate the observations here against the predictions of PT claims (see Alhawary 2003, 2009a, 2009b; Nielsen 1997; for a review of other Arabic L2 studies testing processability claims, see Alhawary 2009a; for other counter evidence to PT based on French and Spanish data, see Dewaele and Véronique 2001; Farley and McCollam 2004, respectively).[32] In addition to L1 transfer, other factors may contribute to L2 grammatical development. In fact, Lui (1991), Tarone and Lui (1995) and Tarone (2007) argue that social contexts can influence SLA to the extent of forcing a stage to be skipped, contrary to PT predictions. Longitudinal data from English L2 acquisition from a five-year-old show that the participant child skipped a stage 3 structure (WHX-front without inversion: "Why you do that?") and produced structures at stages 4–6, including pseudo inversion ("Where's the monkey?"), aux-2nd ("What are you doing?"), and question tag ("You don't like green, are you?"). The child later produced the stage 3 structure. The study was based on Pienemann and Johnston's (1987) framework, a precursor of PT.

7.7 Summary and Areas of Future Research

The data reported on in the foregoing chapters are directly relevant to current models and proposals in the SLA literature. The data seem to provide evidence to usage-based as well as crosslinguistic typological effect accounts in that the processing of nominal gender agreement construction, in absence of the gender agreement feature, is expectedly more entrenched in the Chinese participants than their Russian counterparts, where only the L1 of the former does not exhibit the gender feature. Similarly, the null-subject use data over time seem overall to reflect an attentional or processing bias from the Russian participants' L1s. However, counterevidence for typological effects and usage-based accounts seems to be yielded from the verbal gender agreement data where no such effects are detected and no group differences are found, although Russian distinctly exhibits verbal gender agreement in the past tense whereas Chinese does not.

By the same token and of all current L1 transfer accounts, the full transfer / full access model seems to provide the closest adequate explanation, especially if an additional refinement is added: the presence or absence of a feature in L1 plays a role in L2 acquisition, even when no obvious complexity of feature realization (entailing a challenging learning task to figure out the (re)assembly or (re)configuration of features in L2) is observed (i.e., contra the feature reassembly hypothesis). The data accordingly yielded three conclusions. First, the maintained advantage exhibited by the Russian participants over their Chinese counterparts on nominal (noun–adjective) gender agreement points to the robust role of L1 transfer, which seems to extend to even the advanced/third-year level of Arabic (intensive and nonintensive) instruction. The robust role of L1 also seems to be evident in the different patterns of null-subject use, where the Chinese L1 participants seem to converge on dropping subjects more freely than their Russian L1 counterparts; the latter seem to converge on dropping subjects rather conservatively. Second, the role of L1 transfer seems to be overridden or decreased by increasing input exposure or proficiency, at least as far as nominal (noun–adjective) gender agreement is concerned, where due to the (double) extra input exposure, the beginner Chinese L1-A participants (Group 1) were able to minimize the impact resulting from absence of the gender feature versus the Chinese L1-B participants who could not (for a similar conclusion about the extent of the role of L1, see Hopp 2010; Ionin and Montrul 2010). Third, the full transfer / full access model predictably allows for full attainment or acquirability of the feature in adult L2 acquisition as evident in some of the interlanguage systems of some of the Chinese L1 and Russian L1 participants, in evidence of temporary rather than permanent impairment (e.g., contra the representational deficit / interpretability hypothesis). However, the full transfer / full access model does not seem to readily account alone for the verbal gender agreement data and the lack of asymmetry in the performance of the participants (on par with that of nominal gender agreement) without recourse to additional contributing factors such as the nature of the target forms. Although more research needs to be conducted to confirm this conclusion, not taking into account other contributing acquisition factors such as the exact nature of target forms might make the process of (L1) transfer appear superficially or randomly selective. Other factors such as perceptual salience must also be considered in order to account for the acquisition of word order within the Arabic noun phrase.

The above findings are taken into account in absence of any significant or clear L2 transfer effects, where it is quite unlikely that L1 transfer effects were superseded by L2 transfer effects. Upon examining individual performance of participants in all groups, no particular evidence of L2 transfer effects (including of English L2 and other languages) could be detected with respect to the participants' production of nominal (noun–adjective) gender agreement and null subjects. Similarly, individual performance of participants' production of other target forms, such as verbal gender agreement and tense/aspect, did not reveal any clear patterns. Individual cases where participants had knowledge of other L2s were contradictory and too few to reveal any significant effect for L2 transfer of languages other than English, and despite the fact that L2 transfer effects from English is possible (especially in relation to the production data of tense/aspect), L1 transfer effects from (L1 Chinese and L1 Russian) could not be ruled out. Accordingly, the findings (at least those related to nominal (noun–adjective) gender agreement and null subjects) leave little doubt that the role of L1 transfer is far more robust than admitted by any of the current L2 transfer models and provide concomitantly some counter evidence to their claimed predictions.

The present data are also relevant to the notion of speech processing prerequisites posited by PT (Pienemann 1998, 2005). Based on the participants' performance on nominal gender agreement versus verbal gender agreement, the findings seem to provide mixed evidence. On one hand, the data seem to be in support of the hypothesized speech processing prerequisites since the beginner Chinese L1 and beginner and intermediate Russian L1 participants seem to find nominal gender agreement less difficult than verbal agreement in the past tense. On the other hand, the beginner and intermediate Chinese L1-B and Russian L1-B groups seem to find nominal gender agreement more difficult than verbal gender in the present tense, contrary to the prediction made by the hypothesized speech processing prerequisites. Moreover, the detected asymmetry (where the Russian L1 participants seem to maintain an advantage over their Chinese L1 counterparts) in the acquisition of nominal (noun–adjective) gender agreement cannot be accounted for by PT's prediction. Thus, PT claims related to the presence of a speech processing hierarchy in L2 acquisition cannot fully account for the present data. Instead, the data can be better explained by an L1 transfer account such as the full transfer / full access model. In addition, the participants seem to process verbal agreement in the present tense more accurately than verbal agreement in the past tense (based on the accuracy percentages by the different groups), which indicates that there may be other acquisition factors involved such as perceptual salience where the agreement prefix (in the present tense) may have been more salient for those participants than the agreement suffix (in the past tense). In fact, even other additional factors may also be involved in L2 grammatical development such as social context (see Lui 1991; Tarone and Lui 1995; Tarone 2007).

Further research will be useful to be conducted on Arabic L2 participants with (1) different language pairings such as those employing participants of an L1 (such as Indonesian) that exhibits neither verbal agreement nor tense features (in order to isolate the processing of verbal agreement from tense), and (2) similar language pairings to those in the present study (i.e., by Russian L1 and Chinese L1 speakers learning Arabic as an L2) as well as previous studies (e.g., Alhawary 2009a) with English L1-, French L1-, Spanish L1-, and Japanese L1-speaking learners of Arabic at more advanced or near-native levels.

Such studies should also take into account additional variables, as is done here, such as exposure time or proficiency and input frequency. For replication purposes, spontaneous production data should be relied upon rather than other measures, such as grammaticality judgment tasks or writing completion tasks and other similar ones, since such measures are metalinguistic in nature and do not necessarily reflect the underlying unconscious knowledge of the target forms in the learner's interlanguage. When examining Arabic L2 data against usage-based claims, it will be also crucial to rely on comprehensive statistical frequencies of the target forms (e.g., Lin and Alhawary 2018).

Notes

1. Apart from Lightbown's (1980) study, which focused on the acquisition of the relative frequencies and order of certain French question forms in child French L2 acquisition, these studies were mainly in the context of English L2 morpheme accuracy and order acquisition studies.

2. Other frequency research covered vocabulary acquisition (e.g., Rott 1999; Vermeer 2001; Brown, Waring, and Donkaewbua 2008; Kweon and Kim 2008; Joe 2010; cf. Hawkins and Casillas 2008; Bley-Vroman 2002). Bley-Vroman argues against frequency/usage-based accounts altogether because they do not explain why "many" rare forms, including those encountered once, are readily noticed, processed deeply, and incorporated into linguistic knowledge due to some aspects of saliency "which remains largely mysterious" (2002, 213).

3. Proficiency is somewhat loosely used here based on number of years of study (first through third year, corresponding to beginner, intermediate, and advanced), reflecting the accumulated years of study and exposure to Arabic L2. Although there was no independent measure for proficiency, based on the elicitation interviews (thirty to forty-five minutes), participants in their different years of enrollment did signal noticeable differences in L2 development (e.g., in terms of quantity, quality, and speed of their output production). In addition, the terms "beginner," "intermediate," and "advanced" were also designated to the years of study (first through third year) by the home institutions of the participants. More importantly, the use of general proficiency tests would have limited value, since such tests do not necessarily test the participants' knowledge of the target structures.

4. The main assumptions include the notions of structural latency in language usage, Zipfian frequency patterns, semantic coherence, and form–function contingency. Ellis, O'Donnell, and Römer (2013, 34) explain the assumptions of this statistical learning approach thus: "Psychology theory relating to the statistical learning of categories suggests that constructions are robustly learnable when they are (1) Zipfian in their type-token distributions in usage, (2) selective in their verb form occupancy, (3) coherent in their semantics, (4) with a high contingency between form and function."

5. The demonstrative agreement data may presumably pose a slight problem to

this line of reasoning. Recall, the Russian L1-A Groups 2 and 3 seem to maintain a lead (though not statistically significant) over their Chinese L1-A counterparts (section 3.3.2, chapter 3). However, the advantage in accuracy rates was limited to feminine agreement only (i.e., to the exclusion of masculine agreement) and no such advantage was maintained by the Russian L1-B participants over the Chinese groups (tables 3.10 and 3.12, section 3.3.2, chapter 3). Moreover, since there is a close interaction, whether between a demonstrative pronoun and a following modified noun within a DP (as in *hāðihi ʔal-tˤālib-a ʔal-ʤadīda* "this new female student") or between a predicate noun and a demonstrative subject within a nominal sentence, this may trigger the checking or processing of the demonstrative gender feature or help make the gender feature of Arabic demonstratives more salient for the Russian L1 participants than for their Chinese L1-A counterparts. This would entail the presence of different acquisition factors and would consequently render the learning task (involved in demonstrative agreement) not the same for the two groups of participants with different L1s. This learning task seems to be facilitated by extra input exposure as evident in the observation that the Russian L1-B groups, who received about half the input exposure time than the Russian L1-A groups, do not display a similar advantage over the Chinese L1 groups.

6. Rather, differences in performance here seem to be, at least in part, attributed to the quality and timing/schedule of input presentation of tense (see chapter 5).

7. See also Han (2014) and Tarone (2014).

8. The latter approach seems to resemble the contrastive analysis hypothesis from the 1960s in its primary focus on features and their reassembly in L2 rather than parametric feature setting, calling into question the proliferation of parameters and their (non)explanatory adequacy (contrary to the data and predictions where, for example, a given parameter is stipulated to be part of a cluster of features/forms, the setting of which would trigger the setting of all the structures of the cluster but that such a prediction was not borne out), thereby calling for paradigm shift (Lardiere 2008, 2009a, 2009b).

9. In minimalist terms, proponents of the representational deficit / interpretability hypothesis assume that operations such as "merge" or "agree" (in narrow syntax) are available in L2 but place different emphasis on interpretable versus uninterpretable features. Interpretable features are assumed to be visible at LF because they are intrinsic for semantic interpretation whereas uninterpretable features are considered extrinsic features (i.e., not visible at LF and restricted to syntactic derivation) and remain unvalued until they enter into an "agree" relation with interpretable features (e.g., Tsimpli and Dimitrakopoulou 2007).

10. There are at least two other compatible hypotheses that were advanced in the 1990s: the valueless feature hypothesis and the local impairment hypothesis. The valueless feature hypothesis claims that both lexical and functional categories and the linear orientation of the L1 grammar transfer in L2 acquisition but that the feature values (strength) associated with functional categories do not (Eubank 1993–94, 1996). The local impairment hypothesis assumes that functional projections are attainable in L2 but that features associated with functional heads are

permanently impaired (or "inert") irrespective of L1 (Beck 1997, 1998; Eubank et al. 1997; Eubank and Beck 1998). Accordingly, no transfer of (abstract) feature strength from L1 takes place and on such accounts UG is partially unavailable in L2.

11. In addition to claiming that L2 learners already have access to lexical categories and that functional categories develop upon exposure to L2 input, the minimal trees hypothesis assumes that development of functional projections takes place in successive stages: a verb phrase stage, an underspecified functional projection stage, grammatical agreement stage, and a complementizer phrase stage, in this order. It is also claimed that the trigger for functional projection in L1 may not be the same in L2. Following Newport (1990), morphological processing capacity in L2 is assumed to undergo a quantitative shift due to critical period effects, accounting for the developmental differences between L1 and L2 acquisition (Vainikka and Young-Scholten 1994, 1996, 1998).

12. Cf. researchers who instead argue for limited or no UG access (without being able to acquire new parameter values) and appeal for universal cognitive principles or constraints accessed by L2 learners (e.g., Meisel 1983, 1991; Clahsen 1984; Clahsen and Muysken 1986, 1989; Felix 1985; Bley-Vroman 1989, 1990; Schachter 1989).

13. The missing surface inflection hypothesis claims that the feature system is temporarily impaired at the morphophonological (surface) level due to complexity in mapping between surface forms and underlying abstract features, that morphology and syntax can develop independently, and that the presence or absence of a feature in L1 is irrelevant (Lardiere 1998, 2000; Prévost and White 2000; Bruhn de Garavito and White 2002; Prévost 2008). The nature of impairment, according to this proposal, depends on the L2 learner figuring out the mapping complexity and spelling it out properly. This proposal is in line with the full transfer / full access model (Schwartz and Sprouse 1994, 1996; Schwartz 1998). The missing surface inflection hypothesis seems to be now subsumed by the feature reassembly hypothesis, and doubt about the status of the former has already been expressed by White (2009).

14. Following Chomsky (2001b), acquiring "functional morphology" or assembling the "functional lexicon" is not viewed as an easy task in L1 in the first place (Hwang and Lardiere 2013, 57–58). Acquiring a grammar, à la minimalism, involves selecting relevant features from a universal inventory, composing such features into matrices for functional categories, and assembling them into lexical items—a process that is mediated by a universal computational system/module.

15. Moreover, in fact the Chinese L1-A participants received more instructional exposure time than their Russian L1-A participants did (see table 2.1, chapter 2).

16. In the case of nominal (noun–adjective) gender agreement within the Arabic noun phrase, functional feature strength seems to license N raising (over the adjective) for proper noun–adjective word order placement and for the feature gender to be checked. However, within the reformulation of the representational deficit/interpretability hypothesis, the exact status of the acquirablity/unaqcuirability of

functional strength is not clear. As discussed in chapter 3, the Russian L1 and Chinese L1 participants seem to have all acquired and adjusted to Arabic noun–adjective word order with all groups producing an insignificant number of prenominal adjectives ranging from zero to three tokens per group, except for participants in the beginner L1-Chinese L1-B and Russian L1-B groups, who produced forty-seven and twenty-one tokens, respectively (see table 3.5, chapter 3; see also Alhawary 2009a for similar findings based on data from English L1, French L1, and Japanese participants). This finding may be problematic for the representational deficit/interpretability hypothesis, which would otherwise predict greater variability (or optionality) in noun–adjective word order use, especially by the Chinese L1 participants in whose L1 feature strength is set to [-strong] (see chapter 3, section 3.1). The hypothesis is silent about why such participants were able to reset feature strength to [+strong] for their Arabic L2 although their L1 (Chinese) does not share the same feature specification with that of Arabic (for a similar treatment and crosslinguistic evidence for resetting the nominal feature strength and word order in L2, see also White 2003, 133–35). However, this uncertainty may also be due to uncertainty in the generative framework since Russian does not exhibit N raising even though it exhibits (like Arabic) rich gender agreement and the gender feature is set to [+strong]. If it may be the case that feature strength does not need to necessarily trigger movement (see Lightfoot and Hornstein 1994), it is not clear how this concept and its pairing between Arabic (as an L2) and Russian (as an L1) exactly applies, with the surface word order in both languages being distinct. Of course, other factors may be at play here, such as the notion of "salience" according to which word order may be considered more salient than an inflectional feature and may have therefore contributed to the participants' noticing and acquiring the strong inflection feature that licenses N raising from early on (see Corder 1978; Slobin 1973).

17. An example of such features is the accusative case realization on the predicate of *kāna* and *laysa* (for a detailed discussion and analysis, see Alhawary 2009a, 161).

18. Bruhn de Garavito and White (2002), White et al. (2004), and Franceschina (2005), among others, all point out that the generalization of the endings {*-o*} and {*-a*} as masculine and feminine gender markers, respectively, is misleading in Spanish and insufficient to account for many other obscure cases. For example, there are some feminine nouns that end with {*-o*}, numerous and common masculine nouns that end with {*-a*}, and many (invariant) adjectives that lack overt gender agreement. Following Harris (1991), several authors consider these endings as word markers rather than gender markers, hence justifying—and perhaps correctly so—their attributing the problems of their participants with respect to nominal gender agreement to the mapping problem between surface and underlying abstract forms rather than to L1 transfer (see especially Bruhn de Garavito and White [2002], citing the mapping problem involved with Spanish nominal gender agreement in support of the missing surface inflection hypothesis; see also note 13, above). Such observations indeed suggest that the input related to gender

agreement in Spanish DPs that the participants of such studies received is in fact obscure. It is worth noting here that under the full transfer / full access model (Schwartz and Sprouse 1994, 1996), learning problems are predicted to occur in the event input is obscure.

19. A similar effect for input exposure was found in previous findings of Japanese L1 learners of Arabic who, despite the fact that they were significantly outperformed by their French counterparts, outperformed their English counterparts significantly. Although neither Japanese nor English exhibits gender demonstrative agreement (unlike French), negative L1 transfer effects seems to have been mitigated by the extra input received by the Japanese participants (see Alhawary 2009a).

20. See note 5, above.

21. See Alhawary (2009a, 163–67; 2007b) for another proposal where the mechanism of feature checking of verbal agreement may interact with that of the feature tense and where, in this case, both Russian and Chinese exhibit the feature tense, hence the proposal against what came to be known as the split-INFL hypothesis or the call for separate projections for tense and agreement, among others.

22. This methodology has been criticized for its many limitations (e.g., Ellis 1990, 1991; Lantolf 1990; Goss, Ying-Hua, and Lantolf 1994).

23. There was no evidence for or against the clustering effects since this question has not been investigated.

24. In attributing parametric variation to strength of functional features, standard minimalist assumptions are adopted here. On this account, due to rich verbal agreement features, both Arabic and Russian are analyzed with the functional feature strength set to [+strong], especially with respect to past tense, while functional feature strength in Chinese is set to [-strong]. More recent reformulations of null subjects such as radical pro-drop (à la Neeleman and Szendrői 2007) are not adopted here since such proposals would lump together languages such as Arabic [+null], Spanish [+null], and English [-null] as nonradical pro-drop languages as opposed to Chinese [+null] and Japanese [+null] as radical pro-drop languages (for a similar criticism, see Lardiere 2009a; cf. Liceras 2009).

25. Syntactically, both Arabic and Russian also exhibit nominal/verbless sentence structure.

26. Like Russian, Polish only exhibits verbal gender agreement in the past tense.

27. For a brief account of LFG and how it fits into PT, see Pienemann (1998, 93–98); for a comprehensive account of LFG, see Bresnan (1982, 2001).

28. This claim is similar to Krashen's (1977, 1985) concept of optimal input stated within the input hypothesis (IH) that the L2 learner will make progress if the level of the input is at i+1.

29. There seems to be an ambiguity as to whether formal instruction can be demonstrated to be beneficial, affecting the falsifiability of the claim in (7) (see Krashen 1993). In addition, it is not clear from the model how the notion of "functional need" can be controlled for in order to test the hypothesis.

30. Data from intermediate participants may be necessary since beginner

participants may encounter problems learning and recalling vocabulary, and therefore the data from beginner participants alone may be too limited to reach valid claims (from such a cross-sectional design).

31. In addition, recall (from chapter 5) that there was an asymmetry in the performance of the Chinese L1-B, the Russian L1-A, and Russian L1-B participants on past versus present tense due likely to input effects (i.e., quality and timing of input of the target present and past tense). Most studies that have attempted to test PT claims do not seem to take input factors into account, whether for or against confirming the predictions.

32. In addition to the Arabic studies that have tested PT claims and are reviewed in Alhawary (2009a), two other studies (Husseinali 2006, 2016; Al Shatter 2008) claimed their findings confirmed PT predications. Based on data collected quasi-longitudinally (over two semesters) and cross-sectionally from three participants (a beginner, an intermediate, and an advanced Australian English L1–speaking learner of Arabic), Al Shatter (2008) claims that his study provides evidence in support of PT's prediction. However, the study relies on three types of structures: (1) lexical procedures (where learners are able to produce pronoun suffixes with verbs without agreement with a given subject), (2) interphrasal procedures (where learners are able to apply agreement between the subject and the verb), and (3) interclausal procedure (where learners are able to observe agreement between a relative pronoun and a preceding noun occurring as an object of a verb). There are at least three limitations with the study. First, the three target forms are too coarse-grained, allowing for wide and predictable structural gaps between them. Since lexical procedures are stage 2 and interphrasal procedures are stage 4, more robust testing of PT predictions would have followed from target forms occurring consecutively with no stage gaps between them (such as stage 2 and 3 or stage 3 and 4 structures). Second, the target forms do not seem to take into account the schedule of input exposure and whether emergence of form is subject to exposure timing rather than speech processing constraints, which is the case with relative clauses, which are usually introduced later than verbal agreement in almost all syllabi. Third, based on the examples provided (Al Shatter 2008, 294–97), which included many different suffixes (including those for third person singular feminine, third person singular masculine, third person plural masculine, third person dual masculine, third person dual feminine, first person plural, and first person singular) in both past and present tense contexts, it is not clear how data elicitation and production/emergence of agreement involving such forms were tracked among the participants. It is also unclear as to how participants/learners are assumed to produce pronoun suffixes on verbs without taking agreement with a subject (as an explicit noun/pronoun or an implicit subject in the discourse) into account.

Similarly, Husseinali (2006, 2016) claims that his study "confirms the implicational hierarchy of processing stages," that "variation was found between structures belonging to the same stage (intraphrasal variation)," and that there was no evidence of "stage skipping" (Husseinali 2016, 104). The study was based on data from six participants (two first-year, two second-year, and two third-year

American English L1–speaking learners of Arabic) collected from two interview sessions (one at the end of the first semester and another after six weeks of the second semester). However, based on the data provided (and relevant to the present data), while some data seem to be either evidently inconclusive and insufficient for the conclusions drawn, other data seem to be clearly in violation of the hypothesized implicational hierarchy, contrary to the stated conclusions. For example, noun–adjective agreement (between the attributive adjective and head noun processable at stage 3) is already found to have emerged together with subject–verb agreement and noun–predicate adjective agreement, both of which are processable at stage 4) in the interlanguage systems of both first-year participants (Husseinali 2016, 63, 66; tables 6.1–6.3) and one of the two second-year participants (Husseinali 2016, 70; tables 6.5 and 6.6). As for the other second-year participant, the data show the participant was not able to acquire noun–predicate adjective (processable at stage 4) in either interview session even though the data show she had already acquired verbal agreement (processable at stage 4) in both sessions (Husseinali 2016, 74–75; tables 6.7–6.8). According to processability, gender agreement in both forms should emerge at the same time, a prediction not validated by the data (see Alhawary 2009b for data from French L1 and English L1 participants on similar target forms providing evidence against PT predictions). Moreover, one of the two third-year participants did not show evidence that noun–adjective agreement (processable at stage 3) emerged in the first interview session even though she has shown clear evidence that she has already acquired subject–verb agreement and noun–predicate adjective agreement (both of which are processable at stage 4), an observation in clear violation of PT's implicational hierarchy of processing stages (Husseinali 2016, 78; table 6.9). Husseinali (2006, 2016) claims that the "results and conclusions of Alhawary (1999) were stretched beyond the point warranted by the data" (Husseinali 2016, 6; 2006, 6) and states that he "counted all the verbs and all the adjectives presented in the vocabulary list at the beginning of each unit of the twenty units in the textbook that Alhawary reported to have been used with his subjects. . . . It turned out that there were far more verbs than adjectives in those lists. There were a total of 114 (none repeated) verbs and only 22 adjectives" (Husseinali 2016, 30; 2006, 59). Needless to say, vocabulary lists alone are not indicative of the number of occurrence of forms in any given lesson. Rather, the number of occurrence of forms can only be reliably determined based on their occurrence in passages/texts and drills within lessons, as noted throughout beneath tables listing input schedules of target forms (e.g., Alhawary 1999, 2003, 2009a), a method that was also oddly adopted wholesale by Husseinali himself (e.g., Husseinali 2016, 34).

Chapter 8

Pedagogical and Applied Implications

This chapter discusses implications and practical applications for the findings in a number of subfields of Arabic applied linguistics, including Arabic curriculum design, Arabic foreign language pedagogy and teacher preparation, and Arabic proficiency testing. Crucial to these areas are findings to do with acquisition tendencies or patterns, in particular, and second language acquisition factors, in general. Specific Arabic SLA tendencies are first discussed, followed by explanation and examples of subfields that can be informed by Arabic SLA findings.

8.1 Acquisition Tendencies of the Target Structures

From a sound observational perspective, conclusions about the emergence of acquisition trends about target forms should be made only in conjunction with information about the timing and amount of input exposure of such forms. In other words, for such conclusions to be warranted, the forms should be introduced and should subsequently maintain reasonable presence in the input. Against the backdrop of input scheduling and its maintenance we can also make claims about other contributing factors such as language transfer. The observations made about the target forms here are based on this rationale.

8.1.2 Gender Assignment on Nouns

Based on the instructional input of the participants of the present study with respect to gender assignment on nouns, we can speculate that both Russian L1 and Chinese L1 speakers learning Arabic as an L2 are likely to produce the feminine {-*a*} and masculine {-*0*} gender features correctly on nouns and without noticeable difficulty (as reported in chapter 3), suggesting that they are able to acquire gender assignment on nouns from early on. Although participants from both L1 backgrounds produced tokens where nouns were inflected for the wrong gender (see sections 3.3.1.2 and 3.3.2.2, chapter 3), such tokens were either too small to be significant or were produced by a few participants. It is possible that the participants of the present study may have learned and produced nouns initially based on instance learning of the stem noun and inflection as a monomorphemic chunk as attested during the initial stage of L2 acquisition. Notwithstanding this general observation, the main conclusion here is that gender assignment on nouns does not seem to constitute a noticeable learning problem for Chinese and Russian speakers. This is, in fact, consistent with previous data from English L1, French L1, and Japanese L1 speakers learning Arabic as an L2 (e.g., Alhawary 2009a).

8.1.2 Gender Assignment on Adjectives

Unlike gender assignment on nouns, the findings of the present study indicate that, for Chinese and Russian L2 learners of Arabic, the main learning problem posed by nominal gender agreement is gender assignment on adjectives, uniformly more so by the Chinese than the Russian speakers, although both learners may tend to use the singular masculine as the default form (see chapter 3, section 3.3.1). Provided that adjectives (inflected for the masculine and feminine gender, especially those following head nouns within the noun phrase) are available and maintained in the input from early on, Russian L1 speakers are likely to acquire (especially feminine) gender assignment on adjectives more robustly than Chinese L1 speakers. The latter are able to mitigate the influence of their L1 (due to the lack of the gender feature in their L1) through intensive instruction at the early stages, but in the long run they are likely to encounter more difficulty and make more errors in their production of adjectives even at later stages (e.g., third year) of learning. This is congruent with previous findings where speakers of a language similar to Russian (such as French, which exhibits the gender feature) find gender assignment on adjectives less difficult than speakers of languages similar to Chinese (such as English and Japanese), which do not exhibit the gender feature (e.g., Alhawary 2009a).

8.1.3 Gender Agreement Involving Demonstrative Pronouns

As for the acquisition tendency of gender agreement involving Arabic demonstrative pronouns, Chinese L1 and Russian L1 speakers learning Arabic as an L2 tend to find gender assignment on demonstrative pronouns as well as agreement involving demonstratives difficult to acquire due to absence of the gender feature in both languages, and they tend to use the singular masculine as the default form (see section 3.3.2, chapter 3). However, as is the case with gender assignment on adjectives, with intensive input exposure from early on, for Chinese and Russian speakers, errors of gender agreement involving demonstrative pronouns can be mitigated, but Chinese speakers are likely to encounter more difficulty and make more errors in later stages (such as the third year) than Russian speakers. The latter tendency may be due to the Russian speakers being more sensitive to the gender feature in nominal constructions in general.[1] By the same token, previous findings indicate that speakers of languages (such as French) that exhibit gender demonstrative agreement do not find demonstrative gender agreement problematic, as do speakers of languages (such as English and Japanese) that do not exhibit such agreement (see Alhawary 2009a, 2009b).

8.1.4 Verbal Gender Agreement

As long as verbal agreement is present and maintained in the input, Chinese and Russian L2 learners of Arabic tend to acquire verbal agreement from early on and continue to improve their performance over time. They may exhibit more feminine than masculine agreement errors in their production of verbal agreement during and beyond the early stages of Arabic L2 exposure (section 4.3, chapter 4). Thus, learners with different L1s may not exhibit (significant) differences in performance.[2] This is consistent with previous findings, where English, French, and Japanese L2 learners of Arabic were found to improve their performance with length of exposure and exhibited more feminine than masculine agreement errors (see Alhawary 2009a).

8.1.5 Tense/Aspect (Past and Present)

Not unlike the acquisition tendency of verbal agreement and provided that past and present tense input is maintained throughout, Chinese and Russian L2 learners of Arabic are likely to acquire both tenses from early on and continue to improve their performance over time without exhibiting significant differences in performance between past and present tense. Thus, the ability to narrate within past and present time frames is expected to improve equally among all these learners with more time and exposure to the target language. However, in addition, acquisition of tense seems to be subject to input exposure timing, where past tense is acquired before present tense if the former is presented before the latter and conversely. By the same token, if both tenses are presented together, both tend to be acquired at the same time (see section 5.3, chapter 5). Previous findings, especially based on English L2 learners of Arabic, point to the same conclusion where past tense was acquired before present tense, as the former was introduced before the latter (Alhawary 2009a; see also section 5.4, chapter 5). The above observation is true so long as all previous Arabic L2 studies have been conducted on participants whose L1s exhibit a tense distinction between past versus present/non-past.

8.2 Contributing Acquisition Factors

Based on the data presented in the foregoing chapters, a number of crucial contributing acquisition factors are at play. The most crucial of such factors are the role of input frequency and that of L1 transfer (in relation to typological and structural proximity or lack thereof), both of whose effects are evident in all of the acquisition tendencies discussed above.[3] In addition, two other factors seem to be crucial to the present data: perceptual salience and motivation. Perceptual salience is most evident in the ability of both the L1 Chinese and L1 Russian learners of Arabic to acquire noun–adjective word order. Although in Arabic noun phrases the adjective occurs postnominally, almost all participants acquired and were able to adjust to the Arabic word order from early on, despite the fact that in both Chinese and Russian the adjective occurs prenominally. It has long been suggested in the literature that word order may be considered more salient than an inflectional feature and may have therefore contributed to the participants' noticing and acquiring the proper noun–adjective word order (see Corder 1978; Slobin 1973). Previous data from participants whose L1s that are both similar (such as French) and different (such as English and Japanese) from Arabic provided even stronger evidence for perceptual salience where such participants produced a very small number of tokens with prenominal adjectives (e.g., Alhawary 2009a).[4] As for motivation, its impact was detected in most of the Chinese L1 and some of the Russian L1 participants, especially those who scored 100% correct in nominal gender agreement and who seemed particularly motivated to learn Arabic. This was immediately evident to the researcher and was confirmed by participants' teachers as belonging among the more motivated learners (see section 7.3 and figure 7.1, chapter 7).

8.3 Subfields of Arabic Applied Linguistics Informed by Arabic SLA

8.3.1 Arabic Curriculum Design: Scheduling Learning Objectives and Input Recycling

One subfield in Arabic applied linguistics that can beneficially be informed by Arabic SLA findings is Arabic curriculum design and construction. Understanding Arabic second language acquisition tendencies or patterns helps the Arabic textbook writer determine the scheduling of learning objectives of forms (i.e., what and when to introduce forms) and their recycling in the input. For example, despite being among high-frequency forms, nominal gender agreement seems to be particularly problematic for certain Arabic L2 learners such as L1 Chinese (and L1 English and L1 Japanese) learners of Arabic and, therefore, should be introduced from early on and subsequently recycled for such learners for an extended period of time.[5] This may be counterintuitive for some since basic and high-frequency forms may be assumed to occur often in the input (inside and outside of the classroom) and may not, therefore, need as much attention as low-frequency and more complicated items. However, the present findings indicate that (due to L1 transfer and lack of the feature gender in L1) Chinese L1 speakers are more likely to encounter problems with nominal gender agreement (than do others, such as Russians), and their performance may decline at later stages (see section 3.3.1, chapter 3). This is supported by similar findings on French L1 (similar to Russian) speakers versus English L1 and Japanese L1 speakers learning Arabic as an L2 (e.g., Alhawary 2009a).

On the other hand, other forms that do not seem to be particularly problematic such as verbal agreement and tense can be introduced when needed (i.e., with no difference as to whether the aim is to develop the learner's ability to narrate in present tense before past tense or vice versa) but should nevertheless be recycled reasonably in the input. Accordingly, such forms are not likely to have any particular (negative) consequence for the Chinese L1 versus the Russian L1 speakers learning Arabic as an L2. The same is true of previous findings with respect to French L1 versus English and Japanese L1 speakers (see Alhawary 2009a). Additionally, based on previous findings, forms that do not seem to be particularly complex, such as the various negation particles, should also be introduced as soon as their prerequisite tenses are introduced.[6] Recycling such forms in the input is also necessary for acquisition of such forms, as evident in the acquisition of the present tense negation with *lā* versus past tense negation with *mā*, where the former seems to be acquired more readily, probably due to more consistency in input recycling (Alhawary 2009a, 125–39). However, forms that are too complex due to form–function relationships may not be beneficial to introduce and focus on from early on as L2 learners may not be developmentally ready to acquire or produce such forms, and as a result Arabic L2 learners may adopt avoidance strategies to not produce the forms altogether. In this case, instruction time would be wasted and the L2 learners discouraged. This is true, for example, for focusing on case endings associated with *laysa* and *kāna* constructions at an early stage (for a detailed discussion of these forms, see Alhawary 2009a, 142–45). However, once introduced, such forms should receive a good amount of recycling in the input and different types of activities implemented in order to enhance learners' awareness of such forms in the input (perhaps à la Sharwood Smith 1981, 1991).

8.3.2 Arabic Foreign Language Pedagogy and Teacher Preparation

Another area that can beneficially be informed by Arabic SLA findings is Arabic foreign language pedagogy and classroom teaching. Awareness of L2 acquisition factors and tendencies provides the teacher with prior expectations in the classroom in order to adopt strategies and design and implement effective techniques for reinforcing textbook input and offering effective feedback and error correction. For example, by being aware that Chinese (and English and Japanese) L2 learners of Arabic may encounter learning problems with nominal gender agreement even through their third year of learning the language, the novice or in-training teacher can recognize the need to tolerate learners' errors and adopt effective and indirect ways of error correction. Such teachers can equally become cognizant of the need to reinforce or enhance classroom input by incorporating additional drills and activities on nominal gender agreement to supplement textbook input (should it fall short of recycling the form consistently) or to raise the learner's consciousness about gender or other grammatical features (e.g., Sharwood Smith 1981, 1991). Last, but not least, realizing that the highest performance is achieved by highly motivated learners, the teacher can also aim for the highest levels of learner success by nourishing and nurturing learners' motivation throughout the different stages of language learning (Alhawary 2009a).

8.3.3 Arabic Foreign Language Proficiency Testing

A third subfield of Arabic applied linguistics that can be greatly informed by Arabic SLA findings is Arabic second language testing, including refining the rubrics of the different proficiency levels and training raters and testers. Despite the several updates of the ACTFL Proficiency Guidelines for the different proficiency levels (ACTFL 1989, 1999), current ACTFL Proficiency Guidelines (ACTFL 2012) contain various vague rubrics and descriptors. For example, in referring to grammatical elements, the current guidelines for speaking contain the following general and vague descriptors (extracted from ACTFL [2012] Speaking Proficiency Guidelines):

- Novice High:
  - Syntax may be strongly influenced by the first language
- Intermediate Low:
  - Syntax . . . strongly influenced by first language
- Intermediate Mid:
  - Difficulty manipulating time and aspect
  - Limitations in grammar and/or syntax
- Intermediate High:
  - Can narrate and describe in all major time frames . . . but not all the time
  - Failure to carry out fully the narration or description in the appropriate major time frame
  - Interference from another language may be evident (e.g., use of code-switching, false cognates, literal translations)
- Advanced Low:
  - Ability to narrate and describe in all major time frames of past, present, and future
  - Some control of aspect
  - Sufficient accuracy
  - Marked by a certain grammatical roughness (e.g., inconsistent control of verb endings)
- Advanced Mid:
  - Ability to narrate and describe in the major time frames of past, present, and future
  - Good control of aspect
  - Much accuracy
- Advanced High:
  - An imperfect grasp of some forms
  - Ability to explain in detail and narrate fully and accurately in all time frames
- Superior:
  - Virtually no pattern of error in the use of basic structures
  - Sporadic errors, particularly in low-frequency . . . and in complex high-frequency structures.

Since the limitations of such vague descriptors were discussed and problematized in Alhawary (2009a, 179–81)—which include absence of specific grammatical forms to aid the tester in identifying test taker's level, heavy emphasis of functions over forms, treatment of structures as static and irrespective of speakers' L1s, and lack of clarity as to what "basic" and "complex" structures mean or what those structures are—some minor updates have been added to the current guidelines (ACTFL 2012) in the form of "specific annotations."

However, despite the addition of "specific annotations" to some of the rubrics and errors identified for specific levels, the annotations are either considerably vague themselves or problematic altogether. Table 8.1 provides some examples of the annotations as they relate to the errors and patterns of errors identified for the sublevels. Vague annotations include those for the Novice High level (where it is not clear why or if the entire verbal agreement paradigm in the present is targeted at this stage rather than a few conjugation forms related to the most immediate personal needs of the speaker at this level, which include first person singular) and for the Advanced Mid level (one of which simply states that speakers at the level exhibit "a noticeable increase in errors"). As for the problematic annotations, these include the ones for the Advanced High and Superior levels, where "gender and number" errors are stated to "persist" in the Advanced High level and that such structures are considered low frequency. It is not at all clear how structures involving gender and number are considered low frequency since every single noun, adjective, and verb in the Arabic language exhibits gender and number features. Such descriptors can be greatly and more accurately informed if they are further based on actual Arabic second language acquisition data. Recall from the present as well as previous findings, there is ample evidence that verbal agreement (which include gender and number) does not pose a problem to learners with different L1s but that nominal agreement (which includes gender and number) constitutes different learning tasks or problems for learners with different L1s.[7] Moreover, if structures involving gender and number are considered low frequency, one wonders what complex high-frequency structures are.[8]

Accordingly, use of vague descriptors and annotations in the current ACTFL (2012) Speaking Proficiency Guidelines still reveal a number of limitations. These include, among others, lack of specificity of what grammatical errors characterize a specific level or free from it; lack of specificity as to the exact structures that are complex, basic, high frequency, and low frequency; lack of inclusion of criteria for such classifications; and treatment of the notion of *complexity* and the learning of structures as constituting the same learning tasks/problems for Arabic L2 learners irrespective of their L1 backgrounds.[9] As a result, the tester is left to decide, based on what seems intuitive from the tester's point of view, what "basic" and what "complex" or "what high frequency"

Table 8.1 Example annotations of ACTFL (Speaking) Proficiency Guidelines (2012)

Level	*Descriptor*	*Specific Annotation*
Novice High	Their language consists primarily of short and sometimes incomplete sentences in the present.[1]	[1] This statement may be partially correct. Unlike Romance languages, the Arabic imperfect verb (i.e. present tense) is more complicated than the past tense morphologically and syntactically. The imperfect verb has 14 conjugations, each with a prefix and a suffix that change with number and person. In addition, it has three moods, two of which are loosely equivalent to the indicative and subjunctive. On the other hand, the past tense has only suffixes that indicate number and person [and gender].
Advanced Mid	[They] demonstrate the ability to narrate and describe in the major time frames of past, present, and future by providing a full account, with good control of aspect.[13]	[13] In Arabic, this point may be equivalent to the control of the moods of the imperfect verb (i.e., the indicative, subjunctive, and jussive).
	the quality and/or quantity of their speech will generally decline [15]	[15] This decline is marked by a noticeable increase in errors.
Advanced High	. . . patterns of error appear [3]	[3] The patterns of error that persist up to this level include gender and number agreement as well as the moods of the imperfect (e.g., the indicative, subjunctive, jussive – المضارع المرفوع و المنصوب و المجزوم). Sometimes, errors in case are also observed.
Superior	Speakers at the Superior level demonstrate no pattern of error in the use of basic structures, although they may make sporadic errors, particularly in low-frequency structures[7] and in complex high-frequency structures.	[7] Low frequency sporadic structural errors include gender and number agreement as well as the use of the wrong imperfect mood of the verb (e.g., the subjunctive/jussive instead of the indicative – ماذا تدرسوا – and the jussive instead of the subjunctive – تصِفْ لي غرفتك).

and what "low frequency" mean. Although the notion of adding "specific annotations" to levels' rubrics and descriptors is a step in the right direction, much more work remains to be done, and here is where SLA findings can inform proficiency testing and make a significant difference. Specifying acquisition tendencies, patterns of emergence and acquisition (by speakers of similar as well as different L1s), and problematic structures (based on SLA findings such as those of the previous, present, and future studies) can inform proficiency testing and mitigate the confusion and ambiguity entailed by current descriptors and annotations and help guide testers away from misidentifying the correct proficiency level of test takers.

Before concluding, consider two specific examples of how SLA data can inform proficiency testing. First, beyond Novice High and Intermediate Low levels, rubrics of other levels do not acknowledge or accurately capture the role of L1 transfer, contrary to the data of the present and previous studies. Recall such studies show that due to L1 transfer, L1 Chinese, L1 English, and L1 Japanese learners (and others with similar L1s) of Arabic are likely to find gender agreement in nominal constructions more problematic than learners whose L1s exhibit nominal gender agreement (such as French and Russian), perhaps even as their proficiency level comes close to Intermediate High or Advanced Low—as they are finishing their third year of language study.[10] Accordingly, current ACTFL rubrics may need to be refined to acknowledge such a difference among different learners as well as acquisition asymmetry patterns even when structures involve similar features (e.g., gender and number) so that they are not lumped together in the same level. Testers can then be cautioned to take into consideration other rubrics of the level before rushing to judgment in determining the level of the examinee. Second, isolating tense and aspect in Arabic (indicating that L2 learners develop "some control of aspect" at Advanced Low whereas they develop "good control of aspect" at Advanced Mid) may not be warranted (pending further future research) since tense and aspect seem to be conflated in Arabic and seem to develop along the same developmental path, along with verbal agreement (for a similar proposal to refine the ACTFL rubrics, see Spinner 2007; see also Spinner 2011). Third, relying on SLA findings can concomitantly help revise and/or add annotations to specify more accurately the exact levels exhibiting certain errors and those that do not.[11]

8.4 Summary and Areas of Future Research

The above discussion is intended to provide some examples and explanation as to how Arabic SLA findings can contribute to subfields in Arabic applied linguistics, such as Arabic foreign language pedagogy, teacher preparation, Arabic curriculum design, and Arabic proficiency testing. The present chapter has been written in the spirit of encouraging further research in Arabic SLA, which has fortunately witnessed more activities and publications in recent years including the emergence of studies on the Arabic heritage learner. More research will further contribute to our knowledge of how the Arabic language is learned by different L1 speakers. Such research should include longitudinal studies, especially those that are conducted for a number of years. More crucially, SLA data at higher proficiency levels (that is, beyond the first three years) as well as the near native level are needed. Finally, such studies should also consider not only the same target forms investigated here but also other inflectional members of the agreement paradigms as well as other structures. Other language pairings should also be considered, employing Arabic L2 learners who are speakers of L1s that are similar and dissimilar, typologically and structurally, to Arabic.

Notes

1. As discussed in chapters 3 and 7, this may be additionally due to the interaction in the syntax between demonstrative pronouns and nominal gender agreement within the determiner phrase in both Russian and Arabic (section 3.3.2, chapter 3; see also note 5, chapter 7).

2. This is true as far as the present and previous Arabic L2 findings are concerned and as long as such L1s exhibit a tense feature (i.e., a distinction is made between past versus nonpast/present tense).

3. For a detailed discussion of the role of L1 transfer of the present data, see chapter 7; see also Alhawary (2009a, 2009b). For detailed discussions of the role of input frequency, see sections 3.3.1.4 and 3.3.2.3, chapter 3; section 4.4, chapter 4; and section 5.4, chapter 5. Previous findings provide additional evidence for the robustness of the role of input. This is evident in the acquisition data of negation structures and mood endings. In particular, although they do not have functional urgency as other forms, mood endings such as those affixed on verbs following *lan* "will not" and *ʔan* "to" emerged in some L2 learners primarily due to their somewhat sustained presence in the input (Alhawary 2009a, 125–46). Moreover, and beyond evidence provided by input- or usage-based accounts cited in chapter 7, the role of input frequency has been widely acknowledged in the SLA literature, especially with respect to morpheme order acquisition. Larsen-Freeman and Long (1991, 91) go as far as stating that, among the factors of acquisition of morpheme order, "only input frequency has much empirical support to date." More recently and based on meta-analysis of a number of morpheme order studies, Goldschneider and DeKeyser (2001) found input frequency to be one of five factors (including perceptual salience, morphological regularity, semantic complexity, syntactic category, and frequency in input) that account for variance in the data. Goldschneider

and DeKeyser conclude that "a considerable portion of the order of acquisition of grammatical functors by ESL learners . . . can be predicted by the five factors" (2001, 37).

4. See also section 7.6, chapter 7, for an analysis where verbal agreement production by the participants tends to be slightly more accurate than verbal agreement in the past tense (based on accuracy percentages alone). Since the former involves a prefix and the latter a suffix, such an acquisition tendency may be due to prefixes being more perceptually salient than suffixes.

5. Regarding being among high-frequency forms, this recommended scheduling happens to be somewhat the same as the one implemented by the authors of the instructional input of the participants (see section 3.3.1.4, chapter 3). The same is true for instructional input of previous studies on English L1, French L1, and Japanese L1 speakers learning Arabic as an L2 (Alhawary 2009a, 57, 88–91).

6. Note that the negation construction involving *lam* seems to require more additional attention and recycling than other negation constructions (Alhawary 2009a, 134–39).

7. Based on data from Arabic L2 learners with different L1s (e.g., English, French, Spanish, Russian, Chinese, and Japanese), this statement must be qualified to be applicable thus far to L1s that exhibit a tense feature. Findings about acquisition tendencies of learners with L1s that do not exhibit a tense feature (in addition to verbal agreement) are not available yet.

8. Furthermore, more problematic is the following descriptor and its related annotation added to the Superior level:

> When appropriate, these speakers use extended discourse without unnaturally lengthy hesitation to make their point, even when engaged in abstract elaborations. Such discourse, while coherent, may still be *influenced by language patterns other than those of the target language* [6] [emphasis added]
>
> [6] One example is the use by a Superior speaker whose sentence structure in Arabic is more typical of English sentence structure which uses relative clauses where the object pronoun in the dependent clause that refers back to the subject noun in the main clause is dropped (e.g., المباريات التي حضروا instead of المباريات التى حضروها).

where such a statement reflects a common misunderstanding that use of resumptive pronouns in object position is obligatory in Arabic and consequently labels such use as evidence of L1 transfer (from English) rather than proper (Arabic) target-like use (see Alhawary 2016, 56).

9. The notion of "complexity" is itself problematic since the notion is vague here and should be explicitly defined.

10. It is not the intention here to equate attainment of certain proficiency levels with strict amounts of exposure time or durations of language study, but most language programs do set such proficiency benchmarks in terms of durations of study.

11. See Bachman and Cohen (1998) and Alderson (2005) for detailed discussions on the interfaces between SLA and language testing and assessment.

Appendix A

Language Background Biographical Data

1. Age: ______________ 2. Gender: ______________ 3. Major: ________________

4. Year at University: ______________ 5. Years or months studying Arabic: ___________

6. Where? ____

7. Is English your native language? Yes ______ No ________

8. If English is not your native language, what is your native language? ___________

9. Knowledge of other languages:

Language 1: Please state what language: ___________________

(please circle appropriate levels of proficiency)

Speaking	native	near native	good	fair	weak
Listening	native	near native	good	fair	weak
Reading	native	near native	good	fair	weak
Writing	native	near native	good	fair	weak

Language 2: Please state what language: _____________________

(please circle appropriate levels of proficiency)

Speaking	native	near native	good	fair	weak
Listening	native	near native	good	fair	weak
Reading	native	near native	good	fair	weak
Writing	native	near native	good	fair	weak

Language 3: Please state what language: ________________________

(please circle appropriate levels of proficiency)

Speaking	native	near native	good	fair	weak
Listening	native	near native	good	fair	weak
Reading	native	near native	good	fair	weak
Writing	native	near native	good	fair	weak

10. Other languages? ____

11. If bilingual, what are the two languages? ________________ & ________________

And what is the more dominant of the two? ________________.

12. Have you traveled briefly to an Arabic-speaking country?
If yes, where? _________________________
How often? ______________ And for how long? ____________________

13. Have you resided in an Arabic-speaking country? If yes, where? __________________

For how long? ________________ Have you taken courses in Arabic there? __________

How many and what courses have you taken there? ______________________________

Appendix B

Tables 1–4

Table 1a Frequency of verbal gender agreement (past tense) occurrence in the textbook of the Chinese L1-A Group 1

	Verbal Gender Agreement (Past Tense)									
Unit[a]	*3. s.m*	*3. s.f*	*3. p.m*	*3. p.f*	*1. s*	*1. p*	*2. s.m*	*2. s.f*	*2. p.m*	*2. p.f*
1										
2										
3	(X)	(/)	(/)	(/)	(/)	(/)	(/)	(/)	(/)	(/)
4	(X)	(/)	(/)	(/)	(/)	(/)	(/)	(/)	(/)	(/)
5	(X)	(/)	(/)	(/)	(/)	(/)	(/)	(/)	(/)	(/)
6	()	(/)	(/)	(/)	(/)	(/)	(/)	(/)	(/)	(/)
7	(X)	(/)	(/)	(/)	(/)	(/)	(/)	(/)	(/)	(/)
8	(/)	(/)	(/)	(/)	(/)	(/)	(/)	(/)	(/)	(/)
9	(X)	(/)	(/)	(/)	(/)	(/)	(/)	(/)	(/)	(/)
10	(/)	(/)	(/)	(/)	(/)	(/)	(/)	(/)	(/)	(/)
11	(X)	(/)	(/)	(/)	(/)	(/)	(/)	(/)	(/)	(/)
12	(X)	(/)	(/)	(/)	(/)	(/)	(/)	(/)	(/)	(/)
13	X	X	X	X	X	X	X	X	X	X
14	[X]	[X]	[X]	[X]	[X]		[X]	[X]		
15	[X]	(X)	(/)			(/)	(X)	(/)	(X)	
16	[X]	[X]	[X]	(/)	[X]	(/)	[X]	[X]	[X]	
17	(X)	[X]	[X]		(X)		(/)	(/)		
18	(X)	(X)			(X)	(/)	(X)	(/)	(/)	
19	(X)	(X)	[X]	[X]	(X)	(/)	(/)	(/)		
20	(X)	(/)	(X)	(/)	(X)	(X)	(/)			
21	(X)	(X)	(/)		(X)	(/)	(X)			
22	(X)	(X)	(/)		(X)	(X)	(/)		(/)	
23	[X]	(/)	(X)		(X)	(/)	(/)		(/)	
24	[X]	[X]	[X]	[X]	[X]	[X]	[X]	[X]	[X]	[X]

[a] The textbook used is *al-Jadīd fī al-Lugha al-ʿArabiyya*, vol. 1 (Guo and Zhou 2002).

X = focused attempt to teach the structure; [X] = indirect focused attempt occurring in conjugation drills; (X) = structure is not the focus of instruction but occurs in the lesson and drills 4 or more times; (/) = structure is not the focus of instruction and occurs less than 4 times.

Table 1b Frequency of verbal gender agreement (present tense) occurrence in the textbook of the Chinese L1-A Group 1

	Verbal Gender Agreement (Present Tense)									
Unit[a]	*3. s.m*	*3. s.f*	*3. p.m*	*3. p.f*	*1. s*	*1. p*	*2. s.m*	*2. s.f*	*2. p.m*	*2. p.f*
1										
2										
3	(X)									
4	(X)	(/)	(/)	(/)	(/)	(/)	(/)	(/)	(/)	(/)
5	(X)	(/)	(/)	(/)	(/)	(/)	(/)	(/)	(/)	(/)
6	(/)	(/)	(/)	(/)	(/)	(/)	(/)	(/)	(/)	(/)
7	(/)	(/)	(/)	(/)	(/)	(/)	(/)	(/)	(/)	(/)
8	(/)	(/)	(/)	(/)	(/)	(/)	(/)	(/)	(/)	(/)
9	(/)	(/)	(/)	(/)	(/)	(/)	(/)	(/)	(/)	(/)
10	(X)	(/)	(/)	(/)	(/)	(/)	(/)	(/)	(/)	(/)
11	(X)	(/)	(/)	(/)	(/)	(/)	(/)	(/)	(/)	(/)
12	(X)	(/)	(/)	(/)	(/)	(/)	(/)	(/)	(/)	(/)
13	X	X	X	X	X	X	X	X	X	X
14	(X)	(X)	(X)	(X)	(X)	(X)	(/)	(/)		
15	[X]	[X]	[X]	(/)	[X]	[X]	(X)	[X]		
16	[X]	[X]	[X]	[X]	(X)	[X]	(X)	[X]	[X]	(X)
17	[X]	(X)	(X)	[X]	(X)	(X)	(X)	[X]	[X]	
18	(X)	[X]	(/)	[X]	(X)	[X]	(X)	[X]	[X]	
19	[X]	[X]	(X)	(/)	(X)	(X)	(/)	[X]	[X]	
20	(X)	(X)	(X)	(X)	(X)	(X)	(/)	(/)	(X)	
21	[X]	[X]	[X]	(/)	(X)	[X]	(X)	[X]	(/)	
22	(X)	(X)	(X)		(X)	(X)	(X)	(/)	(X)	(/)
23	[X]	(X)	(X)		(X)		(X)		(X)	
24	(X)	(X)	(X)	(X)	(/)	(/)			(/)	

[a] The textbook used here is *al-Jadīd fī al-Lugha al-ʿArabiyya*, vol. 1 (Guo and Zhou 2002).

X = focused attempt to teach the structure; [X] = indirect focused attempt occurring in conjugation drills; (X) = structure is not the focus of instruction but occurs in the lesson and drills 4 or more times; (/) = structure is not the focus of instruction and occurs less than 4 times.

Table 2a Frequency of verbal gender agreement (in past tense) in the textbook of the Chinese L1-B Group 1

Unit/ Lesson[a]	Verbal Gender Agreement (Past Tense)										Unit/ Lesson[b]	Verbal Gender Agreement (Past Tense)									
	3. s.m	3. s.f	3. p.m	3. p.f	1. s	1. p	2. s.m	2. s.f	2. p.m	2. p.f		3. s.m	3. s.f	3. p.m	3. p.f	1. s	1. p	2. s.m	2. s.f	2. p.m	2. p.f
1–40											1			(/)							
1											2	(/)						(/)		(/)	
2	(/)										3						(/)				
3	(/)										4	(/)		(/)			(/)	(/)			
4											5	(/)									
5					(/)		(/)				6	(/)		(X)							
6											7	X	(/)				(/)	(/)			
7					(/)						8	(/)	(/)	(/)		(/)	(/)	(/)			
8	(/)										9	(/)	(/)				(/)	(/)		(/)	
9		(X)			(/)		(/)				10	(X)		(/)		X					
10	(X)	(/)	(/)								11	(X)	X	(/)		X		X			
11	(/)	(/)									12	(X)	(/)			X		X			
12	(X)	(/)	(/)	(/)							13	(X)	(/)			(X)		(X)			
13	(X)	(/)	(/)	(/)	(/)						14	(X)				X		X			
14					(/)	(/)		(/)	(/)		15	X	(X)	(/)		X		X			
15	(/)	(/)	(/)								16		(/)			(/)		(X)			
1	(/)																				
2	X																				
3	(X)	(/)			(/)																
4	(/)																				
5	(/)																				

[a] The textbooks used for the left half of the table are *Kitāb al-Qirā'a* and *Mudhakkira 'Iḍāfiyya li-l-Mustawā al-'Awwal* (Saudi Teaching Delegates, n.d.).

[b] The textbook used for the right half of the table is *al-'Arbiyya bayna Yadayk*, vol. 1 (Al-Fawzān et al. 2003).

X = focused attempt to teach the structure; [X] = indirect focused attempt occurring in conjugation drills; (X) = structure is not the focus of instruction but occurs in the lesson and drills 4 or more times; (/) = structure is not the focus of instruction and occurs less than 4 times; shaded area = skipped in *Kitāb al-Qirā'a* and *Mudhakkira* (below the shaded area) was covered instead.

Table 2b Frequency of verbal gender agreement (in present tense) in the textbook of the Chinese L1-B Group 1

Unit/ Lesson[a]	*Verbal Gender Agreement (Present Tense)*										Unit/ Lesson[b]	*Verbal Gender Agreement (Present Tense)*									
	3. *s.m*	3. *s.f*	3. *p.m*	3. *p.f*	1. *s*	1. *p*	2. *s.m*	2. *s.f*	2. *p.m*	2. *p.f*		3. *s.m*	3. *s.f*	3. *p.m*	3. *p.f*	1. *s*	1. *p*	2. *s.m*	2. *s.f*	2. *p.m*	2. *p.f*
1–40	(X)										1	(/)		(/)							
1	(X)										2	(X)	(X)	(/)		(/)	(/)			(/)	
2	(X)	(/)			(/)	(/)					3	(/)				X		X		(/)	
3	(X)	(X)	(X)		(/)						4	(X)	(X)	(/)		X		X	X		
4	(/)	(X)		(X)	(X)						5	X	(X)			X		X	X		
5	(/)	(/)			(/)	(X)					6	X				X		X	(/)		
6					(X)	(/)					7	X	(X)			(X)		X	X		
7		(X)		(/)		(/)					8	(X)	(X)			X		X	(X)		
8	(X)	(X)									9	(X)	(X)			X		X	(X)		
9	(X)					(/)	(/)				10	(X)	(X)	(/)		(X)	X	(/)	(/)		
10	(/)		(/)		(/)	(/)					11	(X)	X			X		X			
11	(/)										12	(X)	(X)			X		X	X	(/)	
12	(/)		(/)								13	(X)	(X)	(/)		(/)		(X)			
13	(/)				(/)		(/)				14	(X)		(/)		(X)	X	(X)			
14											15	(X)	(/)	(/)		X		(X)			
15	(/)				(/)						16	(X)	(/)	(/)		(X)	X	(X)			
1	(/)																				
2	X																				
3	(X)																				
4																					
5	(X)	(X)																			

[a] The textbooks used for the left half of the table are *Kitāb al-Qirā'a* and *Mudhakkira 'Iḍāfiyya li-l-Mustawā al-'Awwal* (Saudi Teaching Delegates, n.d.).

[b] Textbook used for the right half of the table is *al-'Arbiyya bayna Yadayk*, vol. 1 (Al-Fawzān, Hussein, and Faḍl 2003).

X = focused attempt to teach the structure; [X] = indirect focused attempt occurring in conjugation drills; (X) = structure is not the focus of instruction but occurs in the lesson and drills 4 or more times; (/) = structure is not the focus of instruction and occurs less than 4 times; shaded area = skipped in *Kitāb al-Qirā'a* and *Mudhakkira* (below the shaded area) was covered instead.

Table 3a Frequency of verbal gender agreement (in past tense) in the textbook of the Russian L1-A Group 1

Unit/ Lesson[a]	*Verbal Gender Agreement (Past Tense)*										Unit/ Lesson[b]	*Verbal Gender Agreement (Past Tense)*									
	3. s.m	*3. s.f*	*3. p.m*	*3. p.f*	*1. s*	*1. p*	*2. s.m*	*2. s.f*	*2. p.m*	*2. p.f*		*3. s.m*	*3. s.f*	*3. p.m*	*3. p.f*	*1. s*	*1. p*	*2. s.m*	*2. s.f*	*2. p.m*	*2. p.f*
1–10											1–2										
11–20	(X)				(/)	(/)					3–4										
21–30	(X)	(/)			(X)	(X)	(X)	(/)			5–6	(X)	(X)	(X)		(/)	(/)				
31–40		(/)			(/)	(X)	(/)	(/)			7–8	(X)	(X)	(/)					(/)		
41–50	(/)				(/)	(X)	(/)				9–10	(/)	(X)	(/)		(/)			(/)		
51–60	(X)	(X)			(X)	(/)	(X)	(/)			11–12	(X)	(X)	(X)		(X)	(/)				
61–70	(X)	(/)			(X)		(/)				13–14	(X)	(X)	(/)		(/)	(X)				
71–80	(X)	(X)			(X)	(X)		(/)			15–16	(X)		(/)			(/)	(/)			
81–90	(X)	(X)			(X)	(X)	(X)				17–18	(/)	(/)	(/)			(/)				
91–100	(X)	(/)	(/)		(/)	(/)	(X)				19–20	(X)	(X)			(/)					
101–110	(/)	(X)			(X)	(/)	(X)				21–22	(X)	(X)	(X)			(/)				
111–120	(X)	(X)	(/)		(X)	(/)	(/)	(/)			23–24	(X)	(X)		(/)			(/)			
121–130	(X)	(/)	(/)		(X)		(/)	(/)			25–26	(X)	(/)	(/)		(/)					
131–140	(X)	(/)			(X)	(/)		(/)			27–28	(X)	(X)	(/)							
141–150	(X)	(X)	(/)		(X)	(X)	(/)	(/)			29–30	(X)	(X)	(X)							
											31–32	(X)	(X)	(/)					(/)		
											33–34	(X)	(X)	(X)			(/)				
											35–36	(X)	(X)	(X)							

[a] The textbook used for the left half of the table is *Povsednevnyarabskijjazyk* (Franka 2007).

[b] The textbook used for the right half of the table is *Literaturnyarabskyjazyk* (Khanna 2006).

X = focused attempt to teach the structure; [X] = indirect focused attempt occurring in conjugation drills; (X) = structure is not the focus of instruction but occurs in the lesson and drills 4 or more times; (/) = structure is not the focus of instruction and occurs less than 4 times.

Table 3b Frequency of verbal gender agreement (in present tense) in the textbook of the Russian L1-A Group 1

Unit/ Lesson[a]	*Verbal Gender Agreement (Present Tense)*										Unit/ Lesson[b]	*Verbal Gender Agreement (Present Tense)*									
	3. *s.m*	3. *s.f*	3. *p.m*	3. *p.f*	*1. s*	1. *p*	2. *s.m*	2. *s.f*	2. *p.m*	2. *p.f*		3. *s.m*	3. *s.f*	3. *p.m*	3. *p.f*	1. *s*	1. *p*	2. *s.m*	2. *s.f*	2. *p.m*	2. *p.f*
1–10	(/)	(/)			(/)	(X)	(/)				1–2					(X)					
11–20			(X)		(X)	(/)	(/)		(/)		3–4	(/)	(X)	(/)							
21–30	(/)	(X)			(X)	(X)	(X)	(/)			5–6	(/)					(/)				
31–40	(X)	(/)	(X)		(X)	(/)	(X)				7–8	(X)	(/)	(/)		(X)	(X)		(/)		
41–50	(X)	(/)	(/)		(X)	(X)	(X)				9–10		(X)	(/)							
51–60	(X)	(/)			(X)		(X)				11–12	(X)		(/)		(/)	(/)				
61–70	(X)	(X)	(/)		(X)	(X)	(X)	(/)			13–14	(X)	(/)			(/)	(/)				
71–80	(X)	(/)	(X)		(X)	(X)	(X)		(/)		15–16	(/)		(/)		(X)	(/)	(/)			
81–90	(X)	(/)			(X)	(/)	(X)				17–18	(X)	(/)	(/)			(/)				
91–100	(X)	(/)	(/)		(X)	(X)	(X)	(/)			19–20	(X)	(/)								
101–110	(X)	(/)	(/)	(X)	(X)	(/)	(X)		(/)		21–22	(X)	(X)	(/)			(/)				
111–120	(X)	(X)	(X)		(X)	(X)	(X)				23–24	(X)	(/)			(/)		(/)			
121–130	(X)	(X)	(/)		(X)	(X)	(X)		(X)		25–26	(X)	(/)			(/)	(/)	(/)			
131–140	(X)	(/)	(X)		(X)	(X)	(X)	(X)	(/)		27–28	(X)	(/)	(/)			(/)				
141–150	(X)	(X)	(/)		(X)	(X)	(X)	(/)	(/)		29–30	(X)	(X)	(/)			(X)	(/)			
											31–32	(X)	(X)	(/)			(X)		(/)		
											33–34	(X)	(X)	(X)							
											35–36	(X)	(X)	(X)			(/)	(/)			

[a] The textbook used for the left half of the table is *Povsednevnyarabskijjazyk* (Franka 2007).
[b] The textbook used for the right half of the table is *Literaturnyarabskyjazyk* (Khanna 2006).

X = focused attempt to teach the structure. [X] = indirect focused attempt occurring in conjugation drills; (X) = structure is not the focus of instruction but occurs in the lesson and drills 4 or more times; (/) = structure is not the focus of instruction and occurs less than 4 times.

Table 4a Frequency of verbal gender agreement occurrence (in past tense) in the textbook of the Russian L1-B Group 1

Unit/ Lesson[a]	Verbal Gender Agreement (Past Tense)										Unit/ Lesson[b]	Verbal Gender Agreement (Past Tense)									
	3. s.m	*3. s.f*	*3. p.m*	*3. p.f*	*1. s*	*1. p*	*2. s.m*	*2. s.f*	*2. p.m*	*2. p.f*		*3. s.m*	*3. s.f*	*3. p.m*	*3. p.f*	*1. s*	*1. p*	*2. s.m*	*2. s.f*	*2. p.m*	*2. p.f*
1											1	(X)									
2											2	(X)				(/)					
3											3	(X)									
4											4	(X)	(/)								
5	X	X									5	(X)	(X)			(/)					
6	(X)	(X)									6	(X)	(X)	(X)		(/)	(X)			(X)	
7	X	X			X		X	X			7	(X)	(X)	(X)	(/)	(/)	(/)				
8	(X)	(X)			(X)		(/)	(/)			8	(X)	(/)	(X)	(/)	(X)	(/)		(/)	(X)	
9	(X)				(/)		(/)				9	(X)	(X)	(/)		(/)	(/)	(/)		(/)	
10	(X)	(/)			(X)		(/)	(/)			10	(X)	(X)	(X)		(/)	(/)				
11	(X)	(X)			(X)			(/)			11	(X)	(X)	(X)		(X)	(/)			(/)	
											12	(X)	(X)								

[a] The textbook used for the left half of the table is *Vvodno Foneticheskii Koors Arabskovo Yezika* (Semyonova and Lukyanova 2004).

[b] The textbook used for the right half of the table is *Oochebna-Metodicheskoye Possobiye Po Arabskomu Yaziku* (Semyonova and Lukyanova 2005).

X = focused attempt to teach the structure; [X] = indirect focused attempt occurring in conjugation drills; (X) = structure is not the focus of instruction but occurs in the lesson and drills 4 or more times. (/) = structure is not the focus of instruction and occurs less than 4 times.

Table 4b Frequency of verbal gender agreement occurrence (in present tense) in the textbook of the Russian L1-B Group 1

	Verbal Gender Agreement (Present Tense)											*Verbal Gender Agreement (Present Tense)*									
Unit/ Lesson[a]	3. *s.m*	3. *s.f*	3. *p.m*	3. *p.f*	1. *s*	1. *p*	2. *s.m*	2. *s.f*	2. *p.m*	2. *p.f*	*Unit/ Lesson*[b]	3. *s.m*	3. *s.f*	3. *p.m*	3. *p.f*	1. *s*	1. *p*	2. *s.m*	2. *s.f*	2. *p.m*	2. *p.f*
1											1	(X)	(X)			(X)		(/)	(/)		
2											2	(X)	(X)			(X)		(/)	(X)		
3											3	(X)	(X)	(/)		(X)	(/)	(/)	(/)		
4											4	(X)	(X)	(/)	(/)	(X)	(X)				
5											5	(X)		(X)	(X)	(/)	(/)			(X)	(/)
6											6	(X)	(/)	(/)		(/)	(X)			(/)	
7											7	(X)		(X)			(/)	(/)	(/)		
8											8	(X)		(X)		(X)	(X)	(X)	(/)	(X)	
9											9	(X)	(X)	(/)		(X)	(X)	(X)		(/)	
10											10	(X)	(X)	(X)			(/)	(/)		(/)	
11											11	(X)	(X)	(/)		(/)	(/)			(/)	
											12	(X)	(X)	(/)		(/)	(/)				

[a] The textbook used for the left half of the table is *Vvodno Foneticheskii Koors Arabskovo Yezika* (Semyonova and Lukyanova 2004).

[b] The textbook used for the right half of the table is *Oochebna-Metodicheskoye Possobiye Po Arabskomu Yaziku* (Semyonova and Lukyanova 2005).

X = focused attempt to teach the structure; [X] = indirect focused attempt occurring in conjugation drills; (X) = structure is not the focus of instruction but occurs in the lesson and drills 4 or more times; (/) = structure is not the focus of instruction and occurs less than 4 times.

References

Abboud, P., Z. N. Abdel-Malek, N. A. Bezirgan, W. M. Erwin, M. A. Khouri, E. M. McCarus, R. M. Rammuny, and G. N. Saad. 1983. *Elementary Modern Standard Arabic*, vol. 1. Cambridge: Cambridge University Press.

Abd El-Jawad, H., and Issam Abu-Salim. 1987. "Slips of the Tongue in Arabic and Their Theoretical Implications." *Language Sciences* 9:145–71.

Abrahamsson, N., and K. Hyltenstam. 2008. "The Robustness of Aptitude Effects in Nearnative Second Language Acquisition." *Studies in Second Language Acquisition* 30:481–509.

ACTFL (American Council on the Teaching of Foreign Languages). 1989. "ACTFL Arabic Proficiency Guidelines." *Foreign Language Annals* 22:373–92.

———. 1999. "ACTFL Proficiency Guidelines: Speaking."

———. 2012. "ACTFL Proficiency Guidelines: Speaking." www.actfl.org/publications/guidelines-and-manuals/actfl-proficiency-guidelines-2012/Arabic.

Agren, M., and J. Van de Weijer. 2013. "Input Frequency and the Acquisition of Subject-Verb Agreement in Number in Spoken and Written French." *Journal of French Language Studies* 23:311–33.

Al Shatter, G. 2008. "The Development of Verbal Structures in L2 Arabic." In *Processability Approaches to Second Language Development and Second Language Learning*, edited by J.-U. Keßler, 267–99. Newcastle, UK: Cambridge Scholar.

Alderson, J. C. 2005. *Designing Foreign Languages Proficiency: The Interface between Learning and Assessment*. London: Continuum.

Al-Fawzān, A. I., M. A. Hussein, and M. A. M. Faḍl. 2003. *al-'Arbiyya bayna Yadayk*. Riyadh, Saudi Arabia: Arabic for All.

Al-Ghalayyīnī, Al-Sheikh Muṣṭafā. 2000. *Jāmi' al-Durūs al-'Arabiyya*. Sidon, Lebanon: Al-Maktaba Al-'Aṣriyya.

Al-Hamad, M. M. 2003. "Morphological and Syntactic Properties in the Acquisition of Arabic as a Second Language: Implications for the Theory of SLA and for Language Teaching." PhD dissertation, University of Essex.

Alhawary, M. T. 1999. "Testing Pocessability and Effectiveness of Computer-Assisted Language Instruction: A Longitudinal Study of Arabic as a Foreign/Second Language." PhD dissertation, Georgetown University.

———. 2003. "Processability Theory: Counter-Evidence from Arabic Second Language Acquisition Data." *Al-'Arabiyya* 36:107–66.

———. 2005. "L2 Acquisition of Arabic Morphosyntactic Features: Temporary or Permanent Impairment?" In *Perspectives on Arabic Linguistics XVII–XVIII*, edited by M. T. Alhawary and E. Benmamoun, 273–311. Amsterdam: John Benjamins.

———. 2007a. "Null Subjects Use by English and Spanish Learners of Arabic as an L2." In *Perspectives on Arabic Linguistics XIX: Papers from the Nineteenth Annual Symposium on Arabic Linguistics*, edited by E. Benmamoun, 217–45. Amsterdam: John Benjamins.

———. 2007b. "The Split-INFL Hypothesis: Findings from English and Japanese L2 Learners of Arabic." In *Perspectives on Arabic Linguistics XX: Papers from the Twentieth Annual Symposium on Arabic Linguistics*, edited by M. Mughazy, 135–52. Amsterdam: John Benjamins.

———. 2009a. *Arabic Second Language Acquisition of Morphosyntax*. New Haven, CT: Yale University Press.

———. 2009b. "Speech Processing Prerequisites or L1 Transfer: Evidence from English and French L2 Learners of Arabic." *Foreign Language Annals* 42:367–90.

———. 2011. *Modern Standard Arabic Grammar: A Learner's Guide*. West Sussex, UK: Wiley-Blackwell.

———. 2016. *Arabic Grammar in Context*. London: Routledge.

Al-Ḥulwānī, M. K. 1972. *al-Wāḍiḥ fī al-Naḥw wa al-Ṣarf*. Aleppo, Syria: Al-Maktaba Al-ʻAṣriyya.

Anderson, R. 1983. "Transfer to Somewhere." In *Language Transfer in Language Learning*, edited by S. Gass and L. Selinker, 177–201. Rowley, MA: Newbury House.

Avrutin, S., and B. Rohrbacher. 1997. "Null Subjects in Russian Inverted Constructions." In *Proceedings of the 4th Meeting of Formal Approaches to Slavic Linguistics: The Cornell Meeting*, edited by W. Browne, E. Dornisch, N. Kondrashova, and D. Zec, 32–53. Ann Arbor: Michigan Slavic Publications.

Ayoun, Dalila. 2003. *Parameter Setting in Language Acquisition*. London: Continuum.

Bachman, L. F., and A. D. Cohen. 1998. *Interfaces between Second Language Acquisition and Language Testing Research*. Cambridge: Cambridge University Press.

Badry, F. 2005. "Acquisition of Arabic Word Formation: A Multi-Path Approach." In *Perspectives on Arabic Linguistics XVII–XVIII: Papers from the Seventeenth and Eighteenth Annual Symposia on Arabic Linguistics*, edited by M. T. Alhawary and E. Benmamoun, 242–71. Amsterdam: John Benjamins.

Barakāt, I. I. 1988. *al-Ta'nīth fī al-Lugha al-ʻArabiyya*. Al-Manṣūra, Egypt: Dār Al-Wafā'.

Bardel, C., and Y. Falk. 2007. "The Role of the Second Language in Third Language Acquisition: The Case of Germanic Syntax." *Second Language Research* 23:459–84.

———. 2012. "The L2 Status Factor and the Declarative/Procedural Distinction." In *Third Language Acquisition in Adulthood*, edited by J. Cabrelli Amaro, S. Flynn, and J. Rothman, 61–78. Amsterdam: John Benjamins.

Baten, K., A. Buyl, K. Lochtman, and M. Van Herreweghe. 2015. *Theoretical and Methodological Developments in Processability Theory*. Amsterdam: John Benjamins.

Beck, M.-L. 1997. "Regular Verbs, Part Tense, and Frequency: Tracking Down One Potential Source of NS/NNS Syntactic Competence Differences." *Second Language Research* 13:93–115.

———. 1998. "L2 Acquisition and Obligatory Head Movement: English Speaking Learners of German and the Local Impairment Hypothesis." *Studies in Second Language Acquisition* 20:311–48.

Benmamoun, E. 1999. "Arabic Morphology: The Central Role of the Imperfective." *Lingua* 108:175–201.

Berg, T., and H. Abd El-Jawad. 1996. "The Unfolding of Suprasegmental Representations: A Crosslinguistic Perspective." *Journal of Linguistics* 32:291–324.

Berkes, É., and S. Flynn. 2012. "Further Evidence in Support of the Cumulative-Enhancement Model: CP Structure Development." In *Third Language Acquisition in Adulthood*, edited by J. Cabrelli Amaro, S. Flynn, and J. Rothman, 143–64. Amsterdam: John Benjamins.

Berman, R. 1985. "The Acquisition of Hebrew." In *The Crosslinguistic Study of Language Acquisition*, vol. 1, edited by D. Slobin, 255–371. Hillsdale, NJ: Lawrence Erlbaum.

———. 1999. "Children's Innovative Verbs versus Nouns: Structured Elicitations and Spontaneous Coinages." In *Methods in Studying Language Production*, edited by L. Menn and N. Bernstein Ratner, 69–93. Mahwah, NJ: Lawrence Erlbaum.

Bley-Vroman, R. 1983. "The Comparative Fallacy in Interlanguage Studies: The Case of Systematicity." *Language Learning* 33:1–17.

———. 1989. "What Is the Logical Problem of Foreign Language Learning." In *Linguistic Perspectives on Second Language Acquisition*, edited by S. Gass and J. Schachter, 41–68. Cambridge: Cambridge University Press.

———. 1990. "The Logical Problem of Foreign Language Learning." *Linguistic Analysis* 20:3–49.

———. 2002. "Frequency in Production, Comprehension, and Acquisition." *Studies in Second Language Acquisition* 24:209–13.

Boudelaa, S., and W. D. Marslen-Wilson. 2001. "Morphological Units in the Arabic Mental Lexicon." *Cognition* 81, 65–92.

———. 2004. "Abstract Morphemes and Lexical Representation: The CV-Skeleton in Arabic." *Cognition* 92:271–303.

———. 2011. "Productivity and Priming: Morphemic Decomposition in Arabic." *Language and Cognitive Processes* 26:624–52.

Bresnan, J. 1982. *The Mental Representation of Grammatical Relations*. Cambridge, MA: MIT Press.

———. 2001. *Lexical-Functional Syntax*. Oxford: Blackwell.

Brown, R., R. Waring, and S. Donkaewbua. 2008. "Incidental Vocabulary Acquisition from Reading, Reading-While-Listening, and Listening to Stories." *Reading in a Foreign Language* 20:136–63.

Bruhn de Garavito, J., and L. White. 2002. "The Second Language Acquisition of Spanish DPs: The Status of Grammatical Features." In *The Acquisition of Spanish Morphosyntax*, edited by A. T. Pérez-Leroux and J. M. Liceras, 153–78. Dordrecht, The Netherlands: Kluwer Academic Publishers.

Brustad, K., M. Al Batal, and A. Al-Tonsi. 1995. *al-Kitaab fii Taʿallum al-ʿArabiyya*. Washington, DC: Georgetown University Press.

Burton, E., and L. Maharg. 1995. *Going Places 1: Pictures-Based English*. London: Longman.

Bybee, J., and J. Newman. 2006. "Are Stem Changes as Natural as Affixes?" In *Frequency of Use and the Organization of Language*, edited by J. Bybee, 148–66. New York: Oxford University Press.

Cadierno, T. 2008. "Learning to Talk about Motion in a Foreign Language." In *Handbook of Cognitive Linguistics and Second Language Acquisition*, edited by P. Robinson and N. C. Ellis, 239–75. London: Routledge.

Carlson, M. 2009. "The Acquisition of Probabilistic Patterns in Spanish Phonology by Adult Second Language Learners: The Case of Diphthongization." PhD dissertation, The Pennsylvania State University.

Carroll, S. E. 1989. "Second-Language Acquisition and the Computational Paradigm." *Language Learning* 39:535–94.

———. 2001. *Input and Evidence: The Raw Material of Second Language Acquisition*. Amsterdam: John Benjamins.

Carstens, V. M. 2000. "Concord in Minimalist Theory." *Linguistic Inquiry* 31:319–55.

Chernov, P. V. 1995. *Arabic Grammar Guide*. Moscow: Oriental Literatures Press.

Chomsky, N. 1995. "Categories and Transformations." In *The Minimalist Program*, 219–394. Cambridge, MA: MIT Press.

———. 1998. "Minimalist Inquiries: The Framework." *MIT Occasional Papers in Linguistics* 15:1–14. Cambridge, MA: MIT Press.

———. 1999. "Derivation by Phase." *MIT Occasional Papers in Linguistics* 18:1–43. Cambridge, MA: MIT Press.

———. 2001a. "Beyond Explanatory Adequacy." *MIT Occasional Papers in Linguistics* 20:1–28. Cambridge, MA: MIT Press.

———. 2001b. "Derivation by Phase." In *Ken Hale: A Life in Language*, edited by M. Kenstowicz, 1–52. Cambridge, MA: MIT Press.

Clahsen, H. 1984. "The Acquisition of German Word Order: A Test Case for Cognitive Approaches to Second Language Acquisition." In *Second Language*, edited by R. Anderson, 219–42. Rowley, MA: Newbury House.

Clahsen, H., and P. Muysken. 1986. "The Availability of Universal Grammar to Adult and Child Learners: A Study of the Acquisition of German Word Order." *Second Language Research* 5:93–119.

———. 1989. "The UG Paradox in L2 Acquisition." *Second Language Research* 2:1–29.

Commissioned Saudi Teaching Delegates. n.d. *al-Kitāba al-ʿArabiyya*.

———. n.d. *Kitāb al-Qirāʾa*.

———. n.d. *Kurrāsat Tadrībāt al-Khaṭṭ*.

———. n.d. *Mudhakkira ʾIḍāfiyya lil-Mustawā al-ʾAwwal*.

Corbett, G. 1999. "Agreement." *Concise Encyclopedia of Grammatical Categories*, edited by J. Miller, 12–18. Amsterdam: Elsevier.

Corder, S. P. 1978. "Simple Codes and the Source of the Second Language Learner's Initial Heuristic Hypothesis." *Studies in Second Language Acquisition* 1:1–10.

Davis, S., and B. Zawaydeh. 2001. "Arabic Hypocoristics and the Status of the Consonantal Root." *Linguistic Inquiry* 32:512–20.

Dewaele, J.-M., and D. Véronique. 2001. "Gender Assignment and Gender Agreement in Advanced French Interlanguage: A Cross-Sectional Study." *Bilingualism: Language and Cognition* 4:275–97.

Ellis, N. C., 2002. "Frequency Effects in Language Processing." *Studies in Second Language Acquisition* 24:143–88.

Ellis, N. C., and F. Ferreira-Junior. 2009. "Construction Learning as a Function of Frequency, Frequency Distribution, and Function." *Modern Language Journal* 93:370–85.

Ellis, N. C., M. B. O'Donnell, and U. Römer. 2013. "Usage-Based Language: Investigating the Latent Structures That Underpin Acquisition." *Language Learning* 63 (Supp.): 25–51.

Ellis, R. 1990. "Grammaticality Judgments and Learner Variability." In *Variability in Second Language Acquisition: Proceedings of the Tenth Meeting of the Second Language Research Forum*, edited by H. Burmeister and P. L. Rounds, 25–60. Eugene: Department of Linguistics, University of Oregon.

———. 1991. "Grammaticality Judgments and Second Language Acquisition." *Studies in Second Language Acquisition* 13:161–86.

Epstein, S., S. Flynn, and G. Martohardjono. 1996. "Second Language Acquisition: Theoretical and Experimental Issues in Contemporary Research." *Brain and Behavioral Sciences* 19:677–758.

Eubank, L. 1993–94. "On the Transfer of Pragmatic Values in L2 Development." *Language Acquisition* 3:183–208.

———. 1996. "Negation in Early German-English Interlanguage: More Valueless Features in the L2 Initial State." *Second Language Research* 12:73–106.

Eubank, L., and M.-L. Beck. 1998. "OI-Like Effects in Adult L2 Acquisition." In *Proceedings of the 22nd Annual Boston University Conference on Language Development*, vol. 1, edited by A. Greenhill, M. Hughes, H. Littlefield, and H. Walsh, 189–200. Somerville, MA: Cascadilla Press.

Eubank, L., J. Bischof, A. Huffstutler, P. Leek, and C. West. 1997. "'Tom Eats Slowly Cooked Eggs': Thematic Verb Raising in L2 Knowledge." *Language Acquisition* 6:171–99.

Falk, Y., and C. Bardel. 2011. "Object Pronouns in German L3 Syntax: Evidence for the L2 Status Factor." *Second Language Research* 27:59–82.

Farley, A. P., and K. McCollam. 2004. "Learner Readiness and L2 Production in Spanish: Processability Theory on Trial." *Estudios de Lingüística Aplicade* 40:47–69.

Fassi Fehri, A. 1993. *Issues in the Structure of Arabic Clauses and Words*. Dordrecht, The Netherlands: Kluwer Academic Publishers.

Felix, S. W. 1985. "More Evidence on Competing Cognitive Systems." *Second Language Research* 1:47–72.

Ferguson, C., and M. Barlow. 1988. "Introduction." In *Agreement in Natural Language*, edited by C. Ferguson and M. Barlow, 1–22. Stanford, CA: Center for the Study of Language and Information.

Flynn, S., C. Foley, and I. Vinnitskaya. 2004. "The Cumulative-Enhancement Model for Language Acquisition: Comparing Adults' and Children's Patterns of Development in First, Second and Third Language Acquisition." *International Journal of Multilingualism* 1:3–17.

Franceschina, F. 2005. *Fossilized Second Language Grammars: The Acquisition of Grammatical Gender*. Amsterdam: John Benjamins.

Franka, Shkola inostrannykh jazykov Ilji. 2007. *Povsednevny Arabskij Jazyk: Londonsky kurs*. Moscow: AST, Vostok-Zapad.

Franks, S. 1995. *Parameters of Slavic Morphosyntax*. Oxford: Oxford University Press.

Frisch, S., and B. Zawaydeh. 2001. "The Psychological Reality of OCP-place in Arabic." *Language* 77:91–106.

Fuller, J. 1999. "Between Three Languages: Composite Structure in Interlanguage." *Applied Linguistics* 20:534–61.

Gass, S. 1983. "Language Transfer and Universal Grammatical Relations." In *Language Transfer in Language Learning*, edited by S. Gass and L. Selinker, 69–82. Rowley, MA: Newbury House.

Gess, R., and J. Herschensohn. 2001. "Shifting the DP Parameter: A Study of Anglophone French L2ers." In *Romance Syntax, Semantics and Their L2 Acquisition*, edited by C. R. Wiltshire and J. Camps, 105–19. Amsterdam: John Benjamins.

Goldberg, A. E., D. M. Casenhiser, and N. Sethuraman. 2004. "Learning Argument Structure Generalizations." *Cognitive Linguistics* 15:289–316.

Goldschneider, J. M., and R. M. DeKeyser. 2001. "Explaining the 'Natural Order of L2 Morpheme Acquisition' in English: A Meta-analysis of Multiple Determinants." *Language Learning* 51:1–50.

Goss, N., Z. Ying-Hua, and J. P. Lantolf. 1994. "Two Heads Better Than One: Assessing Mental Activities in L2 Grammatical Judgments." In *Research Methodology in Second Language Acquisition*, edited by E. E. Tarone, S. M. Gass, and A. D. Cohen, 263–86. Mahwah, NJ: Lawrence Erlbaum.

Guo, S., and C. Jiang. 2002. *al-Jadīd fī al-Lugha al-'Arabiyya*, vol. 2. Beijing: Foreign Language Teaching and Research Press.

Guo, S., L. Yu, X. Wu, and Q. Xue. 2004. *al-Jadīd fī al-Lugha al-'Arabiyya*, vol. 3. Beijing: Foreign Language Teaching and Research Press.

Guo, S., L. Yu, X. Wu, and H. Zhang. 2006. *al-Jadīd fī al-Lugha al-'Arabiyya*, vol. 4 Beijing: Foreign Language Teaching and Research Press.

Guo, S., and L. Zhou. 2002. *al-Jadīd fī al-Lugha al-'Arabiyya*, vol. 1. Beijing: Foreign Language Teaching and Research Press.

Hammarberg, B. 2001. "Roles of L1 and L2 in L3 Production and Acquisition." In *Cross-Linguistic Influence in Third Language Acquisition: Psycholinguistic Perspectives*, edited by J. Cenoz, B. Hufeisen, and U. Jessner, 21–41. Clevedon, UK: Multilingual Matters.

Han, Z. 2014. "From Julie to Wes to Alberto: Revisiting the Construct of Fossilization." In *Interlanguage: Forty Years Later*, edited by Z. and E. Tarone, 47–74. Amsterdam: John Benjamins.

Harris, J. 1991. "The Exponence of Gender in Spanish." *Linguistic Inquiry* 22:27–62.

Hatch, E. 1974. "Second Language Learning Universals?" *Working Papers on Bilingualism* 3:1–17.

Hawkins, R. 1998. "The Inaccessibility of Formal Features of Functional Categories in Second Language Acquisition." Paper presented at the Pacific Second Language Research Forum, Tokyo, Japan, March 1998.

———. 2001. *Second Language Syntax*. Malden, MA: Blackwell.

———. 2005. "Revisiting *Wh*-Movement: The Availability of an Uninterpretable [wh] Feature in Interlanguage Grammars." In *Proceedings of the 7th Generative Approaches to Second Language Acquisition Conference (GASLA 2004)*, edited by L. Dekydtspotter, D. R. Sprouse, and A. Liljestrand, 124–37. Somerville, MA: Cascadilla.

———. 2009. "Statistical Learning and Innate Knowledge in the Development of Second Language Proficiency: Evidence from the Acquisition of Gender Concord." In *Issues in Second Language Proficiency*, edited by A. G. Benati, 63–78. London: Continuum.

Hawkins, R., and G. Casillas. 2008. "Explaining Frequency of Verb Morphology in Early L2 Speech." *Lingua* 118:595–612.

Hawkins, R., G. Casillas, H. Hattori, J. Hawthorne, R. Husted, C. Lozano, A. Okamoto, E. Thomas, and K. Yamada. 2008. "The Semantic Effects of Verb Raising and Its Consequences in Second Language Grammars." In *The Role of Formal Features in Second Language Acquisition*, edited by J. M. Liceras, H. Zobl, and H. Goodluck, 328–51. New York: Lawrence Erlbaum.

Hawkins, R., and Yuet-Hung Chan. 1997. "The Partial Availability of Universal Grammar in Second Language Acquisition: The 'Failed Functional Features Hypothesis.'" *Second Language Research* 13:187–226.

Hawkins, R., and H. Hattori. 2006. "Interpretation of English Multiple *wh*- Questions by Japanese Speakers: A Missing Uninterpretable Feature Account." *Second Language Research* 22:269–301.

Hermas, A. 2014. "Multilingual Transfer: L1 Morphosyntax in L3 Acquisition." *International Journal of Language Studies* 8:1-24.

Hopp, H. 2010. "Ultimate Attainment in L2 Inflection: Performance Similarities between Non-Native and Native Speakers." *Lingua* 120:901–31.

Huang, C. T. J. 1989. "Pro-Drop in Chinese." In *The Null Subject Parameter*, edited by O. Jaeggli and K. Safir, 185–214. Boston: Kluwer.

Husseinali, G. 2006. "Processability and Development of Syntax and Agreement in the Interlanguage of Learners of Arabic as a Foreign Language." PhD dissertation, University of Texas at Austin.

———. 2016. *Arabic L2 Interlanguage: Syntactic Sequences, Agreement and Variation*. London: Routledge.

Hwang, S. H., and D. Lardiere. 2013. "Plural-Marking in L2 Korean: A Feature-Based Approach." *Second Language Research* 29:57–86.

Hyltenstam, K., and N. Abrahamsson. 2003. "Maturational Constraints in SLA." In *The Handbook of Second Language Acquisition*, edited by C. J. Doughty and M. H. Long, 539–88. Oxford: Blackwell.

IBM Knowledge Center. 2017. *SPSS Statistics 23.0.0*. www.ibm.com/support/knowledgecenter/en/SSLVMB_23.0.0/spss/common/idh_glmu_post.html.

Idrissi, A., and E. Kehayia. 2004. "Morphological Units in the Arabic Mental Lexicon: Evidence from an Individual with Deep Dyslexia." *Brain and Language* 90:183–97.

Idrissi, A., J. Prunet, and R. Beland. 2008. "On the Mental Representation of Arabic Roots." *Linguistic Inquiry* 39:221–59.

Ionin, T., and S. Montrul. 2010. "The Role of L1 Transfer in the Interpretation of Articles with Definite Plurals in L2 English." *Language Learning* 60:877–925.

Jarvis, S. 2000. "Methodological Rigor in the Study of Transfer: Identifying L1 Influence on the Interlanguage Lexicon." *Language Learning* 50:245–309.

Jarvis, S., and T. Odlin. 2000. "Morphological Type, Spatial Reference and Language Transfer." *Studies in Second Language Acquisition* 22:535–56.

Jin, F. 2009. "Third Language Acquisition of Norwegian Objects: Interlanguage Transfer or L1 Influence?" In *Third Language Acquisition and Universal Grammar,* edited by Y-K. I. Leung, 144-61. Bristol, UK: Multilingual Matters.

Joe, A. 2010. "The Quality and Frequency of Encounters with Vocabulary in an English for Academic Purposes Program." *Reading in a Foreign Language* 22:117–38.

Jushmanov, N. V. 1999. *Grammatika Literaturnogo Arabskogo Jazyka.* Saint Petersburg, Russia: Juridicheskijtsentr Press.

Keßler, J.-U. 2008. *Processability Approaches to Second Language Development and Second Language Learning.* Newcastle, UK: Cambridge Scholar.

Kellerman, E. 1977. "Towards a Characterization of the Strategy of Transfer in Second Language Learning." *Interlanguage Studies Bulletin* 1:58–145.

———. 1978. "Giving Learners a Break: Native Language Intuitions as a Source of Predictions about Transferability." *Working Papers on Bilingualism* 15:59–92.

———. 1979. "Transfer and Non-transfer: Where We Are Now." *Studies in Second Language Acquisition* 2:37–57.

———. 1983. "Now You See it, Now You Don't." In *Language Transfer in Language Learning,* edited by S. Gass and L. Selinker, 112–34. Rowley, MA: Newbury House.

———. 1995. "Crosslinguistic Influence: Transfer to Nowhere?" *Annual Review of Applied Linguistics* 15:125–50.

Kempen, G., and E. Hoenkamp. 1987. "An Incremental Procedural Grammar for Sentence Formulation." *Cognitive Science* 11:201–58.

Khanna, J. 2006. *Literaturnyarabskyjazyk: Prakticheskykurs.* Saint Petersburg, Russia: KARO.

Klein, W. 1991. "SLA Theory: Prolegomena to a Theory of Language Acquisition and Implications for Theoretical Linguistics." In *Crosscurrents in Second Language Acquisition and Linguistic Theory,* edited by T. Huebner and C. Ferguson, 169–94. Amsterdam: John Benjamins.

Krashen, S. 1977. "Some Issues Relating to the Monitor Model." In *On TESOL '77 Teaching and Learning English as a Second Language: Trends in Research and Practice,* edited by C. A. Yorio, R. H. Crymes, and H. D. Brown, 144–58. Washington, DC: TESOL.

———. 1985. *The Input Hypothesis: Issues and Implications.* London: Longman.

———. 1993. "The Effect of Formal Grammar Teaching: Still Peripheral." *TESOL Quarterly* 27:722–25.

Kweon, S., and H. Kim. 2008. "Beyond Raw Frequency: Incidental Vocabulary Acquisition in Extensive Reading." *Reading in a Foreign Language* 20:191–215.

Lakshmanan, U. 1994. *Universal Grammar in Child Second Language Acquisition.* Amsterdam: John Benjamins.

Lantolf, J. P. 1990. "Resetting the Null Subject Parameter in Second Language Acquisition." In *Variability in Second Language Acquisition: Proceedings of the Tenth Meeting of the Second Language Research Forum,* edited by H. Burmeister and P. L. Rounds, 429–52. Eugene: Department of Linguistics, University of Oregon.

Lardiere, D. 1998. "Case and Tense in the 'Fossilized' Steady State." *Second Language Research* 14:1–26.

———. 2000. "Mapping Features to Forms in Second Language Acquisition." In *Second*

Language Acquisition and Linguistic Theory, edited by J. Archibald, 102–29. Oxford: Blackwell.

———. 2008. "Feature-Assembly in Second Language Acquisition." In *The Role of Formal Features in Second Language Acquisition*, edited by J. M. Liceras, H. Zobl, and H. Goodluck, 106–40. Mahwah, NJ: Lawrence Erlbaum.

———. 2009a. "Further Thoughts on Parameters and Features in Second Language Acquisition: A Reply to Peer Comments on Lardiere's 'Some Thoughts on the Contrastive Analysis of Features in Second Language Acquisition' in SLR 25 (2)." *Second Language Research* 25:409–22.

———. 2009b. "Some Thoughts on a Contrastive Analysis of Features in Second Language Acquisition." *Second Language Research* 25:173–227.

Larsen-Freeman, D. 1976. "An Explanation for the Morpheme Acquisition Order of Second Language Learners." *Language Learning* 26:125–34.

Larsen-Freeman, D., and M. H. Long. 1991. *An Introduction to Second Language Acquisition Research*. New York: Longman.

Levelt, W. J. M. 1989. *Speaking: From Intention to Articulation*. Cambridge, MA: MIT Press.

Liceras, J. M. 2009. "On Parameters, Functional Categories and Features . . . and Why the Trees Shouldn't Prevent Us from Seeing the Forest . . ." *Second Language Research* 25:279–89.

Lightbown, P. 1980. "The Acquisition and Use of Questions by French L2 Learners." In *Second Language Development*, edited by S. Felix, 151–75. Tubingen, Ger.: Gunter Narr.

Lightfoot, D., and N. Hornstein. 1994. "Verb Movement: An Introduction." In *Verb Movement*, edited by D. Lightfoot and N. Hornstein, 1–17. Cambridge: Cambridge University Press.

Lin, C., and M. T. Alhawary. 2018. "Frequency and L1 Transfer Effects for the Perception and Production of Arabic Lexical Stress by L1 English and L1 Chinese Learners of Arabic as an L2." In *The Routledge Handbook of Arabic Second Language Acquisition*, edited by M. T. Alhawary. London: Routledge.

Lui, G-Q. 1991. "Interaction and Second Language Acquisition: A Case Study of a Chinese Child's Acquisition of English as a Second Language." PhD dissertation, La Trobe University, Melbourne, Australia.

Mahfoudhi, A. 2005. "Morphological and Phonological Units in the Arabic Mental Lexicon: Implications for Theories of Morphology and Lexical Processing." PhD dissertation, University of Ottawa, Canada.

———. 2007. "Roots and Patterns in Arabic Lexical Processing." In *Perspectives on Arabic Linguistics XIX: Papers from the Nineteenth Annual Symposium on Arabic Linguistics*, edited by E. Benmamoun, 123–50. Amsterdam: John Benjamins.

Maiburov, N. A. 2010. *Chitaem i Perevodim Arabskuyu Gazetu*. Moscow: Vostochnaya Kneega.

Majmaʿ Al-Lugha Al-ʿArabiyya. 1984. *Majmūʿat al-Qarārāt al-ʿIlmiyya fī Khamsīna ʿĀman*. Cairo, Egypt: Majmaʿ Al-Lugha Al-ʿArabiyya.

MAXQDA. 2010. *Qualitative Data Analysis Software for Windows and Mac OS X*. Berlin, Ger.: VERBI.

McCarthy, J. J. 1981. "A Prosodic Theory of Non-Concactenative morphology." *Linguistic Inquiry* 12:373–418.

McDonough, K., and Y. Kim. 2009. "Syntactic Priming, Type Frequency, and EFL Learners' Production of Wh-questions." *Modern Language Journal* 93:386–98.

Meisel, J. 1983. "Strategies of Second Language Acquisition: More Than One Kind of Simplification." *Pidginization and Creolization as Second Language Acquisition*, edited by R. W. Anderson, 120–57. Rowley, MA: Newbury House.

———. 1991. "Principles of Universal Grammar and Strategies of Language Use: On Some Similarities and Differences between First and Second Language Acquisition." In *Point-Counterpoint: Universal Grammar in the Second Language*, edited by L. Eubank, 231–71. Amsterdam: John Benjamins.

Mellow, J. D. 2006. "The Emergence of Second Language Syntax: A Case Study of the Acquisition of Relative Clauses." *Applied Linguistics* 27:645–70.

Müller, G. 2006. "Pro-Drop and Impoverishment." In *Form, Structure, and Grammar: A Festschrift Presented to Günther Grewendorf on Occasion of His 60th Birthday*, edited by P. Brandt and E. Fuß, 93–115. Berlin: Akademie Verlag.

———. 2008. "Some Consequences of an Impoverishment-Based Approach to Morphological Richness and Pro-Drop. In *Elements of Slavic and Germanic Grammars: A Comparative View*, edited by J. Witkoś and G. Fanselow, 125–45. Frankfurt: Peter Lang.

Neeleman, A., and K. Szendrői. 2007. "Radical Pro Drop and the Morphology of Pronouns." *Linguistic Inquiry* 38:671–714.

Newport, E. 1990. "Maturational Constraints on Language Learning." *Cognitive Science* 14:11–28.

Nielsen, H. L. 1997. "On Acquisition Order of Agreement Procedures in Arabic Learner Language." *Al-'Arabiyya* 30:49–93.

Odlin, T. 1989. *Language Transfer.* Cambridge: Cambridge University Press.

———. 2014. "Rediscovering Predictions." In *Interlanguage: Forty Years Later*, edited by Z. Han and E. Tarone, 27–45. Amsterdam: John Benjamins.

O'Grady, W., J. Archibald, M. Aronoff, and J. Rees-Miller. 2009. *Contemporary Linguistics: An Introduction*. New York: St. Martin's.

Perlmutter, D., and J. Moore. 2002. "Language-Internal Explanation: The Distribution of Russian Impersonals." *Language* 78:619–50.

Parodi, T., B. D. Schwartz, and H. Clahsen. 2004. "On the L2 Acquisition of the Morphosyntax of German Nominals." *Linguistics* 42:669–705.

Pienemann, M. 1998. *Language Processing and Second Language Development: Processability Theory*. Amsterdam: John Benjamins.

———. 2005. *Cross-Linguistic Aspects of Processability Theory*. Amsterdam: John Benjamins.

Pienemann, M., and G. Håkansson. 1999. "A Unified Approach toward the Development of Swedish as L2." *Studies in Second Language Acquisition* 21:383–420.

Pienemann, M., and M. Johnston. 1987. "Factors Influencing the Development of Language Proficiency." In *Applying Second Language Acquisition Research*, edited by D. Nunan, 45–141. Adelaide, Australia: National Curriculum Research Centre, Adult Migrant Educational Program.

Pienemann, M., and J-U. Keßler. 2011. *Studying Processability Theory: An Introductory Textbook*. Amsterdam: John Benjamins.

Poeppel, D., and K. Wexler. 1993. "The Full Competence Hypothesis of Clause Structure in Early German." *Language* 69:1–33.

Portin, M., M. Lehtonen, and M. Laine. 2007. "Processing of Inflected Nouns in Late Bilinguals." *Applied Psycholinguistics* 28:135–56.

Poulisse, N., and T. Bongaerts. 1994. "First Language Use in Second Language Production." *Applied Linguistics* 15:36–57.

Prévost, P. 2008. "Knowledge of Morphology and Syntax in Early Adult L2 French: Evidence for the Missing Surface Inflection Hypothesis." In *The Role of Formal Features in Second Language Acquisition*, edited by J. M. Liceras, H. Zobl, and H. Goodluck, 352–77. New York: Erlbaum.

Prévost, P., and L. White. 2000. "Missing Surface Inflection or Impairment in Second Language Acquisition? Evidence from Tense and Agreement." *Second Language Research* 16:103–33.

Prunet, J. F., R. Beland, and A. Idrissi. 2000. "The Mental Representation of Semitic Words." *Linguistic Inquiry* 31:609–48.

Ratcliffe, R. R. 1997. "Prosodic Templates in a Word-based Morphological Analysis of Arabic." In *Perspectives on Arabic Linguistics: Papers from the Annual Symposium on Arabic Linguistics*, vol. X, edited by M. Eid and R. R. Ratcliff, 147–72. Amsterdam: John Benjamins.

———. 1998. *The "Broken" Plural Problem in Arabic and Comparative Semitic: Allomorphy and Analogy in Non-Concatenative Morphology*. Amsterdam: John Benjamins.

Redouane, R. 2001. "The Use of Modern Standard Arabic Word Formation Processes by English-Speaking and French-Speaking Adult L2 Learners and Native Speakers." PhD dissertation, University of Toronto.

———. 2003. "Learners' Variability in Coining New Words in L2." *Al-'Arabiyya* 36: 49–80.

Ringbom, H. 2001. "Lexical Transfer in L3 Production." In *Cross-linguistic Influence in Third Language Acquisition: Psycholinguistic Perspectives*, edited by J. Cenoz, B. Hufeisen, and U. Jessner, 59–68. Clevedon, UK: Multilingual Matters.

Rohde, A. 2009. "Input Frequency and the Acquisition of the Progressive." In *Input Matters in SLA*, edited by T. Piske and M. Young-Scholten, 29–46. Bristol, UK: Multilingual Matters.

Römer, U., N. Ellis, and M. B. O'Donnell. 2014. "Second Language Learner Knowledge of Verb–Argument Constructions: Effects of Language Transfer and Typology." *Modern Language Journal* 98:952–75.

Rothman, J. 2010. "On the Typological Economy of Syntactic Transfer: Word Order and Relative Clause Attachment Preference in L3 Brazilian Portuguese." *International Review of Applied Linguistics in Language Teaching* 48:245–73.

———. 2011. "L3 Syntactic Transfer Selectivity and Typological Determinacy: The Typological Primacy Model." *Second Language Research* 27:107–27.

———. 2013. "Cognitive Economy, Non-redundancy and Typological Primacy in L3 Acquisition: Evidence from Initial Stages of L3 Romance." In *Romance Languages and Linguistic Theory 2011: Selected Papers from "Going Romance" Utrecht 2011*, edited by S. Baauw, F. Drijkoningen, L. Meroni, and M. Pinto, 217–48. Amsterdam: John Benjamins.

———. 2015. "Linguistic and Cognitive Motivations for the Typological Primacy Model of Third Language (L3) Transfer: Timing of Acquisition and Proficiency Considered." *Bilingualism: Language and Cognition* 18:179–90.

Rothman, J., and J. Cabrelli Amaro. 2010. "What Variables Condition Syntactic Transfer? A Look at the L3 Initial State." *Second Language Research* 26:189–218.

Rothman, J., J. A. Bañón, and J. G. Alonso. 2015. "Neurolinguistic Measures of Typological Effects in Multilingual Transfer: Introducing an ERP Methodology." *Frontiers in Psychology* 6:1087.

Rott, S. 1999. "The Effects of Exposure Frequency on Intermediate Language Learners' Incidental Vocabulary Acquisition and Retention through Reading." *Studies in Second Language Acquisition* 21:589–619.

Sabourin, L., L. Stowe, and J. de Haan. 2006: "Transfer Effects in Learning a Second Language Grammatical Gender System." *Second Language Research* 22:1–29.

Sauter, Kim. 2002. "Transfer and Access to Universal Grammar in Adult Second Language Acquisition." PhD dissertation, University of Groningen, The Netherlands.

Ṣaydāwī, Y. 1999. *al-Kafāf*. Damascus, Syria: Dār Al-Fikr.

Schachter, J. 1989. "Testing a Proposed Universal." In *Linguistic Perspectives on Second Language Acquisition*, edited by S. Gass and J. Schachter, 73–88. Cambridge: Cambridge University Press.

Schwartz, B. D. 1998. "On Two Hypotheses of 'Transfer' in L2A: Minimal Trees and Absolute L1 Influence." In *The Generative Study of Second Language Acquisition*, edited by S. Flynn, G. Martohardjiono, and W. O'Neil, 35–59. Mahwah, NJ: Lawrence Erlbaum.

Schwartz, B. D., and R. A. Sprouse. 1994. "Word Order and Nominative Case in Non-Native Language Acquisition: A Longitudinal Study of (L1 Turkish) German Interlanguage." In *Language Acquisition Studies in Generative Grammar: Papers in Honor of Kenneth Wexler from the 1991 GLOW Workshops*, edited by T. Hoekstra and B. D. Schwarts, 317–68. Amsterdam: John Benjamins.

———. 1996. "L2 Cognitive States and the Full Transfer/Full Access Model." *Second Language Research* 12:40–72.

Schwartz, M., and P. N. L. Causarano. 2007. "The Role of Frequency in SLA: An Analysis of Gerunds and Infinitives in ESL Written Discourse." *Arizona Working Papers in SLA and Teaching* 14:43–57.

Selinker, L., and U. Lakshmanan. 1993. "Language Transfer and Fossilization: The 'Multiple Effects Principle.'" In *Language Transfer in Language Learning*, edited by S. Gass and L. Selinker, 197–216. Amsterdam: John Benjamins.

Semyonova, V. D., and G. O. Lukyanova. 2003. *Mi Govoreem Po-Arabskii*, vols. 1–2. Moscow: Rossiskii Ooniversitet Droojbi Narodov.

———. 2004. *Vvodno Foneticheskii Koors Arabskovo Yezika*. Moscow: Isdatelstvo Rossiskovo Ooniversiteta Droojbi Narodov.

———. 2008. *Znaesh li ti Arabsuyu Literaturu?* Moscow: Rossiskii Ooniversitet Droojbi Narodov.

Semyonova, V. D., G. O. Lukyanova, K. N. Stepanin, and A. M. Novikova. 2005. *Oochebna-metodicheskoye Possobiye po Arabskomu Yaziku*. Moscow: Isdatelstvo Rossiskovo Ooniversiteta Droojbi Narodov.

Sharwood Smith, M. 1981. "Consciousness Raising and the Second Language Learner." *Applied Linguistics* 2:158–68.

———. 1991. "Speaking to Many Different Minds: On the Relevance of Different Types of Language Information for the L2 Learner." *Second Language Research* 7:118–32.

Sīnī, M. I., I. Y. Al-Sayyid, and M. A. Al-Shaykh. 1990. *al-Qawā'id al-'Arabiyya al-Muyassara: Silsila fī Ta'līm al-Naḥw al-'Arabiyy li-Ghayr al-'Arab*. Riyadh, Saudi Arabia: King Saud University Press.

Slabakova, R. 2017. "The Scalpel Model of Third Language Acquisition." *International Journal of Bilingualism* 21: 651-65.

Slobin, D I. 1973. "Cognitive Prerequisites for the Development of Grammar." In *Studies of Child Language Development*, edited by C. A. Ferguson and D. I. Slobin, 175–208. New York: Holt, Rinehart and Winston.

Sorace, A. 2003. "Near-Nativeness." In *The Handbook of Second Language Acquisition*, edited by C. J. Doughty and M. Long, 130–51. Oxford: Blackwell.

Spinner, P. A. 2007. "Placement Testing and Morphosyntactic Development in Second Language Learners of English." PhD dissertation, University of Pittsburgh.

———. 2011. "Second Language Assessment and Morphosyntactic Development." *Studies in Second Language Acquisition* 33:529–61.

Stedje, A. 1977. "Tredjespråksinterferens i Fritt tal-en Jämförande Studie" [Third Language Interference in Spontaneous Speech—A Comparative Study]. In *Papers from the Conference on Contrastive Linguistics and Error Analysis*, edited by R. Palmberg and H. Ringbom, 141–58. Turku, Fin.: Publications of the Research Institute of the Åbo Akademi Foundation.

Tarone, E. 2007. "A Sociolinguistic Perspective on Interaction in SLA." Paper presented at the 30th Annual AAAL Conference, Costa Mesa, CA, April 2007.

———. 2014. "Enduring Questions from the Interlanguage Hypothesis." In *Interlanguage: Forty Years Later*, edited by Z. Han and E. Tarone, 7–26. Amsterdam: John Benjamins.

Tarone, E., and G.-Q. Lui. 1995. "Situational Context, Variation, and Second Language Acquisition Theory." In *Principles and Practice in Applied Linguistics: Studies in honour of H. G. Widdowson*, edited by G. Cook and B. Seidlhofer, 107–24. Oxford: Oxford University Press.

Thomas, A. 2010. "The Influence of Lexical Aspect and Input Frequency in the L2 French of Adult Beginners." *Nordic Journal of Linguistics* 33:169–96.

Tsedryk, E. 2013. "Internal Merge of Nominative Subjects and Pro-drop in Russian." In *Proceedings of the 2013 Annual Conference of the Canadian Linguistic Association*, edited by S. Luo, 1–14. http://homes.chass.utoronto.ca/~cla-acl/actes2013/Tsedryk-2013.pdf.

Tsimpli, I. M. 2003. "Clitics and Determiners in L2 Greek." In *Proceedings of the 6th Generative Approaches to Second Language Acquisition Conference (GASLA 2002)*, edited by J. M. Liceras, H. Zobl, and H. Goodluck, 331–39. Somerville, MA: Cascadilla.

Tsimpli, I. M., and M. Dimitrakopoulou. 2007. "The Interpretability Hypothesis: Evidence from *Wh*-interrogatives in Second Language Acquisition." *Second Language Research* 23:215–42.

Tsimpli, I. M., and M. Mastropavlou. 2008. "Feature Interpretability in L2 Acquisition and SLI: Greek Clitics and Determiners." In *The Role of Formal Features in Second Language Acquisition*, edited by J. M. Liceras, H. Zobl, and H. Goodluck, 142–83. New York: Lawrence Erlbaum.

Vainikka, A., and M. Young-Scholten. 1994. "Direct Access to X'-Theory: Evidence from Korean and Turkish Adults Learning German." In *Language Acquisition Studies in Generative Grammar*, edited by T. Hoekstra and B. D. Schwartz, 265–316. Amsterdam: John Benjamins.

———. 1996. "Gradual Development of L2 Phrase Structure." *Second Language Research* 12:7–39.

———. 1998. "The Initial State in the L2 Acquisition of Phrase Structure." In *The Generative Study of Second Language Acquisition*, edited by S. Flynn, G. Martohardjiono, and W. O'Neil, 17–34. Mahwah, NJ: Lawrence Erlbaum.

———. 2006. "The Roots of Syntax and How They Grow: Organic Grammar, the Basic Variety and Processability Theory." In *Paths of Development in L1 and L2 Acquisition*, edited by S. Unsworth, T. Parodi, A. Sorace, and M. Young-Scholten, 77–106. Amsterdam: John Benjamins.

———. 2007. "Minimalism vs. Organic Syntax." In *Phrasal and Clausal Architecture*, edited by K. Simin, V. Samiian, and W. Wilkins, 319–38. Amsterdam: John Benjamins.

———. 2009. "Successful Features: Verb Raising and Adverbs in L2 Acquisition under an Organic Grammar Approach." In *Representational deficits in SLA: Studies in Honor of Roger Hawkins*, edited by N. Snape, K. I. Leung, and M. S. Smith, 53–68. Amsterdam: John Benjamins.

Valian, V., and S. Coulson. 1988. "Anchor Points in Language Learning: The Role of Marker Frequency." *Journal of Memory and Language* 27:71–86.

Vermeer, A. 2001. "Breadth and Depth of Vocabulary in Relation to L1/L2 Acquisition and Frequency of Input." *Applied Psycholinguistics* 22:217–34.

Weinreich, U. 1953. *Languages in Contact.* The Hague, The Netherlands: Mouton.

Westergaard, M., N. Mitrofanova, R. Mykhaylyk, and Y. Rodina. 2017. "Crosslinguistic Influence in the Acquisition of a Third Language: The Linguistic Proximity Model." *International Journal of Bilingualism* 21:666–82.

White, L. 2003. *Second Language Acquisition and Universal Grammar.* Cambridge: Cambridge University Press.

———. 2009. "Some Questions about Feature Re-assembly." *Second Language Research* 25:343–48.

White, L., E. Valenzuela, M. Kozlowska-Macgregor, and K. I. Leung. 2004. "Gender and Number Agreement in Nonnative Spanish." *Applied Psycholinguistics* 25:105–33.

Williams, S., and B. Hammarberg. 1998. "Language Switches in L3 Production: Implications for a Polyglot Speaking Model." *Applied Linguistics* 19:295–333.

Index

Tables and figures are indicated by *t* and *f* following the page number.

About the Author

Mohammad T. Alhawary is a professor of Arabic linguistics and second language acquisition at the University of Michigan, where he teaches courses on Arabic language and Arabic theoretical and applied linguistics. He is the editor of *Al-'Arabiyya* journal as well as the *Journal of Arabic Linguistics Tradition* and the author of many works, including *Modern Standard Arabic Grammar: A Learner's Guide* (Wiley-Blackwell 2011), *Arabic Grammar in Context* (Routledge 2016), *Second Language Acquisition of Morphosyntax* (Yale University Press 2009), and *The Routledge Handbook of Arabic Second Language Acquisition* (Routledge 2018).

www.ingramcontent.com/pod-product-compliance
Lightning Source LLC
LaVergne TN
LVHW050151080826
844660LV00002B/166

* 9 7 8 1 6 2 6 1 6 6 4 6 2 *